News from Essex

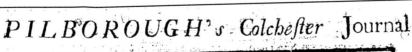

PILBOROUGH's Colchester Journal

Or, ESSEX Weekly Mercury

SATURDAY, MARCH 3 1739   Number 310

The following Account having been sent us by a Person whose Knowledge and Credit may be depended upon, we thought it would be agreeable to our Readers :

 IN the Year 1718, the King of Spain ordered all the Effects of the South-Sea Company in the West-Indies to be feiz'd; which was rigorously executed, and the Goods carried by the King's Officers into his

Ships, in Indigo, Pieces of Eight, and Cochineal ; when the Ship came to Cadiz the Indigo and Pieces of Eight were deliver'd to the Company's Agents, but the Spaniards kept the Cochineal ; so that the Company did not recover of this second Seizure above 150,000 l. and were great.r Losers by this than by the first Seizure.

The South-Sea Company, by their Account deliver'd to both Houses of Parliament, received out of the Produce of the late Directors Estates, upwards of 2,300,000 l.

The Publick has allow'd to the Company

that a Trial at the Common-Pleas Bar, for the real Estate is order'd for the 28th of May next, and to be tried by a Jury of Gentlemen of the County of Kent, where the said Estate lies.

On Monday his Majesty was at the House of Lords, and gave the Royal Assent to the Malt Bill, and to two Naturalization Bills.

On Tuesday his Royal Highness the Prince of Wales went very early to the House of Peers to hear the Debates on the Spanish Merchants, where his Royal Highness stay'd several Hours.

Pip Wright

Copyright © 2013 P. Wright

ISBN 978-0-9564855-5-7

Published by **Pawprint Publishing**
14, Polstead Close, Stowmarket, Suffolk   IP14 2PJ
All rights reserved. No part of this publication may be reproduced, stored in a retrieval system, or transmitted in any form or by any means electronic, mechanical, photocopying, recording or otherwise, without the prior permission of the publisher and the copyright owners.

Other books by Pip Wright

Lydia
Death Recorded
I Read it in the local Rag (pub. by Poppyland Publishing)
Exploring Suffolk by Bus Pass
Exploring East Anglia by Bus Pass
Thomas Slapp's Booke of Physicke
The Watery Places of Suffolk
A Short History of the Village of Cotton

Books by Pip & Joy Wright

**The Amazing Story of John Heigham Steggall,
'The Suffolk Gipsy'**
Newspapers in Suffolk (6 vols)
Grave Reports
Witches in and around Suffolk
Bygone Cotton
The Diary of a Poor Suffolk Woodman
(with Léonie Robinson, pub. by Poppyland Publishing)

Lucky is the Name
(by Alf Burrows, Pip Wright & Michael Anderton)

www.pipwright.com   www.poppyland.co.uk

Contents

32. Yefterday Evening a Gentleman, who lives in Picca-dily, was accofted, by a Woman near the Canal in Hyde-Park, who afked him for Charity; the Gentleman threw her Six-pence and walked on, but had fcarcely gone a Yard, when a Fellow, ftarting from behind a Tree, prefented a Piftol and demanded what Bufinefs he had with his Wife, at the fame time collaring him, and threatening to drag him before a Magiftrate at Kenfington : The Gentleman, in his Surprize, thought it beft to accommodate Matters, and therefore gave the fellow a Couple of Guineas, who feemed perfectly fatis-fied with the Sum, and marched very leifurely with his Doxy a-crofs the Park, to get, as himfelf expreffed it, fome Bread and Cheefe, and a Tankard of Beer.

33. *From the Gen. Ev. Poft of Saturday.* On Monday Af-ternoon a humourous Duel was fought behind King's Col-lege, between two young Gentlemen of the Univerfity of Cambridge, whofe Seconds had charged the Piftols with Pow-der only, which the Combatants difcharged twice each, be-fore the Aggreffor difcovered the Deception. A Blanket be-ing brought by fome of their Acquaintance, under the Pre-tence of conveying home the Wounded, and their popping off the Piftols being ended, it was unanimoufly agreed to tofs the Delinquent in the Blanket, which was accordingly done, to the no fmall Pleafure of the Spectators, as his Behaviour to a young Lady of Fortune and Merit is univerfally con-demned.

Laft Saturday Night as two young Men, on one Horfe, were riding over Wivenhoe Water-bridge, near Colchefter, the Horfe miffed his Footing, fell off the Bridge, and threw both the Men, by which Accident one was drowned ; but the other, by the Affi-ftance of a Boat belonging to a Veffel in the Harbour, was taken up fpeechlefs.

IPSWICH JOURNAL: February 23rd 1765

News From Essex

Chapter 1 - Introduction

In 1736, the first Essex local newspaper was published. It was known as the Essex Gazette, subsequently to be Pilborough's Colchester Journal. It was published for only a few years, its main competitor the Ipswich Journal outlasting it by 170 years or more (By 1736, the Ipswich Journal had already had more than fifteen years to capture a North Essex readership).

It would be later that century before local papers would be published again in Essex. Probably the county's proximity to London rendered them unnecessary. Most eighteenth century 'local' papers carried little local news. For the most part, they offered a digest of what London papers had printed the week before...

from Stanley's News-Letter
They write from Strasburg that on the 23rd of last month, died there a single woman, aged about sixty, whose belly for some years grew up to an immense bigness, without her being sensible of any pain. The Colleges of Physicians tried all the means they could think on to cure her but without success, and allowed her a pension on condition that they should have the liberty to open her when dead, that they might find the cause of so uncommon a disease. Accordingly, they open'd her corps and found a very large serpent in her belly.
IPSWICH JOURNAL: March 2nd 1728

Initially, counties placed farther from London were more successful in finding a market for these new publications. Local papers were published in Norwich almost continuously from 1701, and in Ipswich from 1720.

They slowly grew in popularity. White's Directory for Essex (1848) listed the Ipswich Express & Suffolk Mercury and the Essex Standard (both published in Colchester) and the Chelmsford Chronicle and Essex Herald (both published in Chelmsford).

In 1862, the Post Office Directory for Essex named nine local Essex papers, four published in Chelmsford, three in Colchester and the other two in Stratford and Romford. There were, of course, papers also being published just over the borders in Sudbury, Ipswich and Bishop's Stortford.

By 1870 the list had risen to twenty, and by the end of the century, according to Kelly's Directory, over forty local Essex papers were being marketed, including ones from smaller towns such as Halstead, Maldon, Saffron Walden, Waltham Abbey and Chingford.

Many of the earlier local papers were politically aligned. The Essex Standard and Ipswich Journal were Tory papers through and through. The Essex & Suffolk Mercury and the Suffolk Chronicle were Whig (Liberal) papers. The Chelmsford Chronicle claimed to be in support of no party, but certainly favoured reform in the 1830s when Conservative papers were strongly against it. The Woodford Mail, 1897 had plastered across its front page *'NO POLITICS NO PREJUDICE.'* The Waltham Abbey & Cheshunt Weekly Telegraph claimed to be *'Liberal Conservative'* (a coalition, even in 1870?). But whatever their political standpoint, to be successful, having a broad appeal was vital.

THE LEADING NEWSPAPER IN THE EASTERN COUNTIES.

THE RECOGNISED ORGAN FOR OFFICIAL & LEGAL ADVERTISEMENTS.

THE

EAST ANGLIAN DAILY TIMES

FROM the appearance of its first issue in 1874, has been a most popular Newspaper with all classes in the important and extensive district in which it circulates. It is especially prized by the *elite* of the population of Suffolk, Essex, Norfolk, and Cambridge. Every practicable means are devised to secure its rapid delivery to subscribers resident in country districts. By freely employing special carts and expresses, and by special arrangement with the postal authorities, the very latest Home and Foreign Intelligence is conveyed to thousands of readers in time for perusal at the breakfast table. Equal promptitude is shown in the collection of news from all parts of the large district covered by the paper, a very numerous and able staff of reporters and correspondents being constantly at work, so that the paper is a most valuable combination of Local, National, and Foreign News, brought down to the very latest moment. It has the

LARGEST CIRCULATION OF ANY LOCAL PAPER,

Amongst the Nobility, Clergy, and Gentry; the Legal and other Professions; Investors, Agriculturalists, Shippers, Manufacturers, Tradesmen, and the general community.

An advert from White's Directory for 1885 for a paper that wanted to appeal to everybody.

6

So, sifting through the news that has been published through the years, what might one choose to represent the local news of Essex? When reading through thousands of local rags from Essex and surrounding counties, it is hard to know which stories to select and which to leave out. In the end, it has to be the items that best entertain the reader, the articles that represent the times in which they were written; and above all, those that give us a fuller understanding of the values and concerns of those living in centuries past.

"The principal tradesmen of Dunmow have agreed to close their shops on the day after Christmas Day"

(ESSEX WEEKLY NEWS: December 18th 1868).

"Coggeshall - The tradesmen of the town have agreed to close their shops on the 24th inst. until the 28th inst. in order to afford the assistants the opportunity of spending the interim with their friends."

(HALSTEAD GAZETTE: December 17th 1857)

This was significant at a time just before official Bank Holidays, when postal deliveries were still being made on Christmas Day. The first official Bank Holidays were introduced in 1871.

"We understand that most of the tradesmen at Cheshunt have resolved to close their shops on Whit Monday, that day being one of the Bank Holidays by Act of Parliament." *"During next Monday, as it is a Bank Holiday, the principal tradesmen of Waltham Cross will keep their shops closed."* (WALTHAM ABBEY & CHESHUNT WEEKLY TELEGRAPH: May 18th 1872 and August 3rd 1872)

The same news-paper later that August reported a bank-holiday outing that had taken over 100 employees of the Cheshunt Ordnance Factory by train to Hunstanton for the day. For many, it would have been the first time they'd seen the sea.

As they are today, so were our local papers nearly three hundred years ago: a mixture of international news, national news and (slowly but increasingly), local news. International items took time to reach the press, but the bush-telegraph was well established and stories from within our shores must already have been on the lips of many, by the time they were published.

International news...

STRANGE SEAT - *A more striking conjunction of civilization and barbarism could hardly be given than by the fact related in the following anecdote:* - *An English lady lately passing to Constantinople in a steam vessel, was about to sit down on a convenient looking basket which stood on the deck, when, to her utter astonishment, she was warned by the Commander not to do so, as it contained the head of the Governor of the Dardanelles, on its way to be fixed up before the gates of the Seraglio.*

ESSEX & SUFFOLK TIMES: October 12th 1839

There is always something a bit special about reading tales of almost legendary characters and events...

We beg attention to the following extract of a letter from a gentleman in Louisianna, dated April 12th to a member of Congress...
Colonel [Davy] Crocket was found within the Alamo in an angle made by two houses, lying on his back, a smile of scorn on his lips - a knife in his hand, a dead Mexican lying across his body, and twenty-two lying pell-mell before him in the angle.

ESSEX STANDARD: June 24th 1836

BATTLE OF BALAKLAVA [Charge of the Light Brigade]
...The Earl of Lucan was desired to advance rapidly... From some misconception of the instruction... the Lieut.-General considered he was bound to attack at all hazards and he accordingly ordered Major-General the Earl of Cardigan to move forward with the Light Brigade. This order was obeyed in the most spirited and gallant manner. Lord Cardigan charged with the utmost vigour; attacked a battery which was

firing upon the advancing squadrons, and having passed beyond it, engaged the Russian cavalry in its rear; but there his troops were assailed by artillery and infantry as well as cavalry, and necessarily retired, having committed much havoc among the enemy. They affected this movement without haste or confusion; but the loss they have sustained has, I deeply lament, been very severe, in officers, men and horses, counterbalanced only by the brilliancy of the attack and the gallantry, order and discipline which distinguished it, forming a striking contrast to the enemy's cavalry...

CHELMSFORD CHRONICLE: November 17th 1854

[In other words, Lord Raglan, who wrote this dispatch was doing his darnedest to conjure victory out of utter defeat, conceal to some extent just how great the losses were, and try to cover his tracks. Just over six hundred horsemen had been sent, swords in hand, to attack 5,000 Russians armed with heavy artillery. Though the losses were slightly less than the four hundred first reported, it was seen as a monumental cock-up, whilst being continually represented as a demonstration of true British valour.]

As far as the Victorian newspaper reporters were concerned, heroism did not involve taking avoiding action when the enemy fired at you, as this item from the American Civil War suggests...

A letter describing the 'Battle of Bull's Run' says, 'Orders were given to the men to lie upon their faces when not in motion and menaced by the artillery. However proper this precaution may have been at the time, it afterwards turned out to be one of the most fatal causes of the demoralisation of the division. It was so frequently repeated that some regiments at last could not be made to stand at any point whatever, the least report of cannon or musketry sending them instantly upon their knees. I saw an entire company grovel in the dust at the accidental snapping of a percussion cap of one of their own rifles.'

ESSEX STANDARD: August 16th 1861

Our heroes were supposed to be made of sterner stuff...

The second attempt of Captain Webb to swim across the Channel has been crowned with success after a display of indomitable courage and extraordinary powers of endurance... on Wednesday morning, he touched the sands on the French coast... having remained in the water without even touching a boat on his way, no less than 21¾ hours...
Captain Webb was also accompanied by two small rowing boats in immediate attendance upon himself... one containing his cousin and one of the referees who had been appointed to see fair play...

Nothing occurred particularly worthy of comment until about nine o'clock, when Captain Webb complained of being stung by a jelly fish and asked for a little brandy...

ESSEX STANDARD:
August 27th 1875

National news...

A club of a very whimsical nature is lately established at Maidstone in Kent under the name of the Jiggy Joggies: it is composed entirely of unmarried ladies who alternately meet at each other's houses and never admit anything married or masculine into their society during club hours, which are usually from five in the evening to eleven at night.

CHELMSFORD CHRONICLE: March 22nd 1765

There was lately taken out of the Hackney River a monstrous creature of a fish which has four eyes, its head like a jack, two arms like a child, paw'd like a bear, claws like an eagle and a tail like an eel, hath a crown on his nose and is six foot in length.

PILBOROUGH'S WEEKLY COLCHESTER JOURNAL: January 31st 1736

The other day, a laughable circumstance occurred at Barnsley, in the cottage of a labouring man named Gibbins. The story runs thus - a relation of Gibbins, who lives in Manchester, sent him a goose. Its appearance led Gibbins to believe that goosy was ready for the spit. After it had hung before the fire about twenty minutes, a neighbour of Gibbins popped in to have a peep at his present, who soon discovered by the appearance of the gravy that all was not right. Gibbins, who had not previously observed it, was struck with the same impression, and had it immediately taken away from the fire and opened, when the following articles were found inside the goose, which had been put there with a view, no doubt, to save expense. The first article met with was a letter directed for Gibbins, one for his sister and a third for a distant relation, 30s for a half-year's rent, a set of knitting needles, a print of Her Majesty going in procession to Whitehall, two Godfrey bottles, and six hanks of whitey-brown thread, a receipt for making ginger beer, a new set of Christmas hymns and some confectionery.

ESSEX & SUFFOLK TIMES: January 5th 1838

The reigning winter dress among young men of fashion will be lapelled cloth frocks, the colour brown, with an intermixture of scarlet, and large stand-up collars of crimson sattin: white cashmere waistcoats, the button-holes worked or embroidered with different coloured silks. White ribbed silk stockings, under close Spanish leather boots, rising no higher than the calf of the leg, with turning down tops, will be a distinguishing part of tasty dress.

CHELMSFORD CHRONICLE: December 3rd 1790

Saturday morning, a filthy maniac known about the markets by the name of Mad Moll seized a young gentleman in Fleet Market, declaring he was her husband, and insisting on the rights of her assumed condition. The poor youth expostulated in pain; she swore nothing again should separate them, and had nearly suffocated him with caresses when some persons interfered and rescued him.

ESSEX UNION: November 17th 1809

National disasters received full attention from the local press, sometimes in a rather contradictory way.

Yesterday morning an express was received at the Admiralty from Lord Howe with the melancholy tidings of the loss of the Royal George, of 100 guns... It appears that her lower deck ports were not lashed in and the ship thwarting on the tide, with a squall from the north-west filled her with water and she sunk in the space of about three minutes. Her masthead remains just above the surface, but it is generally thought it will be impossible ever to buoy her up. She was a fine ship and was built at Woolwich in 1756. In addition to the above

unfortunate event, it is with the greatest regret we inform our readers that... upwards of 400 men and 200 women perished in her.

[Only officers were named. The final figure would be more than 800 drowned.]

IPSWICH JOURNAL: September 7th 1782

One of the country's largest warships had sunk at Portsmouth whilst undergoing routine maintenance. Later in the same article, the large number of females would be explained... *"...Of these the bulk were of the lowest order of prostitutes: but not a few, the wives of the warrant and petty officers."* Also was added... *"We are assured from very good nautical authority that the Royal George ought to have been broken up at least 3 years ago."* [Hang on; you've just described her as a fine ship!]

Local news...

The Faithless Wife and Unfortunate Gallant - *One night last week, a labouring man went to his lodgings in George Yard, Saffron* [Walden] *Hill, when he found the room door locked, and there being a light in the room, he saw through the keyhole a man's clothes lying on the ground, when he swore if his wife did not open the door he would force it, and would kill any man he should find. He then went downstairs to get an implement to effect his purpose, and during his absence, the gallant jumped from the window (two stories), broke his leg, and otherwise so injured himself as to be taken to St. Bartholemew's Hospital without hopes of recovery.*

                    COUNTY CHRONICLE: July 7th 1812

Edward Clarke one of the unfortunate men upon whom the punishment of death was inflicted at Chelmsford for their violation of the laws, yesterday se'nnight, left a request in writing, drawn up on the morning of his execution, in the following terms - "I, Edward Clarke, now in a few hours expecting to die, do sincerely wish as my last request, that three of my fingers be taken from my hands, to be given to my three children as a warning to them, as my fingers were the cause of bringing myself to the gallows and my children to poverty." - Two persons were then named whom he exhorted to see this extraordinary injunction carried into effect, and it was strictly complied with.

COLCHESTER GAZETTE: August 20th 1814

Colchester - *This day, a numerous and riotous mob assembled, and on account of the dearness of corn, said they would stop all wagons that brought corn or flour into the town, and make them unload it and sell it at such prices as they should think proper. This determination they began between eight and nine o'clock in the morning, and stopped the wagon of Mrs. Parmenter of Wormingford on North Hill and so abused the drivers they abandoned their wagon and horses. Application was made to the Recorder, who immediately with a manly courage himself entered into the thickest of the mob, with his own hands secured several of the ringleaders, and committed them; and by a judicious address to the others, prevailed on them to disperse. Thus by a spirited and sensible conduct of an active magistrate, this town has been rescued from a threatened violence, and peace restored.*

CHELMSFORD CHRONICLE: July 31st 1789

Ship Launch At Wivenhoe

This most riveting spectacle which was announced for Monday night, drew together an immense number of persons. The frigate intended to be launched was named the Pearl; she carries 22 guns, and was built by Mr. Sainty. At the appointed time, when it was expected she would have been embraced by her natural element, some defects arose, and great disappointment ensued. At this time, we are told, two hundred persons were on board. The fatal accident at Manchester was not then known among them. The cradle which had been prepared to guide the ship, got on one side, owing, we are told, to her great weight and the soil of the foundation giving way. Great apprehensions were in consequence manifested by the builder, that she would not reach her destination with safety; he, therefore, in preference to so great a risk, concluded to postpone further operations until Monday next, the 17th March.

CHELMSFORD CHRONICLE: 14th March 1828

Ambrose Witney [a gipsy] *was charged by Mr. Alston, farmer of Lt. Bromley with stealing a quantity of sallows for the purpose of making linen pegs... The prisoner was sentenced to 2 months hard labour.*

IPSWICH & COLCHESTER TIMES: February 18th 1859

[Shortly afterwards, this weekly paper would become the East Anglian Daily Times]

In January1852, the Ipswich Express reported a case that had been brought to court in Essex involving a boat that had run aground in St. Osyth Creek, thereby damaging the oyster bed. Damages were being claimed, but the case was unsuccessful as the oyster fishermen, in spite of paying for the right to fish for oysters, the judgement was that they could not claim ownership of what was considered to be a public highway. Protection of their livelihood by certain groups of Essex fishermen would be a topic that would re-emerge some years later.

ALLEGED PIRACY ON THE ESSEX COAST

What is described as 'an act of piracy' took place near the Bench Head Buoy, off Brightlingsea on March 9th. Several Burnham smacks were on the open cultching grounds there, the men having been engaged in securing a cargo of cultch and shell for use in the private fishing grounds on the Crouch. This practice has caused much ill feeling, the fishermen of Tollesbury and neighbourhood contending that the taking of the shell destroys the spat which in the season affords a living to them. On several occasions they have threatened to run down Burnham boats engaged in the work unless they desisted, and although they have never put this threat into execution, they proceeded on Friday to take the law into their own hands with a vengeance. The Emiline, the Alma, the Wonder and the Rose, all from Burnham were on the point of finishing their cruise, when three Tollesbury vessels, each apparently armed with two or three hands were seen to be bearing down upon them...

In this article, Captain Barker of the Emiline describes how... *"20 or 30 men, armed with sticks and shovels... told us they would do for us this time. We could do nothing but keep our mouths shut and see them throw our cargo overboard. They told us never to come there again or it would be the worse for us."*

However, not all of the Burnham boats submitted without a fight... *Ambrose* [Captain of the Rose] *had gone into the cabin for a gun which he loaded and with which he threatened to blow out the brains of any man who attempted to board the Rose. As none of the Tollesbury men desired to meet this fate, the Rose was allowed to escape with her cargo of Cultch.*

SOUTHEND ON SEA OBSERVER: March 22nd 1894

Burnham-on-Crouch

Early attempts by Burnham to persuade magistrates to issue warrants against the Tollesbury men for piracy proved problematic. It is doubtful if the magistrates had ever encountered a situation like this and they were unsure just how far their jurisdiction extended. However, within a week, Col. Lucas, J.P. of Witham had issued summonses against twelve Tollesbury men. Questions were asked in the House of Commons. The protection of the local oyster fishery was fast becoming a major issue.

But in the meantime, there was a legal case to answer...

Great was the interest shown in the case by the mariners and fishermen of the places concerned. They literally swarmed into the court. Two hundred turned up from Tollesbury, a hundred from Mersea, and a number from Burnham. Mr. Warburton, the learned counsel for the

16

prosecution, who is an Essex man... began by drawing a graphic picture of piracy in the olden days when gentlemen sailing under mysterious flags with pistols in their belts, bucket boots upon their legs and slouched hats on their heads roamed the seas seeking what ships they might plunder and what sailors they might subject to terror or death. The Mersea case, he admitted, was of a milder order... but... there had been the spirit of the old buccaneer shown by the Tollesbury fishermen, who disputing the right of the Burnham men to dredge for cultch off the Mersea coast, bore down upon their ships, boarded them twenty-eight strong, armed with thick sticks and shovels... threw out their cargo and threatened the sailors that if they weren't civil they would pitch them bodily after it.

ESSEX COUNTY CHRONICLE: April 13th 1894

Though the Tollesbury men claimed in their defence they were only trying to '*preserve from destruction the most valuable oyster fishery in the world,*' this could not prevent five of the men being sent for trial at the County Assize. So it was that in July 1894, Jas Lazzell, Chas. Potter, William Crabb, John Taylor and Stephen Appleton were listed for trial on a charge of '*Piracy on the high seas.*' Mr. Justice Day was not impressed... "*This case in the Blackwater,*" he remarked, "*if it was an offence at all, it was one of a most trumpery and ridiculous character!*" [ESSEX COUNTY CHRONICLE: June 22nd 1894]

It may have been ridiculous but it was successful. Later that year, local papers reported Parliament's successful introduction of '*The Shellfish Bill*' enabling Mersea and Tollesbury to pass by-laws forbidding any further removal of their valuable oyster beds.

From the very earliest days of the local press, publishers realised that to sell papers, you had to entertain your audience. So, many wonderful tales have appeared through the years…

On Tuesday night last, John Sommerford, a sawyer, (who came into the upper gallery in Covent Garden at the latter end of the play), was pressing forward in order to get a better place. He was pushed by a person who took disgust at his standing before him, and he tumbled over into the pit (the depth of thirty feet) between two rows of the audience, without receiving any damage. He got up immediately, and begging the people to let him pass, swore he would bring the fellow down with the d___l to him, which he accordingly did, and carried him before a magistrate who bound him over. When the sawyer fell down, one of his legs hit Mrs. Gunter on the head, which stunn'd and frighted her very much, but a surgeon, being in the house, let her blood immediately and she was afterwards perfectly well. After the performance was over, Sommerford went to Mr. Rich and facetiously told him that he had made himself free of the gallery and hoped he should have the liberty of going into it whenever he pleased. This Mr. Rich consented to, provided always that he did not come out of it in the same abrupt manner - to which proviso, the sawyer readily agreed.

PILBOROUGH'S COLCHESTER JOURNAL: February 10th 1739

The following is an alarming evidence of the progress of the photo-graphic art... a lady last week had her likeness taken by a photographist and he executed it so well that her husband prefers it to the original.

BRAINTREE & BOCKING ADVERTISER: July 11th. 1860

By some extraordinary mistake, the Sheriff appointed for Huntingdon and Cambridge has been dead more than twelve months.

COLCHESTER GAZETTE: February 25th 1815

Nearly every tenth Scotsman is a bastard. The registration returns for 1858 show that 9, 256 births against 94, 939 were illegitimate.

STRATFORD TIMES & S. ESSEX GAZETTE: March 4th 1859

A very singular discovery has been made at Colchester regarding the sex of a servant who had lived 30 years in a family in that town as housemaid and nurse. Having lately paid the debt of nature, it was discovered on examining the body that the deceased had been a male. No reason is assigned for his having assumed the female garb; and he had never excited suspicion, or been the subject of bets or law-suits.

SUFFOLK CHRONICLE: April 13th 1811

[IPSWICH JOURNAL]

Mark's Tey, Oct 29, 1729,

Whereas Henry Miller, aged about 15 Years, with lank brown Hair, a freckled Complexion, and of low Stature, a Covenanted Servant to the Rev. Mr. William Bree, Rector of Mark's Tey, did run away from his Service on the 25th Day of laft September; all Perfons are hereby forbid to entertain the faid Henry Miller; and whoever fhall apprehend the faid Henry Miller, and bring him to his Mafter at Mark's-Tey near Colchefter, fhall receive a fuitable Reward from me

WILLIAM BREE.

A householder in a village between Stamford and Uppingham, in filling up his Census schedule, under the column 'Where born?' described one of his children as born 'in the parlour' and the other 'upstairs.'
ESSEX STANDARD: June 6th 1851

The following laconic epistle may be seen in the window of a coffee-house in Featherstone Street, City Road... "Stolen from this window, a china cup and saucer: the set now being incomplete, the thief may have the remainder a bargain."
ESSEX & SUFFOLK TIMES: October 12th 1839

And of course, you can never beat a bit of scandal...
CANON BAYNES, who was for some time Rector of Toppesfield, Essex... the reverend dipsomaniac who was convicted last year of obtaining money under false pretences and who was charged about ten days ago at Bow Street with being drunk and disorderly, has been sent to prison at Bristol for four months for stealing luggage at the railway station there. It is to be hoped that some of Mr. Baynes' relatives or former friends will endeavour, when he comes out of gaol to place him under some kind of restraint, or at least take steps to prevent him from again getting into trouble... The crisis of Mr. Baynes' clerical career occurred at Folkestone, where he was Vicar at Holy Trinity. There had been unpleasant reports about him for some time, but no open scandal, when one Sunday evening, there being a crowded congregation, he ascended the pulpit in a state of hopeless intoxication, stumbled forward and shouted hilariously, "And now dear friends, let us sing Rule Britannia."
SOUTH WEST SUFFOLK ECHO: March 22nd 1890

Obviously I am not the only one to have beeen both intrigued and entertained by our local rags. Duffield William Coller was a young apprentice shoemaker when he became hooked. In the 1820s, whilst still in his mid-teens, he composed verses which were regularly published by the two local papers of the time. This was one...

Magnetism of a newspaper

Come gentle muse, let's touch a spring
To chase the gloom of care away;
A spark of humour hither bring,
To burnish up an idle lay.

Come let's the 'mighty magic' doff
Full naked to the public eye,
Which forms the very basis of
Newspaper popularity.

Hold - there's no magic in the case;
Newspapers are a looking glass,
Where ev'ry one can see their face,
And their beloved subject pass.

There we can solitary sit,
And see the medley of the world,
By ev'ry passion's frantic fit,
Turn'd topsy-turvey, crisp'd and curl'd

Most readers have a theme apart
For private curiosity;
A subject penn'd upon the heart,
That only can gratify.
The tender virgin tasks her brains,
To learn what lady of sixteen
Is bound in Hymen's golden chains
By stolen trip to Gretna Green.

The widow - she whose youthful bloom
Some twenty years ago was shed,
Leaves weeping o'er her husband's tomb,
To see what neighbour's wife is dead.

The politician marks the flames
That raising laid a city low;
Then points his finger, and exclaims,
'I always said it would be so.'

In short, all classes high and low,
Peruse its columns with delight;
At least they did some time ago,
Ere poverty engender'd spite.

C H E L M S F O R D,

SO named from a Ford through the river Chelmer, over which there is now a beautiful stone bridge. No town in the kingdom can surpass it for taste, convenience, and comfort. The Shire Hall is a magnificent edifice, the beautiful pediment which adorns the front, and the figures of Justice, Wisdom, and Mercy, over the windows, are admired by all travellers. The military officers greatly add to the fashionable pleasures of the town. The four pipes on the four sides of the Conduit, from which the water flows, remind us of the Four Twenty Thousands now ready to flow from the Wheel of Fortune, to the adventurers in the present Grand Lottery. Two Hundred Thousand Pounds in Prizes, and only Five Thousand Numbers, will be drawn in one day, and one Number must gain Eighty Thousand Pounds.

SHARES ARE NOW TO BE HAD OF

H. KELHAM,

PHŒNIX LIBRARY, CHELMSFORD,

Who recommends an immediate purchase, as, from the scarcity of Tickets, they are likely to be much dearer, and it would give him great pleasure to see the Forty Capital Prizes, which will be drawn

On the 14th February, Valentine's Day,

DISTRIBUTED IN THIS COUNTY.

ESSEX UNION:February 2nd 1810

But now they read it with a curse -
The cause I'm quite afraid to quote;
But dip your fingers in your purse,
You'll find it dubb'd - 'a county note.'

ESSEX REVIEW: Vol. IX

D.W. Coller would never finish his apprenticeship. Instead, he would join the ranks of the papers he so loved reading, rising eventually to editing two of Essex's longest running local rags.

Through the years, certain topics have been perennial favourites with Essex readers. Take for example… Stories on the subject of **'Love and Marriage.'**

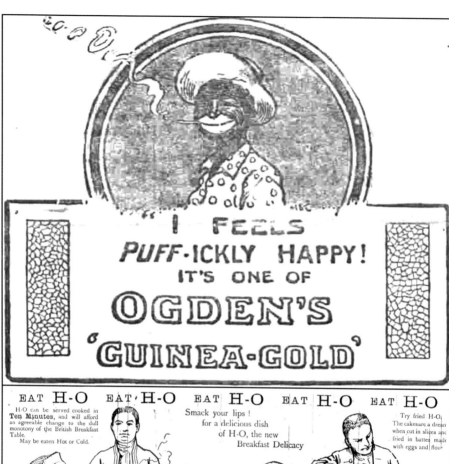

I FEELS PUFF-ICKLY HAPPY!
IT'S ONE OF
OGDEN'S
'GUINEA-GOLD'

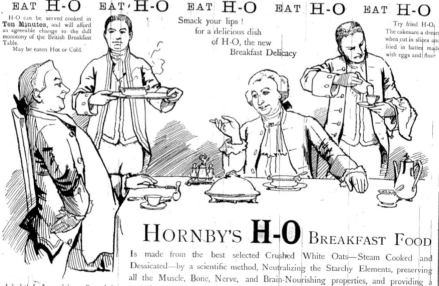

EAT **H-O** EAT **H-O** EAT **H-O** EAT **H-O** EAT **H-O**

H-O can be served cooked in **Ten Minutes**, and will afford an agreeable change to the dull monotony of the British Breakfast Table.
May be eaten Hot or Cold.

Smack your lips ! for a delicious dish of H-O, the new Breakfast Delicacy

Try fried H-O, The cakes are a dream when cut in slices and fried in batter made with eggs and flour

HORNBY'S **H-O** BREAKFAST FOOD

Is made from the best selected Crushed White Oats—Steam Cooked and Dessicated—by a scientific method, Neutralizing the Starchy Elements, preserving all the Muscle, Bone, Nerve, and Brain-Nourishing properties, and providing a delightful Appetizing, Sustaining, and Digestible Article of Healthy Diet, supplying the two main vitalizing needs of existence, viz : heat to maintain the proper temperature of the body, and material to repair the wasted tissue.

A Shilling Packet of the H-O Breakfast Food is sufficient for a week's consumption in an ordinary Family, costing less than a half-penny per meal per person. You can come again and again for delicious H-O, which will be enjoyed with zest by young and old. Entirely supersedes Porridge, Bread and Milk, &c.

22

Chapter 2 - Love & Marriage

A Treaty of Marriage is concluded as far as settlements and content of parties, between the daughter of Lord Howe and the Earl of Altamont, an Irish peer. The lady's fortune is £73,000.
CHELMSFORD CHRONICLE: February 9th 1787

Being able to have a good choice of potential husband was the main reason for thousands of young girls in the mid-nineteenth century being encouraged to emigrate. For one reason or another, Australia had a hugely disproportionate population. How much this had been down to the fact that ten times as many men were transported as convicts than women, or whether the gold-rush and other enticements had been the reason is hard to say. But women were desperately needed, not merely as the adverts suggested, as domestic servants.

FEMALE EMIGRATION - The 18th party of female emigrants under the auspices of the Female Emigration Fund left Blackwall on Monday, accompanied by their friends and the committee to join their destined ship, the Northumberland, in which they are to embark for Port Phillip, the future scene of their labours,

> ## EMIGRATION to NEW SOUTH WALES
>
> THE Agent-General for the Colony will provide approved applicants with passages to Sydney in first-class steamships, on payment of the undermentioned REDUCED RATES :—
>
> Married Couple not exceeding 40 years, £6.
> Single Men not exceeding 35 years, £4.
> Single Women   do   do.   £2.
> Children of 3 and under 14 years £1 ; under 3 years free.
>
> Farmers, Agricultural and Railway Labourers, Vine Dressers, and Female Domestics, are much required.
>
> Further information may be obtained from the Emigration Department, New South Wales Government Offices 5, Westminster Chambers, S.W. ; or of the Local Agent, THOS. B. GRUBB, Long Melford

and let us hope successful ones. The Northumberland made a similar voyage last year, with 62 emigrants. This time, she is to carry 36 additions to our colonies, most of them young girls.
ESSEX STANDARD: July 25th 1851

23

Royal Mail Steamers to

UNITED STATES & CANADA.
FROM LIVERPOOL.

CIRCASSIAN.....For QUEBEC .... Oct. 30
NOVA SCOTIAN.For HALIFAX & BALTIMORE. Nov. 4
POLYNESIAN ...For HALIFAX & PORTLAND. Nov. 6
PERUVIAN ......For HALIFAX & BALTIMORE Nov. 13
HANOVERIAN...For HALIFAX & BALTIMORE Nov. 18
SARDINIAN ......For HALIFAX & PORTLAND. Nov. 20

OCEAN RATES:
Saloon, 12 to 21 GUINEAS ; Intermediate, £7 7s. ;
STEERAGE AT LOWEST RATES.
Through Tickets at special rates to Montreal, Toronto,
Chicago, and to all parts of Canada and the Western
States.
☞NOTE.—The best, quickest, and cheapest route for
Manitoba and the Great North West is by the Mail
Steamers of this Line.
ASSISTED PASSAGES TO CANADA.
☞ Passengers landing at Halifax, Portland, or
Baltimore, and going inland, are accompanied on the
Railway by the Company's special conductors.
PAMPHLETS on Canada, Manitoba, and the Western
States free on application.
Full Particulars from ALLAN BROTHERS and Co.,
James Street, Liverpool ; or
    THOS. J. RALLING,
1857   Essex Standard Office, Colchester

Weddings could be hurried affairs. In some cases, time was of the essence, and a quickly arranged marriage essential, usually to ensure the first child would not be a bastard. However, the reason for speed here was very different.

We are informed of the following extraordinary wedding: Thomas Ashman if Lidhurst in the New Forest, Hants, aged 89 was lately married to Mother Springer of Minsted in the forest, aged 103. It seems these two old people had such juvenile inclinations that they could not stay till Lent was over and therefore had a dispensation to play the fool.
PILBOROUGH'S COLCHESTER JOURNAL: April 7th 1739

Not everyone who married was totally satisfied by his choice. If your wife displeased you, then you could always sell her to someone else. The Ipswich Journal of July 19th 1729 reported that George Wyatt, a shoemaker from Blackfriars, sold his wife to George Chiddington for a full pot of beer. Others demanded a slightly higher price.

Thursday, a butcher at Halstead sold his wife to a wealthy farmer in that neighbourhood for three guineas and a good supper; the woman acceding to the bargain, the farmer immediately took her home and seemed very well pleased with his bargain.

IPSWICH JOURNAL: February 8th 1777

A remarkably detailed wife auction in Devon appeared in the Chelmsford Gazette, just after Christmas 1822. The public, we are told, were attracted to Plymouth in consequence of a notice previously posted that a man was intending to dispose of his wife by public auction.

The lady was not only young and handsome, but she rode to town in the morning on her own horse of her own free will and accord and with consent of her husband who was to act the part of the auctioneer on the occasion.

The husband put the article up at once and asked for bidders. 'Five shillings' was the first offer - 'ten' - the next, 'fifteen' - and so on until the ostler aforesaid bade 'three pounds,' when, to the evident disappointment of the auctioneer, as well as of the lady, two Constables took charge of 'the goods,' and with them the auctioneer, and carried them both directly to the Guildhall, where the chief Magistrate was sitting.

CHELMSFORD GAZETTE: December 27th 1822

Wife-selling was, of course, and always had been, strictly illegal, even with the consent of both parties. The couple had only lived together for a short time after their marriage, she having given birth to two children by other men. Believing the auction was legal and having been advised that a man from Plymstock called Kane would offer £20 for her, they had agreed on this course of action. However, Kane had not turned up and they had paid the Ostler of the nearby Inn to bid up to £20 for her to ensure she should not be sold too cheaply. The two were bound over to appear at the next Court Session, though as neither had any money left, their promise to appear had to suffice.

On Saturday last, a man named Feake led his wife into Chipping Ongar Market, Essex by a halter, and there exposed her for sale. She was soon purchased by a young man, a blacksmith of High Ongar at the price of 10s. Her person was by no means unpleasing and she appeared to be about 25 years of age. The collector of the tolls actually demanded and received from the purchaser the customary charge of 1d which is always paid upon livestock sold therein per head.

BURY & NORWICH POST: December 31st 1823

Unfortunate Purchase of a Wife.—On Monday, one Casmore, of Cow-cross, sold his wife, to whom he had been married ten years, in Smithfield-market, to a dustman, for 12s. to whom the lady, nothing loth, was delivered in due form, viz. with a halter round her neck, and so far all parties seemed content; but as love is a fleeting passion, the spirit of turbulence found little difficulty in banishing it from the fair one's breast, and in consequence of some contradiction from her new inamorato, while passing down Field-lane, in the course of the afternoon, she fairly knocked him down. The Man of Dust was preparing, like another Petruchio, to tame his Shrew, by arguments of an equally forcible nature, when, fortunately for her, a Jack Tar espoused her cause, towed her off triumphantly towards Wapping, and left the forsaken swain to brood over his lost money, exclaim against the fickleness of the sex, and seek consolation in the best manner he could, for the effects of his drubbing.

If however, your wife left you, then an advert like this might be necessary...

Whereas Elizabeth, the wife of James Harrington constable at Burnham hath absconded from her said husband, he hereby gives notice that he will not be answerable for any debts she may contract.

CHELMSFORD CHRONICLE: March 4th 1808

In an 1888 account in the Essex Telegraph, a man arrested for blacking a woman's eyes and knocking out her teeth gave as his excuse, *'It was dark and he thought she was his wife.'*

When William Rayner was brought for trial at Halstead Petty Sessions for assaulting his wife, she proved to be rather more formidable than she first appeared. Constables Johnson and Kemp arrived at the Rayner's house one Saturday night after receiving news of a disturbance. Johnson... saw Mary Rayner and her five children in the street crying (It was raining quite fast), who said she was obliged to leave her house for her husband had been beating her and said he would kill her and the children. Johnson... met Rayner and took him into custody to prevent any mischief being done. Rayner was bound over to keep the peace towards his wife for three months... His wife, thinking the sentence was not sufficient, became very boisterous, said she would never live with him again, and gave him a child she had in her arms and told him to take all the children, for she intended to leave him for ever. Her abuse ran so fast that the Bench were obliged to order her to be turned out of the room. The husband promised never to beat or contradict her any more and said in future she should always have her own way.

ESSEX STANDARD: January 11th 1834

Last week, the following odd affair happened in Shadwell: a shop-keeper and his wife, having had words together, at last came to blows, and in the battle the woman had the worst of it, which so highly exasperated her that she took her husband up with a warrant and had him before a Justice who, on the wife's complaint, thought it necessary to bind him over to his good behaviour: and whilst the Constable had him in custody, waiting for security, the artful slut slipt home, stripp'd the house and shop of the most valuable effects and mov'd off with them, whereby she has entirely ruined her husband, who is now forced to abscond for fear of his creditors.

PILBOROUGH'S COLCHESTER JOURNAL: February 10th 1739

For some, getting married at all could prove rather more difficult than you might expect...

Monday last, a couple who had been out-asked in Marybone Church, went thither to be married. As the Rev. Clergyman was reading the ceremony, when he came to the words, "Wilt thou have this man to thy wedded husband?" the woman answered, "No!" Upon the minister's asking the reason, the woman said, "I have told him several times I would not marry him." The clergyman then asked her why she came to the church. She replied, "I came to tell you I will not marry him," and immediately went away with two men who came to attend the ceremony, leaving the disappointed bridegroom in the church.
CHELMSFORD CHRONICLE: September 28th 1764

The Rev. Agassiz of Gt. Clacton was marrying a couple the other day at St. Osyth in the absence of the incumbent, when requiring the bridegroom to repeat after him the words, "I take thee to be my lawful wedded wife, for better or worse" etc, when the man with ill timed levity altered the formula to "I'll take her for better but not for worse": the Rev. gentleman immediately closed the book and quitted the church.
BURY & NORWICH POST: October 16th 1865

Saffron Walden - *...A buxom lady of some 60 summers , having once tasted the bliss of wedded life fancied that she should feel more comfortable with a second partner to help her on in the remainder of her journey through this vale of tears, and having in some manner, secured the affections, notice or consent of a gentleman whom she considered suitable for her hand and heart forthwith put aside the feminine modesty usually displayed by the 'weaker vessels' on such occasions and put in the banns herself so that there should be no delay.* (WALTHAM ABBEY & CHESHUNT WEEKLY TELEGRAPH: November 16th 1872)

Unfortunately, what the lady didn't know was the man in question already had a wife and four children. He was highly embarassed to hear his name read out in church, but it *"caused no small amount of amusement in the neighbourhood."*

Some evenings since, a young woman named Esther Parker accompanied a sailor who had for some time paid his addresses to her, to a public house, the sign of the Town of Ramsgate, near the London dock. During the evening, the sailor, with characteristic gallantry paid more attention to another girl than the love-sick Esther could endure, and suddenly rising from the table, she rushed out of the room and plunged into the lock. A boatman who saw her leap into the water, with great humanity followed, and at the peril of his life, saved hers. The giddy tar felt as a man should do on the occasion, and on the morning after took the necessary steps to have the marriage banns proclaimed.

ESSEX UNION: November 17th 1809

Halsted - About the average number of valentines, 10,000 or 12,000, passed through the Halsted office, the large influx on Friday causing a delay of an hour in the morning delivery.

MALDON EXPRESS: February 20th 1879

St. Valentine did not lack votaries in Maldon this year, for the letters and packets which passed through the Maldon Post Office... reached between 5,000 and 6,000.

More than 2,000 valentines passed through the Ongar Post-Office on Thursday night.

ESSEX NEWSMAN: February 22nd 1873

Marriage in Lapland - It is death in Lapland to marry without the consent of her parents or friends. When a young man has formed an attachment to a female, the fashion is to appoint their friends to meet to behold the two young parties run a race together. The maid is allowed in starting, the advantage of a third part of the race, so that it is impossible except willing of herself that she should be overtaken. If the maid overrun her suitor, the matter is ended; he must never have her, it being penal for the man to renew the motion of marriage. But if the virgin has an affection for him, though at the first, she runs hard, to try the truth of his love, she will... pretend some casualty and make a voluntary halt before she cometh to the mark or end of the race. Thus, none are compelled to marry against their own wills; and this is the cause that in this poor country, the married people are richer in their own contentment than in other lands where so many forced matches make feigned love and cause real unhappiness.

CHELMSFORD GAZETTE: August 30th 1822

CURIOUS ANECDOTE - *Mr. Coke, of Longfield in the County of Derby is the father of several amiable and accomplished daughters. One of the tenants on his estate a young farmer of respectable address and attainments, had by the depression of the times become in arrears for his rent; his landlord sent for him and expostulated with him on the subject, and hinted to him, that with his handsome person he might easily obtain a wife amongst some of his richer neighbours, that would soon enable him to pay off his arrears and place him in better circumstances in the world. The young farmer listened to the advice, looked thoughtful, and departed. In a few days he returned again, and told his landlord he had been reflecting seriously on their conversation, and would his counsel. At this interview one of the daughters of his wealthy landlord was present. In a short time afterwards, it was discovered that the young farmer had effectually taken the hint, and by an elopement to Gretna-Green, had become Mr. Coke's son-in-law.*

CHELMSFORD GAZETTE: December 6th 1822

[This story originated in the Birmingham Chronicle, but was taken up by countless other regional papers, including the Ipswich Journal]

In all likelihood, these last two items are as improbable as they sound. But they make for good reading nevertheless. As can be seen, a bit of **humour** was important to Essex readers, and there are plenty of examples of old newspaper items that seem to justify their place merely by way of entertaining the reader...

Chapter 3 - Humour

In May 1739, a number of non-conformist preachers were drawing huge crowds. These included Charles Wesley and Rev. Mr. Whitefield (pictured below). But all of their followers may not have been as devoted as they may have liked...

Among such constant attendants on Mr. Whitefield, Shock Egerton, the most dextrous pickpocket about town, lately return'd from Transportation [from America], *never fails to be a constant hearer, and no doubt makes a better collection than can be found in any of the plates handed about.*

PILBOROUGH'S COLCHESTER JOURNAL: May 26th 1739

Grantham: *A few days ago, four bucks assembled at an inn in this neighbourhood to drink a glass and play a game at cards. The glass circulating very briskly, before midnight they became so intoxicated that not one of them was able to determine how the game stood.; and several disputes interspersed with a considerable number of oaths ensued, till they agreed to let the cards lie and endeavoured to drink themselves sober. Shortly after they resumed the game, and each man* *imagining himself capable of directing the rest, they soon came again to very high words; when the waiter, fearful that some bad consequences might ensue, let them know that it was near three o'clock and if any of the gentlemen pleased, he would wait on them home. But instead of complying with his request, the geniusses looked upon it as an indignity offered them and declared, with the most horrid imprecations, that not one of them would depart till daylight. In the height of their anger, an uncommon noise in the chimney engaged their attention when, looking towards the fireplace, a black spectre made its appearance, and crying out in a hollow menacing tone, "My father has sent me for you, infamous reprobates!", they all in the greatest fright, flew out of the room without staying to take their hats, in broken accents confessing their sins and begging for mercy. - It appears that the master of the inn, finding that he could not get rid of his troublesome guests, and having a chimney-sweeper in the house, sweeping some chimneys, gave the boy directions to descend into the room as above related, while he stood at a distance and enjoyed the droll scene of the bucks' flight.*

CHELMSFORD CHRONICLE: March 29th 1765

On Thursday afternoon an immense concourse of people congregated on the meadows between Quay lane and Lady's bridge at Sudbury to witness an exploit of a clown in John Powell's equestrian troupe, John Garrad. He announced his intention to sail on the river in a common tub drawn by four geese: amid cheers he started and an accomplished the distance of near a mile in half an hour. He gratified a large crowd.

SOUTH SUFFOLK & ESSEX FREE PRESS: February 18th 1858

The following is the wording used to address a letter which passed through Baythorne End post office.

Run postman run
And deliver this letter
Ovington is the place of abode
Near the Kicking Dickie [a pub at Gestingthorpe]
On the Halstead road.

SOUTH SUFFOLK & ESSEX FREE PRESS: March 8th. 1860

SUBURBAN ESSEX

A ROMANTIC CAREER.

WOMAN'S LIFE OF DISGUISE.

In the office of the woman's ward of West Ham Workhouse, in the presence of the master, Mr. D. W. Morgans, and a nurse, Catherine Coombes related the circumstances under which for forty-two years she has dressed and worked as a man. Catherine Coombes, or Charles Wilson as she would rather be called—came to the West Ham Union on Saturday night with an order from the relieving officer at Canning Town, Mr. Lewis. Dressed in man's clothing, neat, clean, and respectable, she looked like a clerk or artisan, and went to the men's ward. Then she asked to see the matron and doctor, and begged respectfully to make a statement. Then she made the startling remark, "I am a woman."

In fragments Mrs. Coombes told her story, answering questions in a quiet, pleasant voice. She said, "I was born at Axbridge, in Somerset, in 1834, and received a very good education at the Cheltenham Ladies' College. Unfortunately I left school at sixteen and married my first cousin, a man twenty-three years older than myself, to whose ill-treatment was due my adoption of men's clothes. He ran away to London and wrote to me to say that he had a situation in Chelsea. When I reached London he pawned my clothes and finally said we must walk to Cheltenham. We did it, and I remember those roads to this day. At home again he wished to live on my mother and myself, so I ran away to my brother at Hillstop,

West Bromwich. Mr. Tozer was a painter and decorator, and helping him I learned the trade. But my husband followed me and persuaded me to open a school at Hazenville. Again he ill-treated me, and I returned to Hilltop, but at-tending the funeral of a cousin I met him again, and he said he would never leave me. That de-cided the matter. I went to Birmingham again, took lodgings, bought a suit of boy's clothes, and by taking lodgings at a coffee-shop on Snow-hill, for my brother, managed to make the change of clothes. I did my own up in a bundle and addressed them to my brother. Then I came to London, where I have worked ever since. I am a member of the Painters' Union, and well known as a good 'clean' painter. Everyone knows Charley Wilson. I worked thirteen years for the Peninsular and Oriental Company, living for seven years with my niece at 7 Camden-terrace, Custom House. For twenty-two years she kept house for me. Two years ago she left me, and I believe she has a situation in St. Denis, in France.

The poor woman had followed her occupation as painter and decorator until July last, and her application for admission to the workhouse arose rather from destitution, a result of being unable to get work on account of fracturing ribs in a fall from a scaffold, than a desire to seek medical aid. She is, indeed, convalescent, and is in the body of the house. While employed at Canning Town she did the best of decorative work for the Peninsular and Oriental Company, earning, with her extras, some £2 weekly. She is an intellectual person, and her husband, spoken of as having been a curate, is supposed to be dead.

ESSEX COUNTY STANDARD: October 8th 1897

Amongst amusing entries from the South West Suffolk Echo, published at Haverhill (January 2nd 1892), the following story appeared...

"Hullo Henry. What makes you look so blue this morning?"
"I've just had a tiff with my wife and she is packing to go home to see her mother."
"Pshaw! That's nothing. I've had a tiff with my wife and she has sent for her mother to come and stay with us."

A pedagogue threatened to punish a pupil who had called him a fool behind his back. "Don't, don't," begged the boy. "I won't do so again sir, never: I never will speak what I think agin in my life."
IPSWICH EXPRESS & ESSEX & SUFFOLK MERCURY: January 28th 1852

Under the headlines, *'HANNINGFIELD CLERIC AND HIS DOGS'* and *'MR. THOMAS KEMBLE'S LITTLE JOKE'* [and it was a *little* joke], in 1900 appeared the following item...

At Chelmsford on Friday, the Rev. James Prendergast of South Hanningfield was summoned for keeping a dog without a licence. P.C. Jacobs said defendant, who had two retrievers told him (witness) he had only taken out one licence because he intended leaving the parish in June. Witness replied, 'Then you intend to keep your dog for six months for nothing?'
The Chairman, Mr Kemble then proceeded to hand out the standard fine of 10s with 8s 6d costs, commenting that should he find difficulty with that he could always opt for seven days hard labour. When reminded by the Clerk that he could not award hard labour, he commented, 'Oh well, we'll omit the hard labour.'
This brought laughter in the court as did the Assistant Clerk's final comment, 'First-class misdemeanant, Sir.'

A novel shipping berth - *The crowded deck of an American packet.*
- A Californian to the skipper of ditto: *I should like to have a sleeping berth neow if you please.*
Skipper: *Why? Where have you been sleeping these last two nights since we left?*
Californian: *Wal, I have been a-sleeping a-top of a sick man, but he's got better neow and won't stand it no longer.*

A frizeur who resides within a short distance of Aldgate pump has a board with the following insciption:- 'Hair cut fashionably, philosophically and anatomically.'

ESSEX COUNTY STANDARD: April 15th 1831

But of course, nothing is ever quite so funny as the misfortunes of others...

EARLS COLNE - CURIOUS ACCIDENT

On Thursday evening last, a young man named Henry Rawlinson, son of John Rawlinson, boot-maker of this place met with a curious accident in the following manner. He was indulging in a warm bath in close proximity to a tortoise range (then in use) and whilst standing in the bath, his feet slipped, causing him to lose his balance, and falling over the

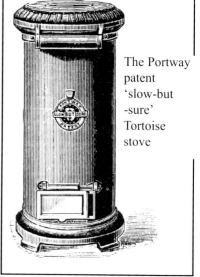

The Portway patent 'slow-but -sure' Tortoise stove

side of the bath, he was fairly seated upon the hot range, although he was off again as quickly as possible, yet he was so much burnt that he was compelled to take to his bed for some days, but under the skilful medical treatment of Mr. J. Taylor, surgeon, he has thus far progressed favourably.

SUFFOLK & ESSEX FREE PRESS: March 17th 1886

On the night of Monday the 23rd, the premises of Mr. Armstrong, Eastgate St., Bury were entered and a couple of ducks stolen. On Thursday morning, the skin of a rabbit was found on the premises, with the following note between the ears - Sir, i am very much oblige to you for the 2 Ducks And Rabbit - i shall Come after the Pig a week before Christmas. pleas to fat all your

fowls and Rabbits for the Ducks was very good but the Rabbit was tough.

HALSTEAD GAZETTE: November 19th 1857

SERVED HIM RIGHT - *A quiet looking gentleman walked down the platform in search of a place in a train which was almost full. He stopped before a carriage in which there was a vacant seat - no, not quite vacant; on it stood a small black handbag. A stout person sat next beside it in the corner.*
"Room here?" demanded the quiet gentleman.
"No," growled the stout one.
"No one is sitting there," pointing to the handbag.
"Got out - coming back - his handbag!" growled the stout passenger.
The newcomer had his own views as to how far this statement was trustworthy, for he said in his quiet tone, "I will sit there until your friend returns."
The train began to move. "Your friend is late," said the quiet one.
The train was fairly in motion. "Your friend has lost the train!" exclaimed the quiet one in a tone of sympathy. "But," he added, "...he shan't lose his property." And he hurled the black bag out of the window. The stout traveller made an ineffectual effort to save the bag,

and then burst into language not that of blessing.
The bag was, of course, his own.
SUFFOLK & ESSEX FREE PRESS: February 3rd 1886

An unusual and indecent exhibition *- On Monday last, some excitement was created in the High Street by a man appearing there without any clothes whatever. On inquiry, it was found that he had been bathing in some of the ditches at the back of the church and that his clothes had been taken away, unobserved by him. After promenading about in this primitive fashion for some minutes, the man was lent some old clothes.*
GRAYS & TILBURY GAZETTE: August 16th 1884

EXCITING SCENES IN ROMFORD MARKET PLACE
On Thursday December 29th, the Market-Place at Romford was the scene of great excitement in consequence of the refusal of the Romford Local Board to allow the Lady of the Manor (Mrs. McIntosh) to affix a weigh-bridge which the new Act, which came into force on January 1st, requires to be placed in or near every market-place in the kingdom... During last week, Messrs. Avery & Co. of London and Birmingham forwarded the iron-work, which was deposited in the market-place. On Thursday morning, five men in the employ of the firm commenced to dig out the foundations for the weigh-bridge. In about an hour, Mr. Turvey,

the Surveyor to the Local Board, arrived on the scene with a similar number of men [and two carts]*, who at once commenced to throw back the earth that had been excavated. A large crowd soon collected and watched the proceedings with keen interest and amusement. The men of the Board quickly filled up the hole made, and as fast as the excavators shovelled out the earth, the Board men threw it back... Things went on this way for some time... A well-known character (Toasty Finch), was sent round with the bell, crying, "Great excitement in the Market-Place!" and this quickly increased the crowd. About three o'clock, the opposition succeeded in covering the site with a number of planks on which they placed the two carts and tipped them up. This effectively put a stop to the work.... Mr. Baker* [Agent for Mrs. McIntosh] *proceeded to the Police Station and requested Inspector Cooper to have the Local Board's men removed. The Inspector said he could only interfere in the event of a breach of the peace. Mr. Baker returned to the scene of operations and, after a short conference with Mr. Turvey, proceeded to make another attempt to get on with the work. Avery's men seized the shafts of one of the carts, but the Board's men held the wheels and prevented them from doing so. Baffled in every way, Mr. Baker gave up the attempt and proceeded to take the names of the men of the Board. In reply to Mr. Baker, the first man interrogated stated that his name was 'Billy Bumper.' (laughter) Mr. Baker, having warned the men they 'were only making it worse for themselves,' proceeded to obtain the names of the others. One said his name was 'Kilrain,' the next, 'Johnny O'Brien,' and another, 'Sullivan the Smasher.' Another refused to give any name and said he lived 'next door to the Workhouse.'*

...About ten o'clock the same evening, the Toll Collector... proceeded to the site with about a dozen men, who at once commenced to remove the carts. The alarm was raised, and the Local Board's men were quickly on the spot, when a struggle ensued between the parties for possession of a crow-bar, which the Toll collector and his men had secured. At times, it looked as though the result would be a hand-to-hand fight, but fortunately the dispute seemed to be taken in good humour, and any serious result was averted... A final struggle for the crow-bar ended in it being secured by Mr. Turvey Jun. and carried off in triumph. This practically brought an end to the proceedings and the Toll

Collector and his men retired very shortly afterwards. Early next morning, Mr. Turvey had a quantity of sand shot down over the site... Mr. Baker sent several men to remove the sand... Mr. Turvey was quickly on the spot with his men, who shovelled back that which the others had dug up. COLCHESTER GAZETTE: January 29th 1822

Eventually, the Board got their way. If a weigh-bridge ever was erected, it wasn't there. The ground was levelled and Romford Market Place reverted to the way it had been before all the fuss and bother.

In Dunmow, an ancient tradition existed. It may date back to before the Norman Invasion of 1066. Certainly records survive from fifteenth and sixteenth centuries stating that a 'flitch or gammon of bacon' was being presented (presumably annually) to the couple providing the most perfect example of wedded bliss. Never a row for at least a year and a day! This tradition and its accompanying ceremony had all but died out between 1750 and 1850, until the idea of reviving it was taken up in 1855. Items in the East Anglian magazines for September 1949 and April 1955 suggest there had been opposition to the tradition's revival from the Lord of the Manor and the Clergy. But they were in the minority.

Dunmow

The London paper, The Era on 22nd July 1855 reported a great gathering of people in Dunmow to such an extent that all lodging houses were full. On July 20th, many thousands assembled at the Windmill field where a *'spacious pavilion had been erected around an elevated stage.'* The winners on this occasion were James and Hannah Barlow of Chipping Ongar whose *'connubial felicity'* was much admired.

However, problems were already on the horizon...

40

DUNMOW - THE FLITCH OF BACON

The aspirants who were sharpening their wits and their carving knives for the promised flitches of 1859 are doomed, we find, to wait rather an indefinite period for their rashers. A circular has been issued, stating it is the general wish of the committee and the inhabitants of Dunmow, that the ceremony 'should be postponed till the railway is completed from London to Dunmow.' But how far this will be agreeable to the candidates who will be compelled to carefully bottle up the rising connubial squabble till the parliamentary battle has been fought and won, and the pickaxe has paved a way of iron to the ancient rill, is somewhat a matter of doubt.

IPSWICH & COLCHESTER TIMES: December 31st 1858

Towards the end of the nineteenth century, there seems to have been a rebirth of old traditions that had somehow lost their original historic significance. It was claimed that at Rochford in Essex, in the 17th century, some tenants of an unpopular Lord of the Manor had gathered with the intention of doing him great harm. As a punishment, a strange penance was devised that had continued, but waned in importance through the years. This was the Lawless Court, or Whispering Court, which was held... *"the Wednesday after Michaelmas at cock-*

crow... the people whispered there. There was no candle there or pen or ink, only a coal, and if any man owing a suit or service did not appear, he forfeited double his rent." (Grantham Recorder: June 24th 1876)

Rochford must have revived this around 1875, as it was picked up by a number of national and local papers. The Chelmsford Chronicle in October 1875 reprinted a story first published in the Daily News, describing how eerie it had all seemed by torchlight. In a fine, but lengthy article in the London Standard of October 1877, it becomes clear that the nineteenth century version of the ceremony was altogether better supplied with food and vittles than was ever intended by the unpopular Lord. Those involved met, after feasting well, at midnight, at the house known as King's Hill. And so as... *"the atmosphere was raw with the chill October breath of the marshes"*...they all seem to have eaten, drunk, had a lot of fun until... *"a clamour of cock-a-whoops in all keys known at a poultry show, and some that are not... the throng made its way higgledy-piggledy back to the market square."*

Clearly, no-one was going to wait for cocks to crow. They just did it themselves, *"piled their torches in a bonfire, shared another bowl of punch and... peacefully went home to roost."*

LONDON STANDARD, repr. CHELMSFORD CHRONICLE: October 19th 1877

According to the Essex County Chronicle, Essex Magistrates in January 1892 received the following invitation...

The Justices of the Beacontree Division request the pleasure of your company at the Court House, Stratford at 2:30 p.m. on Saturday 23rd January, where there will be a discussion on 'The wrongs and remedies of wives.' It was suggested that the reason the Mayor did not receive an invitation was *'because his wife had no wrongs.'*

THE SCHOOLMASTER EXAMINED - *A respectable proprietor of a large academy at Halesworth, Suffolk was recently examined at Ipswich, when the Counsellor, Mr. A. chose to attempt to be witty. The following questions and answers occurred -*

Question: (The Counsellor throwing his gown about) What are you?
Answer: I keep an academy.
Question: (Giving the gown another swing) An academy?
        That is a school. You are a schoolmaster?

Answer: Yes.
Question: And you teach A,B,C?
Answer: Yes.
Question: Anything else?
Answer: Yes.
Question: What?
Answer: and D.
The prompt schoolmaster now goes by the name of 'Mr. ABC - and D.'

THE SICKLE: December 11th 1828
[The Sickle was a paper briefly published in Manningtree, but by 1829 had merged with the Colchester Courier.]

Possibly my favourite of these stories is this which I feel deserves to appear in its entirety. It carries a marvellously mocking tone throughout the report.

The deuce to pay at Dedham - *At the sitting of the Magistrates in*

Colchester Castle on Saturday sen'night, Thomas Nunn Esq., a gentleman of fortune residing near Manningtree was present to complain of an assault. From the statement of Mr. Nunn, it appeared that he and a friend went to the last Dedham Ball, having previously engaged beds

at the Sun Inn, [pictured on previous page] *kept by Mr. Catchpool.*

About four o'clock in the morning, they went to the Inn and had supper, wine &c. &c. They made some remark to Mr. Catchpool, and he returned it with abuse. Mr. Nunn ordered his bed to be warmed, when the landlord brought up a coal-scuttle instead of a warming pan. This excited the wrath of Mr. N. but he only civilly explained the difference between a coal-scuttle and a warming pan. Mr. Catchpool became sarcier than before and refused to harbour his guests any longer. Mrs. C., hearing her husband's musical voice, came up the stairs and turned his solo into a duet. From the vocal, she soon changed into the instrumental and with pro aris et focis *let fly at poor Mr. Nunn with her fists. Mr. N. seized her by the wrists and in the most polite manner possible, thrust her out of the room, but during the performance of the operation, she rubbed a little of the skin from one of her hands. The landlord, seeing this, invoked his household Gods - John Ostler and Tom the waiter - to assist him, but the allied forces were unable to remove complainant and his friend, and they eventually got possession of their beds. In the morning, when they left the house, they encountered further abuse.*

It now came to Mr. Catchpool's turn to speak and as there are always two sides to a story, he put a very different complexion on the affair. He stated that after supper he went into the room and found that the bones of a picked chicken were strewn about the floor, which certainly was not the genteel thing. Next, on taking in some wine and water agreeably to order, Mr. Nunn called him a "G__d__d fool," which was another very ungenteel thing. Complainant then asked for coals and the landlord, thinking they were wanted for the sitting room, brought in a coal-scuttle, the contents of which Mr. N. very quickly and dexterously, kicked all over the room so that the black diamonds being intermingled with the bleached bones of the departed chicken made the floor look like a piece of ancient or mosaic pavement. This was the third ungenteel thing. Mr. Nunn then made a sally - bore down upon Betty the Chambermaid, Molly the Cook and other appendages of the household and chased them upstairs and downstairs into my lady's chamber, where Mr. Catchpool's daughter lay in bed marvelling and trembling at the uproar. Nay, so fiercely did Mr. N. pursue the damosels that one maid of the Inn crept under a bed to escape his fury. Mrs. Catchpool, being of course much scandalised at this invasion of the sanctuary, went upstairs and, on remonstrating with the gallant Mrs. C., he seized her, tore her hand with his nails and twisted her arm in a most unmerciful manner. She was also struck in the face and received a black eye, which was now visible to the court.

After the perpetration of these ungenteel things, Mr. Catchpool considered he was more sinned against than sinning and that, but for the march stolen on him by Mr. Nunn, he (Mr. C.) ought to have been the complainant. It was subsequently stated that Mr. Nunn's anger extended to inanimate things, for he took down one of the servant's bonnets and kicked it about the passage in a most barbarous and inhuman manner, for which he made a recompense in the shape of half a sovereign. This state-ment was partly supported by other witnesses and Mr. Catchpool said that if time were given, he would bring forward his female servants to prove how they were hunted from pillar to post by the complainant. The magistrates, after some consultation, agreed to postpone the decision of the case till next Saturday, intimating that perhaps in the meantime, the affair might be arranged between the belligerent parties.

ESSEX HERALD: April 26th 1831

I'm sure it wasn't meant to be funny, but you had to laugh.

The West Ham Herald in March 1893 reported a lively dispute over a legacy left by an Oxford vicar. He had left £2,000 to the Diocesan Curates' Aid Society. No such society existed, but three others all claimed the legacy had been meant for them. After a somewhat unseem-ly legal scramble, the Oxford Diocesan Spiritual Help Society were duly awarded the money.

Another feature of our old local papers was sentimentality. In Britain, we've always been drawn to a good **animal** story. In past times, they loved items like these...

The heronry at Wanstead Park, pictured in an early
Journal of the Essex Naturalists Society

Chapter 4 - Animal Stories

Thomas Graham of Scattergate, Appleby has at this time a cow and a pig, so strongly attached to each other that they are never separated; the former will not suffer herself to be driven to any place without the company of her little attendant for whom she acts as a careful safeguard; for in her way to grass, she has every day to pass through the town, when the grunter is frequently assailed by dogs, who pay dear for their temerity in attacking it. After a conflict of this kind, the cow and the pig never fail to congratulate each other on their victory, by stopping and rubbing their noses together in a most loving manner. And when they again begin their march, the pig will take its post close by the side of its protector, wagging its short tail with the greatest contentment.

CHELMSFORD GAZETTE: October 11th 1822

THE PORKOFORTE - This is the name of a new musical instrument, said to have been invented in Cincinnati. It is a long box divided into compartments, one for each note... into each division a pig is placed and the tails of the porkers through holes in the side of the box, arranged like the keys of a piano. The tails are pinched by a sort of spring and lever machinery and the effect is said to be delightful. If the pigs are well selected, they will wear about three years without tuning.

ESSEX & SUFFOLK TIMES: August 3rd 1939

THE SAGACIOUS CAT - A cat which, disgusted at having her kittens frequently drowned, and having learned by sad experience that having been discovered with the usual number, 2 of them must be sacrificed at once on the altar of economy, took the precaution to carry off and deposit two of them under an old out-building, keeping the one and the two separate and apart, and nursing and caressing them alternately, day and night... until they had nearly arrived to the state of cathood, when this clever trick of feline strategy was brought to light.

STRATFORD TIMES: July 22nd 1859

On Friday night last, the duckery belonging to the Hon. Gen. Henniker of Dunmow was robbed of six ducks of a very superior breed. [Obviously superior people had to have superior ducks] *A reward of forty guineas was offered for the apprehension of the offenders.*

ESSEX UNION: November 27th 1809

Amongst such superior people, the species known as the 'sportsman naturalist' abounded in the nineteenth century. These were men of breeding who sought out rare birds and animals… and shot them.

One of those very rare birds, the Amphelis Garrulus, or Bohemian Chatterer, [Waxwing] *in very fine plumage, was taken alive on Thursday last in the garden of John Leathes Esq. of Bury. And on the following day, another fine specimen was shot by a gentleman at Bramford near Ipswich.*

CHELMSFORD GAZETTE: January 17th 1823

Coggeshall: *A beautiful specimen of that noble and rare bird, the Peregrine Falcon was shot in this neighbourhood the other day.*

HALSTEAD GAZETTE: November 26th 1857

Swan hunting at Brightlingsea from 'The Graphic' 1893

On Tuesday se'nnight, a sea-eagle was shot at Rollesby in Norfolk, which measured from tip to tip of his wings when expanded, seven feet six inches.

COLCHESTER GAZETTE: February 11th 1815

On Saturday last, was caught in the River Orwell between Harwich and Ipswich, a swordfish measuring nine feet in length, nearly as large as a man's body and weighs about 3 cwt. with a singular pointed beak upwards of three feet long, somewhat in the shape of a sword and toothed or jagged on the sides. This is a most formidable weapon with which it attacks its enemy.

COLCHESTER GAZETTE: October 15th 1814

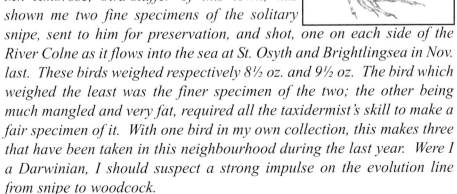

A fine and beautiful specimen of the bittern, [pictured right] *was recently shot on the Belchamp Walter estate of the Rev. J. M. St.Clare Raymond. The bittern is a bird but rarely found in these parts.* [Hardly surprising, really!]

S. SUFFOLK & N. ESSEX FREE PRESS:
January 31st 1867

Mr. C.R. Bree M.D., of Colchester, writing in the Field, says...
Mr. Ambrose, bird-stuffer of this town, has shown me two fine specimens of the solitary snipe, sent to him for preservation, and shot, one on each side of the River Colne as it flows into the sea at St. Osyth and Brightlingsea in Nov. last. These birds weighed respectively 8½ oz. and 9½ oz. The bird which weighed the least was the finer specimen of the two; the other being much mangled and very fat, required all the taxidermist's skill to make a fair specimen of it. With one bird in my own collection, this makes three that have been taken in this neighbourhood during the last year. Were I a Darwinian, I should suspect a strong impulse on the evolution line from snipe to woodcock.

ESSEX STANDARD: January 14th 1882

A few days ago, as some gentlemen were coursing on the Downs near Guildford they by chance found a white hare which they soon after killed: its eyes were encircled with a perfect ring of a very deep red, its ears and legs of the same colour, and what was most extraordinary, one of the two legs both behind and before was shorter than the other, yet it seemed to run very well and afforded excellent sport. This extraordinary animal was stuffed and may now be seen at Guildford.

CHELMSFORD CHRONICLE: January 10th 1783

Of course, not every creature that once attracted a sportsman's gun has become rarer...

A RARE BIRD - *A few days since, a Canada Goose was shot from a group of six by Mr. J.J. Hawkins, not far from Middle Wycke* [near Burnham-on-Crouch]

MALDON EXPRESS: December 13th 1879

Some creatures didn't even need shooting...

The reward of dishonesty - a goldfinch was discovered suspended by the neck with a single hair upon the branch of a plum tree in a garden

in this town [Chelmsford]. *There is, it appears ample evidence to prove that the unfortunate bird which, when found, was quite dead, had entered his neighbour's nest with a felonious intent and, in attempting to steal some of the materials, met with summary punishment. The poor bird is now exhibited in the state in which it was found, the victim of crime.*

ESSEX HERALD:
April 26th 1831

Fortunately, not all news-worthy wild life ended up stuffed...

Two young otters, about half grown with one of the old ones have been captured alive by the Stour near the mill at Baythorne [pictured below] *by two young men named White. The animals are still alive and feed well on small roach.*

SOUTH-WEST SUFFOLK ECHO: December 18th 1890

Last Friday, as a poor man, who resides in the neighbourhood of Walthamstow, was strolling through Epping Forest, near Wanstead, he met with what he supposed to be a snake. He trod on its head with the intention of killing it. On taking it up he discovered it was an adder. It was still alive and it stung one of his fingers. He sucked the wound; his tongue began to swell and also other parts of his body. He immediately went to a medical man at Walthamstow, and from thence he came to Stratford and saw two or three others, who advised him to go the London Hospital, and with the assistance of the police he was taken there. The symptoms at first were very unfavourable and but faint hopes were entertained of his recovery; but from subsequent information, we are enabled to add that the reports are of a more satisfactory nature.

ESSEX STANDARD: May 12th 1848

Queer nesting place - *A pied wagtail has built her nest on the rower's seat of the Ferry Horse Boat, laid 4 eggs and brought the young off all alive.*
BURNHAM-ON-CROUCH & DENGIE HUNDRED ADVERTISER: May 21st 1904

A STRANGE RAILWAY TRAVELLER AT CLACTON-ON-SEA

In a hole, one inch in diameter, in one of the buffers of railway carriage No. 79, the property of the Great Eastern Railway Company, which makes daily excursions between Thorpe and Clacton on Sea, a tomtit has made its nest, laid its eggs and is at the present time sitting upon them. This is a remarkable position for the incubatory process, especially as the buffer - as its name indicates, is often in violent concussion with other carriages. Notwithstanding this fact, the bird is always to be found in its nest. At the end of the day's work, the carriage is shunted at Thorpe for the night and at that period, the male bird invariably pays a visit to its mate. THE NEWSMAN: June 7th 1884

A pig was on Thursday se'nnight seen sailing down the River Thames between Westminster and Blackfriars Bridge, on a large fragment of ice with great gravity. He occasionally shrieked with peculiar shrillness, which a waterman construing into a call for a pilot, he put off and, after a long contest with the floating masses of snow, succeeded in delivering the swinish navigator from his perilous situation.
COLCHESTER GAZETTE: January 22nd 1814

A WHALE IN THE THAMES - *About nine o'clock on Wednesday morning, as four of the Leigh smacks were busy fishing above the Chapman Head lighthouse, the men were alarmed by the sight of a moving object which resembled an unrigged barge, but upon closer inspection was found to be a whale. The monster seemed to be enjoying himself in a very lively manner and spouting up water in the way common to these animals.*
MALDON EXPRESS: May 8th 1979

In a vessel lately arrived at Havre from Manilla, 2,000 rats were found, notwithstanding the sailors had eaten a great many during the voyage.
ESSEX HERALD: May 18th 1830

On Friday, the master of an English vessel, lying in Wexford harbour was alarmed in the middle of the night by a noise on deck. Thinking it proceeded from some person wanting to rob the vessel, he called up the hands, and after a strict search, they discovered a fox hid under some of the sails in the forecastle... marlinspikes, oyster-baskets &c. were instantly put in requisition, but every attempt to take poor Reynard dead or alive proved fruitless. After a chase of 20 minutes... he jumped overboard and swam for the shore, pursued by the sailors in a small boat, where he arrived in safety and... his pursuers soon lost sight of him. Sportsmen are at a loss to account for the manner in which the fox got on board as the vessel was upwards of 400 yards from the quay.

ESSEX UNION: May 23rd 1809

As labourers were excavating on the Stour Valley line at Lamarsh they discovered embedded in the gravel the head and tusks of a mammoth or fossilised elephant. Teeth of a mammoth have also been discovered in the ground at Brundon Hall.

SUDBURY POST: March 9th 1848

In what was largely an agricultural county, vermin had to be controlled. In the latter part of the nineteenth century, Sparrow Clubs formed. Competitions were held between their members, and prizes awarded to the person killing the most sparrows. The Essex & West Suffolk Gazette of December 19th 1862 reported Crawley Sparrow Club's winner as having trapped 1,477 of the birds. However, an article in the same newspaper just under a year later was condemning the practice, as poisoned grain was being used, and all manner of songbirds were being killed as well as the troublesome ones.

The strange, bizarre and exotic drew the attention of local newspaper editors...

A shire mare belonging to Sir Walter Gilbey at Blount's Farm, Thaxted gave birth recently to a foal with two heads, one body, two hind quarters and four legs behind and three in front. The monstrosity did not live.

SOUTHEND-ON-SEA OBSERVER: February 1st 1900

There is a singular circumstance connected with Bideford Bridge, Devon: the tide flows so rapidly that the bridge cannot be repaired by  *mortar. The Bridge Corporation therefore keep boats in employ to bring muscles [by which they mean 'mussels'] and the interstices of the bridge are filled by hand with those muscles; and it is supported from being driven away by the tide entirely by the strong threads these muscles fix to the stone work; and by an Act or Grant, it is a crime, for which the punishment is transportation to any person who shall remove those muscles, unless in the presence and by the consent of the Corporative Trustees.*

CHELMSFORD GAZETTE: Decenber 6th 1822

I did doubt this last story when I first read it, wondering perhaps if it ought to be dated April 1st, but it appears to be perfectly true. A man was arrested for taking mussels from the bridge as recently as 1941 (he was not transported). Equally odd was this story which appeared in papers throughout the country...

On the 18th inst., Cambridge was visited by an ant cloud, the rare phemomenon occurring about six o'clock in the evening, and causing considerable annoyance to persons in the streets, the ants falling in countless millions about the pavements, and in the gardens and college courts. MORNING POST: August 22nd 1874

Mr. A. Peacock of Hockley, Essex has at this time in his possession, a turkey hen under 2 years old which, for the last season, layed more than 100 eggs, hatched 90, and brought to real perfection 75.

IPSWICH JOURNAL: January 28th 1804

Chelmsford

CHELMSFORD - *Wednesday night last, the George Inn in this town and adjoining houses narrowly escaped destruction by fire through rats, in the following singular manner. The maid-servant put the children to bed and left a lighted candle set safe in the room: towards the latter part of the evening, the washer-women had occasion to pass through that room with a basket of clothes which had been washed that day, when the candle stood safe. But on their return through the same room, they discovered the candle-stick was beat down and the candle missing, and in it something disagreeable like singed hair. They informed Mr. Dench thereof, who knowing the house to be pestered with rats, immediately judged they must have taken the candle alight into their hole, which on further search was found to be the case. He then poured down the hole such a quantity of water as was supposed sufficient to prevent any further consequences. Soon after, Mrs. Lee of the next house went to look in every apartment of her premises to see if everything was safe before she went to bed, when she saw a small light shine from the joist of Mr. Dench's house. She supposed some person was going to bed and that it was the light from their candle, but could not be easy till she went again to look at the light before she went to bed, when she found it had* *become considerably larger. On this she alarmed Mr. Dench who immediately got at the place and after unroofing a few tiles, found the candle had fired the joist in such a manner that had it not been discovered, the house must in a short time have been in flames.*

IPSWICH JOURNAL: July 3rd 1790

People in the nineteenth century loved their pets much as they do now. People liked to think of the dog as man's best friend. This story has an air of 'Greyfriars Bobby' about it...

FIDELITY OF THE DOG - A person of the name of Johnson, who resides at Hatfield [Peverel] and held a situation in the excise, after being missing for several days, was found dead on Sunday morning, in a secluded spot in the parish of Little Baddow, Essex with his throat cut; he was also stabbed in various parts as if with a pen-knife. The body was discovered by means of a little dog, which frequently accompanied the deceased on his rounds, having returned home in the most meagre and reduced condition. The circumstances led to suspicion and induced the owner to watch the conduct of the dog which, as soon as his hunger was satisfied, again left his home, faithful even in death, to watch over the remains of his lifeless companion. In that situation he was found, placed by the side of the body, which had ceased to breathe for several days and was fast approaching decomposition.

BURY & NORWICH POST: September 20th 1826

Even mythical creatures found their way into our local papers. From time to time, the subject of 'mermaids' was tackled, often by way of letters to the editor. In 1809, a widely respected school-master in Thurso in Scotland wrote a most detailed account of his encounter with one of these creatures...

...When I was parochial schoolmaster at Reay, in the course of walking on the shore... my attention was arrested by the appearance of a figure resembling an unclothed human female, sitting upon a rock extending into the sea and apparently in the act of combing its hair which flowed around its shoulders and of a light brown colour. - The resemblance which the figure bore to its prototype in all its visible parts was so

striking that had not the rock on which it was sitting been dangerous for bathing, I should have been constrained to have regarded it really as a human form, and to an eye unaccustomed to the situation, it must undoubtedly appeared as such... It remained on the rock for three or four minutes after I observed it... and then dropped into the sea... from whence it did not reappear to me.
ESSEX UNION: September 15th 1809

This inevitably sparked a lively correspondence from those offering historic references as well as first-hand experiences and sightings. Mr. Munro's account was backed up by the Rev. Mackay, Minister of Reay, who also claimed seeing a group of mermaids on the coast of Caithness, noting their smooth skin and webbed fingers. (His letter was published in a number of local papers including the

Kentish Gazette)

In answer to a request from a reader, the very first editor of the Ipswich Journal offered his own remarkable set of explanations for their existence...

...some think 'em not to be creatures, but monsters... got since by un-natural copulation: some think 'em to be very devils from the strange effects attributed to 'em; some, that when the angels fell, those that light into the sea were turned into mermen; and some that the devils begat them of fishes; some that fishes generating in the deluge [Noah's flood] *and seeing drowned men, by strength of imagination, got something like 'em. But we see no reason but that they were created at first amongst that infinite number of other fishes which bear some resemblance to the creatures on Earth.*
IPSWICH JOURNAL: May 27th 1721

From the late eighteenth century, travelling menageries began to appear in a our towns and villages. Local newspapers carried advertisements and reports of their visits. The greatest of these was George Wombwell, whose shows were truly spectacular, if the reports are anything to go by. However, with dangerous animals around, things could go horribly wrong. In 1834 this story from the Northampton Herald was published in the Essex Standard (It was common for good stories to be passed around among local papers).

ESCAPE OF A LION AND TIGRESS FROM WOMBWELL'S MENAGERIE - FOUR LIVES LOST

A melancholy accident ocurred at Wombwell's Menagerie, in consequence of the Lion Wallace and a large tigress escaping from the caravan at Wirksworth on Tuesday night last on the way to Newhaven Fair. It appears that the drivers were putting the vans into the yard of the White Lion Inn, when a carriage laden with timber came in contact with the one in which the celebrated lion Wallace and a very large tigress were kept and staved in the whole side of the vehicle. Every pains possible were taken to prevent the beasts obtaining their liberty by repairing the van as well as circumstances would permit and by closing the gates of the yard, but in the course of the night the beasts, being by nature restless, by some means removed one of the broken panels and succeeded in making their escape by the back-yard into the fields where the tigress attacked a number of sheep and killed three. The lion, finding himself at liberty, was by no means idle, but falling in with some cows belonging to Mr. Wilson, killed one and severely wounded two others. The bleating of the sheep, the lowing of the cows and the roaring of the lion roused the keepers and several of the inhabitants, whose instant pursuit was made by the whole body in order to kill or, if possible, to retake them. The first discovered the lion about three or four fields distant, feeding on the cow which had fallen a victim to his irresistible fury. They immediately fronted him as well as their fears would admit and several shots were fired, though contrary to the orders of the keeper, by which the lion was severely wounded. The infuriated animal suddenly rushed upon a man who was at some distance from him, and before assistance could be rendered, he unfortunately killed him. He

58

then dashed into a cow shed where, by the well-known voice of the keepers, and by their able management, he was secured and lodged in a place of safety without further mischief. The party then went in pursuit of the tigress which had taken another direction and had fallen in with some persons going to work at the brickfields. The animal attacked a woman with a child in her arms and a boy about eleven years of age, all of whom were killed before assistance arrived. On the party coming up, they were horror-struck at the spectacle. Every exertion was made to secure the animal, but it was not before she was so dangerously wounded as not to be expected to recover that the object could be effected. On the following day, an inquest was held when, after a patient investigation, a verdict of Accidental Death was returned; deodand [see page 103] *£10 on the beasts. Too much praise cannot be given to Mr. Wombwell for the promptness he displayed on hearing the melancholy accident. He expressed the utmost concern, ordered the funerals of the sufferers to take place at his expense, and promised to make good all damages arising from the melancholy event.*

ESSEX STANDARD: March 1st 1834

But several aspects of this story do not make sense. Apart from the unlikely lodging of a male lion and a tigress together, how George Wombwell turns out to be the hero of the hour is hard to explain. Maybe the story should have appeared exactly one month later. Just a week after publication, this short explanation received rather less prominence, having been reprinted from the Shrewsbury Chronicle.

A hoax has been this week practised upon nearly all the London and County newspapers, they having given a detailed and dreadful account of a lion and a tiger belonging to Mr. Wombwell's Menagerie having broken loose and devoured women, children and cattle at Worksworth, Northants. Two months ago, this same horrible tale was printed verbatim in this town and sold for one penny to each of the simpletons who bought it.

Even though this may have been a story conjured from nothing, accidents did happen when big cats were around. George Wombwell was the main witness at the inquest on the death of Richard Haynes in

March 1839. He had received a small bite from a leopard on his knee, but in spite of treatment with a bread and water poultice, it had festered and Haynes had died. The verdict was accidental death.

As to the Northamptonshire story of the escaped lion and tigress, whose hoax was it? I might venture a suggestion. George Wombwell was the great show-man of his age and he knew that where his business was concerned, there was no such thing as bad publicity - quite the opposite; the more dangerous his animals appeared to be, the more people wanted to pay to see them. The celebrated Wallace, born in captivity was, by repute, toothless and as tame as a kitten, but that was not the way Wombwell wanted the public to see him.

When Wallace (pictured here) died in captivity in 1838, he was stuffed and presented to the newly-opened Saffron Walden Museum, where he can still be seen today.

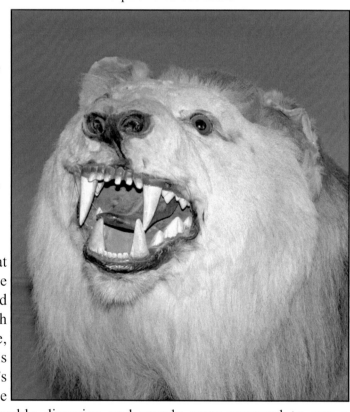

In a world that for much of the time was dull and predictable much of the time, entertainments like Wombwell's menagerie offered a memorable diversion and people were prepared to pay a disproportionate amount of their meagre salaries on being entertained. So, it is to **entertainment** we turn next...

Chapter 5
Sport & Entertainment

Sport in the eighteenth century was all about betting - not just the obvious sports like horse-racing, but almost any 'athletic endeavour'

 would be staged as a means of having a gamble. Both amateur and semi-professional sportsmen often made a good living out of challenges and bets they might make, trusting in their own ability.

A very respectable farmer living not one hundred miles from Pond Farm in West Bergholt laid a wager that he would run one mile backwards in ten minutes - This undertaking was performed and two minutes to spare, staying on the road and taking a glass of wine with a friend.
ESSEX STANDARD: April 15th 1831

A few evenings ago, a person in the corn trade undertook to drive his horse in a Windsor Chair from his house in Leather lane, London to Colchester in six hours and a half, which he won by eight minutes. It is computed to be 55 miles, and what makes it more extraordinary is he drove at night. One person won 132 guineas on the performance, between Witham and Colchester.
CHELMSFORD CHRONICLE: May 17th 1765

A man for a wager of a guinea, broiled a steak on the roof of a house in Tottenham Court Road and then ate it.
IPSWICH JOURNAL: April 23rd 1808

The Essex Newsman in August 1889 described a wager whereby Mr. A. of Romford bet he would kill 15 pigeons in 25 shots, backing himself for £5 and a leg-of-mutton supper for twenty sportsmen. He only needed 16 of his 25 shots to win.

The Stratford Times, in April 1859, described a successful bet of $1,000 to $50 paid to Signor Gaspa Morelli, formerly of Barnum's circus, who manged to stilt-walk acoss the Niagara River.

Herculean Task - *A celebrated pedestrian is matched to stand on one foot for 3 hours and during that time to shave himself, eat his supper and to pull off both his shoes and stockings six times and put them on again without any other support than the foot on which he stands.*

ESSEX STANDARD: April 3rd 1835

A novel swimming match took place on Saturday at Fisher Row [Edinburgh] between a barber and Mr. Downie's dog, Maggie for £5 a side. The distance was three-quarters of a mile. The barber took the lead and was soon overtaken by his canine opponent, which, after a good struggle, went in winner by about ten yards.

ESSEX STANDARD: September 22nd 1858

BRAINTREE - *On Saturday evening, a young man named Patmore, whilst in company at a beerhouse, undertook for a wager to eat a tobaco pipe - an achievement which he had partly accomplished when he was taken ill and*  *had to be removed to the Infirmary at the Workhouse where, for a time, he was in a critical condition. He soon, however, 'came round' and is now convalescent.*

ESSEX TELEGRAPH: April 28th 1888

As has been shown, before 1850, most sport seems to have involved prize money or betting or both. Prize fights were common, bloody and often looked down on by those writing for the newspapers.

FIGHT BETWEEN NED NEAL AND YOUNG DUTCH SAM

This long protracted battle... took place at Bumpstead in the county of Essex. The place appointed for the battle was a large field at Borough Green within six miles of Newmarket. At twelve o'clock, Neal arrived... when suddenly the appearance of Mr. Eaton, a magistrate in the neighbourhood put all into confusion. This gentleman expressed his determination not to permit the fight either in the counties of Cambridge or Suffolk and, after useless appeals to his good nature, a move became inevitable. At the suggestions of the 'knowing ones', the county of Essex was fixed, and the town of Haverhill, a distance of eight miles was named as the point of rendezvous. Thither, immediately horse and foot then proceded at a rapid pace, the whole line of road presenting an extraordinary scene of bustle and excitement... At 32 minutes after three, the men set-to, and fourteen rounds were fought, and then Neal was

completely beaten. We shall not sully our columns with the coarse details of this black-guard and disgusting exhibition. Neal was put to bed at an adjoining public house.

ESSEX STANDARD:
January 21st 1831

This picture shows a famous fight reported in the Ipswich Journal in April 1750 between Jack Broughton & John Slack. Broughton appears to have won with ease.

At the King's Head Inn in Colchester, on Tuesday 2nd April, will be a severe Trial of Manhood between the Persons under mention'd, for Twenty Pounds, viz:

I George Stevenson, commonly called The Fighting Coachman, well known for my Skill and Intrepidity in the Art of Boxing, not fearing the boasted Abilities of Mr Anthony Jones, the Colchester Champion, do hereby invite him to meet me at the Time and Place above for the Sum aforesaid, when I will fully convince him I am much his Superior.

G. Stevenson

I Anthony Jones, accept the above Challenge, and will not fail to meet him; when those Gentlemen who have hitherto entertained a Good opinion of me, may again fee my valiant and resolute Behaviour, not withstanding the Menaces of Mr Stevenson, who will not find me easily defeated, being determin'd rather to sacrifice my Life than submit.

A. Jones

IPSWICH JOURNAL: 2nd April 1745

We are informed by a correspondent from Saffron Walden that the following circumstance happened lately in that town: Eleven fenmen from the Isle of Ely, being employed by Sir John Griffin in training a part of his park at Audley End, went one evening to the inn called the Hoops to drink. After getting a little spirited, they told the maid they would give her six pence each to fetch them as much beer as they could drink in single half-pints out of the cellar: if they tired her, she was to pay for the liquor; if she tired them, they were to pay for the whole. The girl accepted the bet although she had been washing all the day and drew them 517 single half-pints before they gave out, which were all drank by the said men. The distance from the room where they sat to the tap was measure, from which it appears she walked near 12 miles in fetching it, and the quantity of liquor drank by each man was about three gallons in three hours. The above is a real fact.

POLICE GAZETTE: February 17th 1775

Pedestrianism extraordinary - *On the 6th instant, Mr. Thos. French, fishmonger of this town* [Chelmsford] *undertook for a wager of one sovereign to run one mile in 6 minutes and ¾ on the Broomfield Road,* *he wearing at the time a heavy great coat, a close coat, a blue apron, a heavy market apron and a pair of water boots. He completed the task in 10 seconds under the given time to the surprise of all present.*

KENT & ESSEX MERCURY: February 12th 1828

Capt. L. Parry's match - *This pedestrian started from Whitechapel church on Tuesday morning at one o'clock to go on foot 108 miles in 24 hours for 100 sovereigns. He travelled the first 22 miles to Ingatestone in 3 hours and reached Witham on the Ipswich Road, 37 miles at half past seven o'clock, and breakfasted on fowl. He completed half the distance, to and fro over 3 miles of measured ground towards Colchester in eleven hours. He reached Ingatestone on his return at a quarter before eight o'clock, the worse for his journey. He started with five hours to go the 22 miles in, and by astonishing perseverence, he reached the end of his journey in five minutes within the given time. The task is a great one, but the road is the best out of London.*

COLCHESTER GAZETTE: April 10th 1824

For many reading the papers, 'sport' meant hunting and shooting. Typical are articles such as *"The pleasures of Partridge Shooting"* (Chelmsford Chronicle: October 18th 1844). Extensive details of Prince Albert shooting 114 hares, 29 pheasants and a snipe in a visit to Stowe near Buckingham appeared in the Chelmsford Chronicle for January 24th 1845. All manner of rather unpleasant 'sports' amused audiences in times past, but as will be shown in Chapter10 of this book, attititudes gradually changed and what had once been acceptable was no more.

Regular accounts of local fox-hunts appeared. Unusually, this seems to have been penned by a man who wasn't entirely impressed by it all...

A bag fox was on Saturday last, turned off before Mr. Tuffnell's hounds at Broomfield. Reynard, being of a domestic turn, it was with some difficulty that he could be persuaded to afford any sport at all, skulking at every opportunity, but at last taking the valley, he crossed the river twice, after which he made for this town and entered the gardens near the church: the horsemen on the other side of the river were at this time thrown out and obliged to cross the town by Springfield Lane. This

afforded a complete race through the streets to the dread of parents and the danger of children. Some horses which were passing through the town with a waggon, affrighted by the snapping of whips &c. turned sharp round, broke off the shafts of the waggon and much injured the fillers by dragging it upon the ground a considerable distance. The fences of the gardens were so high (which however were soon lowered) the hounds could not make the fox off and the first Tally-ho was on perceiving Reynard mounted upon the tiles near the House of Industry to which place the subtle animal appeared to have led his followers. The Nimrods of the town, were by this time sufficiently alarmed... and Reynard was with some difficulty taken in a pig-cote and again bagg'd alive amidst the curses of the women whose fences had suffered. His good fortune did not however stay long with him for being again turned down on the Navigation Wharf, he made for Springfield and again taking to the river, crossed at Mr. Marriage's Mill and was killed near the Boarded Barn in this parish.

CHELMSFORD CHRONICLE: April 10th 1801

Of all the sports reports I have read, this has to be the best. It is the report of a football game between Essex and Norfolk in 1897, apparently written by 'Kickett Forward.'

Individual play rather than combination was the feature of Wednesday's match, Essex v Norfolk, which took place at Chelmsford and ended in a draw of two goals each. Individual play, perhaps, is to be expected rather than combination in a county match, for the men who compose the respective teams are more often used to playing against one another than with one another... Russell, the Essex centre forward was not quite up to concert pitch and the left wing was not infrequently absent when wanted near the Norfolk goal. Altogether Essex played the better game and should have won.

Robert Cook, the Hon. Sec. to the Essex F.A. made the arrangements for the match with his accustomed precision. There seems to be no obstacle he cannot overcome with ease. On Monday, he received a telegram from the Norfolk secretary saying that the kick-off must be at 2:15, instead of 3:15 as advertised, as an alteration in the timetable which had probably been overlooked necessitated the visitors leaving Chelmsford at 4:30.

"Impossible to alter the arrangements," said Robert, and forthwith proceeded to London and induced Mr. R.P. Ellis of the G.E.R. to stop an express train at Chelmsford - one to pass through about an hour later - to pick up the Norfolk men. How's that for smart?

There was only one thing unfavourable to spectators, and that was the confusion caused by each team wearing... chocolate and light blue shirts. If it had only been known that the Norfolk colours were the same as the Essex, the home team would have been put in something else...

...The league match between Braintree and the York & Lancashire Regiment on Saturday resulted as nearly everybody expected it would. Few if any of the most sanguine supporters of the Braintree team thought there was half a chance against the redoubtable military team and most people were prepared for a big defeat. But 'two to one' is not a very bad licking and when the teams meet again and Braintree has had some much-needed practice, this result may be reversed....

...An unfortunate accident befell White in the second half. He split his knickers in such a ludicrous way that the referee had to stop the play, and order him to repair or replace them. White went off home and the game was stopped for a quarter of an hour, but White never showed up again...

...I may say that I was very glad to hear the referee rebuke some spectators, who urged their own players to 'kick him in the ribs' - the 'him' being an opponent. The referee very rightly told them that was not sport and he was sure that even their own team would not wish such advice to be offered.

The London League match Ilford versus Brentford was a fine one, but I am sorry to say, somewhat rough at times. For the roughness, certain of the spectators were to blame. It's the same old story. They lost their heads in their excitement and urged their team to all sorts of dark doings...   ESSEX COUNTY CHRONICLE: October 15th 1897

The original lady football players, said to be chiefly *artistes* from the music hall stage, gave an exhibition of their prowess before a large crowd at Chelmsford on Saturday. The ladies tumbled inelegantly about a slippery field, and one side, supposed to represent the "South," scored three goals, while the "North" failed to score at all. Several of the ejaculations which came from the crowd jarred on the ears of decent people. On the other hand, some observations were highly diverting. The spectators singled out individual players for nicknames, often going by the colour of the lady's hair. "Ginger" was urged to play up, while "Trilby" was many times emphatically requested to "have a shot," and "Louie" was encouraged to "go it." The ladies looked odd enough in their strange costumes, which consisted of tightly fitting jerseys and knickerbockers, these latter in some cases being covered by loose skirts.

CHELMSFORD CHRONICLE: April 27th 1886

Harwich: *Friday last, a match at cricket was played here by John Booth & Giles Wigner for several considerable wagers, which were won by the former... the ages of the two persons put together amount to 160 years.*   IPSWICH JOURNAL: August 7th 1784

It was not only sport that offered diversions from the drabness of most people's lives. By the end of the eighteenth century it had become increasingly fashionable to visit certain seaside resorts...

SOUTH-END - *The jetty which already extends from the shore 600 feet, is rapidly proceeding towards its completion, when it will be one mile*

and a quarter in length, and in width 20 feet. The promenade will be of Roman cement, in imitation of stone, and a neat iron railing on each side will protect the pedestrian whilst he contemplates the sublime scene which surrounds him. Such is the attraction to this most enchanting spot that on Sunday last there were as many as 500 persons of rank and fashion upon the promenade, and it is the opinion of those who have visited many watering places which rank as the most fashionable that they do not possess charms to be compared with those which are to be found here... Southend only requires to be visited in order to discover attractions not to be resisted.

ESSEX HERALD: May 25th 1828

But it would take the coming of the railways to open up seaside resorts to the masses, as this picture from the London Illustrated News shows...

SANGER'S CIRCUS - *It will be seen by advertisement that this well-known equestrian establishment is to visit Colchester next Tuesday, and will be located in the Military Road. At one o'clock, there will be a procession through the principal streets of the town.*

ESSEX STANDARD: October 25th 1884

MILITARY ROAD, COLCHESTER.

TUESDAY NEXT, October 28th.

JOHN SANGER & SON'S

MONSTRE HIPPODROME CIRCUS

AND MENAGERIE.

THE Mighty Monarch of the Road, from Royal Agricultural Hall and Sanger's National Amphitheatre, London. FIVE TIMES LARGER! than any other Exhibition in England ; of Stupendous Cost, Overwhelming Magnitude, and Electrifying Nature.

NOTICE—IMPORTANT.

SNAKE CHARMING

The Greatest Miracle of the Age.

MDLE. DEMAJUTA, from the Royal Aquarium and Crystal Palace, London.

Come and see her Subdue, Play, and Fondle with the Deadly Poisonous and Venomous Reptiles, which astonishes all beholders.

THE GRAND

FREE NOVELTY PROCESSION AT 1 O'CLOCK

A Gorgeous Living Panorama of Moving Splendour.

Worth a hundred miles journey to witness, the whole to be seen at the Encampment on the Ground previous to the Grand Procession.

Reserved Seats (carpeted and select), 3s. ; First Class Seats, carpeted, 2s. ; Second Class, 1s. ; Area, 6d.

Children under 10 years of age Half-price to Reserved Seats and First Class Seats only. Liberal arrangements made with Schools. TWO PERFORMANCES EACH DAY—at Two and Seven o'clock. ADVANCE AGENT,

2977) Mr. J. LEVEY.

Touring circuses and menageries began by attaching themselves to annual fairs, only later expanding to entertainments in their own right as many of these fairs declined. George Wombwell, mentioned in the previous chapter was a regular face at Essex fairs in the 1820s and 1830s. The Essex Standard described his menagerie of 15 huge caravans attending Maldon Fair in September 1834, including *"The Barbary lioness, Charlotte, with her four fine babies."* Similar reports appeared of Wombwell's menagerie at Chelmsford Fair in May 1835.

Annual fairs, many of which dated back to medieval times, drew huge crowds and generally got a bad press. Pick-pockets and shysters abounded, and gradually more and more such fairs were closed down.

FAIRLOP FAIR - *The judicial ban of prescription pronounced against this ancient festival has been unheard, or if heard, unheeded. The fair this year was something more than itself, in regard to gaiety and good humour, as well as in respect to the number of persons who flocked there, not only from all parts of Essex, but from the Metropolis and other more distant places... there were grim-visaged coal-heavers, murky dustmen, greasy butchers and tawny gipsies, all dressed in their appropriate costumes, and forming a striking contrast to the spruce shopman in his best blue and white and the little merry maidens decked in their 'rosy trim.'*

With spirits light and debonair, free from sorrow - free from care,
Each to meat her favoured swain, whom she may not meet again
Until the parson says, 'You're wed.' And the next meeting is in ____;
Whither, we must not repair, further prying is unfair.

...Several travelling menageries, laden with hanimals *of all sorts... arrived the previous evening and were arranged in good order. Among the most wonerfullest of these, and which consequently produced the most money, was an* orang outang, *the* lusus naturae *of Buffon, described by the eloquent showman as* 'lately harrived from the wilds of Hafrica', *measuring* '7 feet 10 inches from his snout to his tail and 8 feet 10 inches from his tail to his snout.' *This strange animal, we afterwards discovered to be a native, not of the* terra incognita *of Africa, but an old acquaintance from Whitechapel, formerly belonging to a party of Morris Dancers, and now dressed up for the occasion in a bear-skin. The White*

Lady, said to be a daughter of Christophe, the Black Prince attracted no small share of attention... but... this fair creature of the silver hair... proved to be a Billingsgate nymph, whose carroty locks were concealed beneath a white wig. So much for the monstrosities by which poor John Bull is cajoled out of his cash The lions and tigers, leopards, panthers and hyenas, with the rest of the forest tribe were all very fierce and very formidable... But there were other perils - a cunning Jew pedlar exposed his tempting wares, and the unsuspecting country girls exchanged real silver for mock gold and painted glass... The games of chance were innumerable; a smiling gay-faced villain begged of you to try your luck... The thimble-rigged gentry played off their vile pranks to a more fatal extent, the stakes being higher and the game more fleet and subtle. One of these fellows was seated in a booth, at high play, when his operations met with a very sudden check by the unwelcome intrusion of Grossmith & Read, two Police Officers of Upton Hall who most impertinently apprehended the Master of the Ceremonies on a charge of robbery and bore him off, in spite of all his threats and entreaties.

KENT & ESSEX MERCURY: July 15th 1828

ESSEX.

Billericay, Aug. 2, Oct 7
Bishop Stortford, Holy Thursday, Trinity Thursday, Oct. 10
Barking, Oct. 22
Braintree, May 8, Oct. 2 and 3.
Chelmsford, May 12, Oct. 12
Coggeshall, Whit Tues. and Wed.
Colchester, July 5, 23, Oct. 20
Dunmow, May 6, Nov. 8
Epping, Whit Tues, Nov. 13
Grays, May 23, Oct. 20
Halstead, May 6, Oct. 29
Harlow, May 13, Sep. 9, Nov. 28
Lachinden, near Maldon, Aug. 27
Maldon, May 1, 2, Sep. 13, 14
Romford, June 24
Saffron Walden, day before Midlent Sunday, Nov. 1
Stanstead, May 12
Stebbing, July 9
Thaxted, Monday before Whit Monday
Waltham Abbey, May 14, Sep. 25.

At Brentwood Fair on Thursday, business was very flat, but the light-fingered gentry were extremely active.
ESSEX & SUFFOLK TIMES: July 20th 1839

A list of Essex fairs published in the Huntingdon, Bedford & Peterborough Gazette in 1837.

In reporting on an annual fair held at Stowmarket in Suffolk in July 1851, the Ipswich Express & Essex and Suffolk Mercury simply wrote...

"The usual gathering of the lowest grades took place, as is usual on the 10th of every July upon the ground opposite to the mansion of the Rev. Edgar Rust."

At Chelmsford Fair... one or two gentlemen who, as we should imagine, had plenty of room for their hands in their own pockets, were detected dipping them, without leave, into those of their neighbours.
ESSEX STANDARD: May 15th 1835

STEBBING: *Proposed abolition of the fair*

The Rev. A.R. Bingham Wright, the vicar, presented a memorial from a number of the parishioners asking for the abolition of the annual fair which takes place on the 10th and 11th of July. The memorial set forth that the fair which had been held annually from time immemorial in the public street had now become useless and unnecessary and was more-over, the cause of grievous immorality and disturbance in the parish.
ESSEX COUNTY CHRONICLE: January 6th 1893

During the past week, roundabouts, swings and a variety of stalls of various descriptions have been located on the piece of waste ground near the Police Station and have been well paronized by the children of the town. Grays Fair, had it not been abolished, would have taken place yesterday, and as the proprietors of the shows still find it profitable to keep up the custom.
GRAYS & TILBURY GAZETTE: May 24th 1884

Wider afield, grander events were attracting huge numbers...

Taking advantage of Whit Monday, nearly 100,000 persons visited the American Exhibition where Buffalo Bill gave three performances. More than 61,000 went to the Crystal Palace, about 70,000 to the Alexandra Palace, upwards of 20,000 to Kew Gardens, 23,000 to the Zoological Gardens and 11,ooo to the South Kensington Museum. Large numbers also visited the Albert Palace, North Woolwich Gardens, the Japanese village and other places of amusement in and around London. The Great Eastern Railway conveyed from its Railway Stations about 95,000 passengers. The larger proportion of the passengers were carried to

Epping Forest (Chingford & Loughton), Broxbourne, Rye House, Alexandra Palace, Clacton-on-sea, Walton-on-the-Naze and Harwich.
ESSEX STANDARD: June 4th 1887

A considerable number of Ilford people have travelled to Stratford every evening this week to witness the performance of Sir Henry Irving and Miss Ellen Terry with the Lyceum Company at the new Borough Theatre.
ILFORD GUARDIAN: September 10th 1898

But most entertainment a century or two ago was much more likely to be home-grown...

CORBETT'S TYE - *A Smoking concert was held at the George hotel on Tuesday evening. The chair was taken by Mr. W. Hock and an excellent programme was performed. Mr. Wood's mandolin solos were much enjoyed. Songs were contributed by Messrs. Thompson, Lazell, Barnard, Fassinedge, Adams, Chester & Bailey. Mr. Gaywood presided at the piano.*

STEEPLE BUMPSTEAD

CHILDREN'S CONCERT - *On Friday last, the children attending the National School gave an entertainment consisting of songs, musical drill and a fairy land play under the conductorship of Miss Walters, the head mistress. A special feature of the evening was a recitation, "Helping Mother," by a tiny girl of the tender age of three years and six months. Another interesting item was "The Milkmaid's Song," given in character by eight of the elder girls, who were prettily dressed. The infants went successfully through a very elaborate musical drill, plainly showing the careful training they had received. Later in the evening, a* *number of old friends arrived from fairy land in order to convince a youthful unbeliever of their real existence: Cinderella, Red Riding Hood, Santa Claus and many others appearing suddenly at the call of the Fairy Queen and performing a most picturesque group, singing sweetly all the time. At the close, the Vicar, the Rev. C.M. Powell proposed a vote of thanks to Miss Walters. The greatest praise is due to her and to her assistants for the admirable discipline that prevails in the school. The room which was artistically decorated was crowded to overflowing.*

SOUTH WEST SUFFOLK ECHO: April 11th 1891

A very jolly little party was held at the London Road Board Schools, Southend on Friday, when the annual soirée of the South East Essex Teachers' Assn. was carried out in a manner that left nothing to be desired. The gathering was capitally organised and the amusements provided were as varied as they were enjoyable. Several members of the Southend School Board, by their presence, marked their sympathy with the teachers, spending a convivial time together at the end of their week's labours; and with so much spirit were the proceedings sustained that it was not until daylight was approaching that the company separated.

SOUTHEND-ON-SEA OBSERVER: February 8th 1894

HATFIELD PEVEREL - The Brass Band have invested in a hussar uniform and no longer present the appearance of a motley crew. They played in the uniform for the first time at a garden party given by the Rev. & Mrs. Toulmin at the vicarage on the 29th ult. They also played for Lady Rayleigh at the Terling Athletic sports yesterday.

ESSEX NEWSMAN: July 8th 1893

Though musical activities could have their dangerous side...

Mr C. Betts of Helions Bumpstead was driving through Carlton when his horse was frightened, it was said, by the Salvation Army Band. The horse rushed onto the bank. Mr. Betts was thrown out and his collar bone was broken. He was taken to Dr. Hargrave's surgery at Haverhill.

SOUTH WEST SUFFOLK ECHO: April 30th 1892

...And there were times, when it was a thin line between what was seen as entertainment, and a riot...

WITHAM - *This town was the scene of a most disgraceful riot on the 5th inst. Last year, the bonfire made in the heart of the town was of such a large size and the heat so great that fears were entertained for the safety of the houses in the immediate vicinity. Public notices were this year circulated, warning persons not to let off fireworks &c. in the streets. Early in the evening, Superintendent Catchpole ordered several of his constables on duty in the streets, who endeavoured to put a stop to the discharge of firearms, fireworks &c., but to no purpose, and from the close of evening until Sunday morning, a constant running fire was kept up. Catchpole and his half-dozen constables tried their utmost to check the fires, but were assailed by the mob and severely handled. Catchpole was knocked down and was struck at several times whilst lying on the ground by ruffians disguised in various costumes and armed with large sticks; and one of the constables had a squib thrust into his face, which burst in his eye, the sight of which it is greatly feared it has destroyed. The police, finding it impossible to contend against the crowd, endeavoured to leave the principal street and were leading the wounded constable home, when they were surrounded and the sticks were freely used against them, several of the constables receiving very severe contusions and they were compelled to seek refuge in the shop of Mr. Mead, Baker, but no sooner was the door closed than a rush was made at it: the glass was smashed and a perfect storm of fireworks of every description were hurled after the police who, passing out at the rear of the house, succeeded in gaining the station. For a time, it was feared that the station would be attacked by the rioters and several were heard in the crowd to suggest such a proceeding, but fortunately it was not acted upon.*

IPSWICH & COLCHESTER TIMES: November 11th 1859

Reading about **crime and punishment** was an entertainment in itself. You only have to see how much column space was given over to it to recognise that it was without doubt the main reason that most people bought their paper...

Chapter 6 - Crime Stories

Whether they be reports of major crimes or trivial misde-meanours, the readership of the county's local rags has long enjoyed reading about the unacceptable activities of bad boys and girls.

EXTRAORDINARY ATTEMPT TO POISON - A man named Lewis, a journeyman butcher has been apprehended at Woolwich charged with attempting to poison fifteen persons! It appears a jury had been impanelled by the Coroner, on view of the bodies of three convicts who had died suddenly. When the business was over, the jury had several pounds of beef-stakes cooked, and after disposing of them, they were all taken ill. On inquiry being made, it was ascertained that the prisoner had purchased some emetic tartar from a druggist's, which he said he had been asked to do by a man in the street who gave him a glass of gin for his trouble! The magistrates thought there was not sufficient evidence to put him on his trial, but required sureties before they discharged him.
                        ESSEX STANDARD: January 1831

On Monday evening last, as Mr. Macro of Barrow Hall near Bury was returning home on foot about eight o'clock in the evening, he was stopped near his own house by a single highwayman mounted on a brown horse with a waggoner's frock on, who with an oath demanded his money. Mr. Macro, seeing a horse pistol in his hand, immediately struck at it with his walking stick but missed his aim. The highwayman fired at him, which providentially only grazed his cheek and singed his coat in the shoulder. It was so near his own house where he was attacked, that the report of the pistol was heard by his family. The highwayman, as soon as he perceived that Mr. Macro was not wounded rode off with great haste into the open fields without his booty, which would have been considerable, as Mr. Macro had been at the Red Lion, collecting the tithes of the parish. Mr. Macro went the next morning to the place to see

if he could find out any marks of a person being that way, when he discovered the track of a horse with a bar shoe, which he traced to Kentford Bull, where he found it in the stable, and the rider in the kitchen, whom he apprehended.

CHELMSFORD CHRONICLE: 10th January 1783

This would only be the beginning of a widely reported story. James Steggles would be tried at the Bury Assize two months later, and though he had failed to commit murder, he was hanged for his recklessness on April 2nd 1783. The picture comes from a popular magazine of the time, the Newgate Calendar.

Though this was serious stuff, most cases reported were extremely petty. The local magistrates' courts around the county, often referred to as the **Petty Sessions**, produced such examples of shocking behaviour as…

On Tuesday, J. Lambert, J. Boyce and Wm. Deacons were convicted before the Mayor of Harwich for disturbing the inhabitants by singing disgraceful songs and were bound over to keep the peace for 12 months and pay expenses.
ESSEX & SUFFOLK TIMES: March 9th 1839

George England was brought up charged with having concealed himself in a railway truck for the purpose of committing a felony. John Strickland, a police constable of the Eastern Counties Railway, said he received information that morning that a man had been found in a truck at the Chelmsford station, containing general goods from London, and on coming down here he found that several parcels were missing. Some time since a package was missed from the platform at the station, and the prisoner, who had been seen lurking about, had absented himself up to the present time. He (witness) therefore requested a remand, in order to allow time for further inquiries. Wade, carman to Mr. Bird, proved that when he untied the covering of a truck that morning between seven and eight o'clock, he saw the prisoner's legs sticking out, upon which he called the station-master, who gave him into custody.
The prisoner was remanded for a week.
CHELMSFORD CHRONICLE: October 20th 1858

Castle Hedingham Petty Sessions - *Ruth Gaskin, a hawker was fined £2 charged with encamping on the highway at Yeldham and with not having her name on her vehicles* [This was before vehicle registration].
SOUTH WEST SUFFOLK ECHO: February 22nd 1890

Mischievous boys - *Wm. Barber, Alfred Barnard, William Lodge, Frederick Reafield, little boys of Squirrell's Heath, for cruelly ill-treating a number of sheep, the property of Mr. William Barnes, cowkeeper of Hornchurch by riding them about in the fold were each fined 6d & 4s 6d costs.*
ESSEX NEWSMAN: March 2nd 1878

At Bardfield Petty Session, Jan 31st, Robert Hardy, labourer of Finchingfield was found guilty of stealing one oak faggot, value 4d. Sentence: 6 months hard labour [compare this with the same penalty for manslaughter in the Sible Hedingham case in Chapter 10].
ESSEX HALFPENNY NEWSMAN: February 5th 1870

Ilford Session: Thomas Rose and Robert Holloway were fined £5 (lowest penalty) or 1 month for throwing mud into the Thames from a barge.
ESSEX HALFPENNY NEWSMAN: February 12th 1870

Geo. Wainwright and Geo. Wright, lads of Halstead were charged with stealing a piece of driftwood, value 1s., the property of Mr. John Alston, farmer of Halstead on the 2nd inst. and were fined 1s. each.
ESSEX STANDARD: January 14th 1882

Samuel Woffen [or Wiffen] *was charged with stealing a padlock from Mr. S. Radcliffe, landlord of the White Hart, West Bergholt. It was the very same padlock he had prosecuted George Bashett for stealing three weeks earlier.* [Woffen was luckier, receiving a conditional discharge: Bashett had been given 14 days hard labour]
ESSEX TELEGRAPH: November 10th 1863

The **Quarter Sessions** handled slightly more serious cases…
Chemsford Quarter Sessions: Elizabeth Knowles, for stealing two geese, the property of Martin Higham, was ordered to be privately whipt and discharged.
CHELMSFORD CHRONICLE: October 5th 1764

Edward Westwood, labourer was indicted for stealing a duck, belonging to John Gurney Fry at Dagenham. Sentence: One month's solitude - The

Chairman remarked that this was a slight punishment, but upon a repetition of the offence, he would certainly be transported.
ESSEX STANDARD: January 11th 1834

HIGH LIFE BELOW STAIRS - *James Gray and Jane Tucker, alias Rout, alias Badham were charged at Marylebone Office on Monday night with various acts of swindling. When apprehended, they were found in a kitchen regaling themselves with a leg of lamb and asparagus and a bottle of champagne.*

John Seeks, alias Green, 14, labourer, pleaded guilty of breaking into the dwelling house of Isaac Smith of Gt. Dunmow and stealing a penny piece.

Both of the above are taken from from the Colchester Gazette and Essex Independent of April 9th 1836. John Seeks, for stealing one penny received a sentence of one year's hard labour. (In spite of its claim to be 'independent', this paper, like a number of others had a strong allegience to a political party; in this case the Liberals).

But if you were really bad, you could find yourself at the twice-yearly **Assizes**. At the Chemsford Summer Assize of 1814, John Clarke and George Markham were found guilty of the rape of girls under the age of ten. In the case of Markham, he *'communicated to a five-year old a terrible malady.'* They received sentences of one and two years' imprisonment. By way of comparison, Charles Barwell, for stealing a watch and Edward Clarke, for stealing three sheep, received sentence of death. Property was more important than people and the punishment meted out proved it. (COLCHESTER GAZETTE: August 6th 1814)

EXTRAORDINARY CASE - *Robert French (21), labourer was indicted for stealing a nightgown, the property of Edward Killenworth at Rochford... There were some singular circumstances attending this case. A rope was fixed across a narrow part of the road leading from Rochford to Stambridge on the night of 14th of February, in such a position that it must strike near the throat of any person passing in a gig. Mr. Grabham, surgeon, was passing with his servant, but their weight, having caused* *the gig to sink rather more than usual, the rope only struck their hats. They immediately gave information to the constable of Stambridge who watched and took the prisoner, when a razor and nightgown were found in his hat; the latter of which had been stolen from the prosecutor's hedge. Guilty. A former conviction was proved. The Chairman said... What could be the prisoner's intention with the razor in his hat, only himself could know, but no-one who had heard the case could think that any man's life would have been safe, who might have met with him on that occasion. The sentence was that he be transported for the term of his natural life, in order to prevent the natural lives of others being sacrificed.*

ESSEX & SUFFOLK TIMES: February 23rd 1839

For some, it could be easier to get into gaol than out of it...
At the last General Quarter Sessions at Chelmsford, John Saunders was discharg'd from the Goal [Gaol was often spelt like this] *there, after having been confined upwards of seventeen years for want of sureties for the maintenance of two bastard children, sworn to him by two women at Coopersale near Epping.*

PILBOROUGH'S COLCHESTER JOURNAL: May 26th 1739

The old Chemsford gaol

On the other hand, you could be lucky…

AN ODD ACQUITTAL - *A girl was tried last week for stealing a pair of black silk stockings; but it being proved upon evidence that they were odd ones, she was acquitted. Arguing that two do not make a pair is as good as the Irish decision that a dead duck was not a duck.* [Actually, this had not been an Irish judgement, but an English one delivered from the Worcester Assizes about two years earlier.]

ESSEX STANDARD: February 1831

... or very unlucky...

THE LATE MR. BARON GRAHAM - *A very singular instance of the Baron's excessive and ill-timed politeness occurred on one occasion after the close of the trials at a county assize. Nine unhappy men were all appointed to receive sentence of death for burglary, highway robberies and other offences. It so happened however that in entering the names of the unfortunate parties, after being convicted, on his own slip of paper, Baron Graham omitted one of them. The nine men were brought up to receive judgement and the eight whose names were on his slip of paper were severally sentenced to death. They then quitted the bar. The ninth stood in mute astonishment at the circumstance that no sentence was passed upon him. The clerk of the court, perceiving the mistake, immediately called aloud to his lordship, just as he was opening the door to leave the court, that he had omitted to pass sentence on one unfortunate man. Turning about, and casting a look of surprise at the unhappy prisoner, he hurried back to the seat he had just vacated, and taking a pinch of snuff (for he was one of the most inveterate snuff-takers that ever lived) and putting on the black cap, he addressed the prisoner in the following strain, giving at the same time a profusion of bows - "My good man, I really do beg your pardon for the mistake; it was entirely a mistake - altogether a mistake, I assure you. The sentence of the court on you is that you be taken to the place whence you came, thence to the place of execution, and there be hanged by the neck until you are dead. And the Lord have mercy on your soul. I do beg your pardon; I am very sorry for the mistake, I assure you." So saying, he gave another low bow and then quitted the court.*

COLCHESTER & CHELMSFORD GAZETTE: March 18th 1837

Crime then was very different from crime now. This can be noted from some activities that were once more frowned upon than they might be today. In July 1893, the East Anglian Daily Times reported the trial of Amos Grant, a greengrocer from Walton-on-the-Naze. He was accused of stealing water from Walton Waterworks. He paid for and received a supply of water by means of a tap in his premises. His daughter living nearby had to rely on a shared stand-pipe in the street. Amos had been observed carrying two or three buckets of water a day to his daughter's house - reasonable, you might think. Not a bit of it. The Chairman of the magistrates in fining him 5s (with 11s costs) remarked, *"in a place like Walton, water was as valuable as milk and it was as bad to steal water as to steal milk."*

About twenty Peruke [wig] *makers of note were convicted at the Assize Office for using and having in their custody hair powder not made of starch.* PILBOROUGH'S COLCHESTER JOURNAL: May 19th 1739

In an April 1848 edition of the Essex Standard, a case was brought against James Howard of Manningtree for smuggling 13 cwts of foreign rope.

COLCHESTER - HEAVY FINE FOR SELLING BUTTERINE
Frederick Thomas Gosling, pork butcher, Long Wyre Street; Charles White, grocer, Magdalen Street; and Philip Belchem, grocer's assistant in the employ of the International Tea Company... were charged before the Mayor with having sold butter of a different quality to that demanded by the purchaser... Mrs Laura Marsh was instructed by the Head Constable to purchase butter at the defendants' shops. She asked for one pound of shilling butter, and was served with the article, a sample of which had been sent to Mr. William Foster M.A.F.C.S., lecturer on Chemistry at the Middlesex Hospital, for analysis.

A certificate was received from Mr. Foster to the effect that the sample submitted to him did not contain any butter. The magistrates fined Belchem £5 and White and Gosling were each fined £2. All three had to pay costs.

SUFFOLK & ESSEX FREE PRESS: March 29th 1885

Products that were not quite all they might be were a real problem. ' The Sickle', in December 1828, described how Cornish flour was often adulterated with white felspar, and how the fraud might be detected.

There are already between 50 and 60 rioters including 20 for machine-breaking for trial at the approaching Chelmsford Sessions. They have been principally apprehended in the neighbourhood of Newport, Clacton & Kirby, which districts remain still much agitated. The magistracy are not insensible to the alarming aspect, which the county has assumed and have been actively engaged in swearing in special constables and mounted patrols.

SUFFOLK CHRONICLE: January 1st 1831

Even the most peaceful of protests was unacceptable in the early nineteenth century…

On Whit Monday afternoon, the Chartists held a meeting at Eye, which was most numerously and respectably attended. The greatest peace and order prevailed. The Tories as usual, did not forget their persecuting spirit, but shewed the black clouds of their little angry souls, and ordered the Suffolk troop of Cavalry, commanded by Sir Edward Kerrison to be in attendance at a short distance from the town.

ESSEX & SUFFOLK TIMES: May 25th 1839

You can see from this just how politically aligned most of our local papers were. This was how a Liberal paper reported it. On the other hand, the Tory Ipswich Journal presented a different view. In a paper published the same day, they reported another local Chartists meeting in an entirely different way...

THE CHARTISTS - On Tuesday afternoon, a Chartist meeting was held at the Lame Dog Bowling Green on the Corporation Marshes. Up to three o'clock, not more than from 20 to 30 persons were assembled, but during the next half hour, the number increased to about 200, when the proceedings commenced. Two delegates were introduced, Messrs. Powell from Birmingham and Osborn from Brighton, who severally addressed the meeting. Though they disclaimed physical force, and outwardly discarded the insinuation of the torch and the dagger, the subject was insiduously referred to and certainly more inflammatory harangues it has never been our lot to hear... The meeting passed off very quietly, but little applause was given to the speakers, though many a laugh was excited by the humourous remarks of Powell in the course of his seditious harangue... The majority assembled took little interest in the proceedings.

IPSWICH JOURNAL:
May 25th 1839

In April 1848, a Chartist meeting at Braintree gave rise to warning placards being published, cautioning the public not to attend, and suggesting that the public peace was being threatened by such demonstrations. The Chelmsford Chronicle for April 21st 1848, in the pursuit of balance, also published the counter-placard put out by the Chartists themselves.

Though violence at most of these gatherings was rather less than

CAUTION
Whereas

Information having been received by the Magistrates that a large Assemblage of Persons is expected to take place at **BRAINTREE**, on **Friday, 21st Inst.** Which creates Alarm in the minds of **Her Majesty's Subjects,**

ALL PERSONS
Are hereby Cautioned

And strictly **ENJOINED**, not to *attend*, or *take part in*, or *be present at, any such Assemblage.*

And all well-disposed persons are hereby called upon, and required, to aid in enforcing the provisions of the Law, and effectually to protect the public peace, and suppress any attempt at the disturbance thereof.

O. SAVILL ONLEY
T. WHITE
S. W. SAVILL
JOHN PAGE WOOD
B. SCALE

April 20th, 1848.

might be experienced at your average election hustings, it was in the interest of the ruling elite to portray the Chartist protesters as an undisciplined and mindless rabble, plotting to overthrow the rule of law.

The Price of a Whisker - *A man lately sued another in the County Court, Lincolnshire for having shaved one side of his face and head while he was drunk; and the practical joker had to pay 20s damages and costs for the trick.* [They had clearly not heard of Stag nights]
ESSEX STANDARD: February 7th 1851

A crime that featured commonly was that of poaching or *'night adventuring'* as it was sometimes called. For the most part, miscreants received light sentences, as this was viewed more as a misdemeanour than a felony. Many families relied on a bit of poaching to survive. However, if you took a pot shot at a gamekeeper, it could be a very different matter. The Essex Herald, reporting from the Chelmsford Assizes in March 1829 described how no fewer than 18 poachers were tried for shooting at gamekeeper Richard Warren *'with powder and shot'* at Chissel Park Woods near Elmdon [close to Audley End]. The outcome here was that 17 of the men were transported to Australia for periods of 7 - 14 years. Although the charge of shooting *'with malicious intent'* had failed to be proved against any of them, the judge made it quite clear he was going to use his maximum powers over the poaching charge.

'Catching a poacher' from The Graphic: October 1874

A more serious case came up for trial at the Essex County Assize in March 1856. Earlier in the year, four men had been trespassing at

Boreham. They were James, William & Thomas Thorogood (brothers), abetted by James Guiver & Ebenezer Chalk. Shots had been fired and William Hales, keeper to Sir J.T. Tyrell, M.P., had been killed. The trial was complicated by a number of factors. One of the poachers, Ebenezer Chalk, turned Queen's evidence and testified for the prosecution. He claimed the killer was James Thorogood. However, the shot and wadding the men had used had been distributed amongst all of them, so it was impossible to be certain who had fired the fatal shot. In the end, Chalk's account of the evening proved unreliable, and the best that the prosecution could manage to achieve was to find just James Thorogood guilty of being an accessory to murder. Nevertheless, this was still enough to call up the black cap and have a sentence of death read. With whom he was supposed to have been an accessory was unclear as the others received four years each for *'night poaching.'* Chalk merely received an admonition from the judge. (ESSEX STANDARD: March 7th 1856)

A month later, the Norfolk Chronicle reported that... *"Her Majesty had been graciously pleased to extend her royal mercy to James Thorogood of being accessory to the murder of Hales, the gamekeeper on condition that he be transported beyond the seas for the term of his natural life."*

Even poachers were meant to behave in a sporting manner. In reporting a Lancashire poacher in November 1872, the Waltham Abbey & Cheshunt Weekly Telegraph was most scathing. The man had been catching fish with the help of dynamite.

Certain crimes stand out as being particularly representative of their time. Such was highway robbery...

They write from Colchester in Essex that last week 9 Robberies were committed by a Highwayman, on the roads between that place and Newmarket in Cambridgeshire, and in particular Mr. Spilsby of Witham, on his return from Sudbury in Suffolk was robbed of £18.13s.
IPSWICH JOURNAL: February 14th 1730

On Wednesday last, Mr. Hammond, a weaver, and another person, coming from Lavenham, in Suffolk, were attacked near the Whalebone, between Ilford and Romford, by a Highwayman, who robbed the latter of 3 guineas, but Mr. Hammond having no more than half a crown about him, the rogue generously refused to take it, and rode off towards Epping Forest. IPSWICH JOURNAL: February 28th 1730

Some farmers in Dengy Hundred, on their return from Maldon market were attempted to be robbed by two footpads; but escaped by being well mounted.
IPSWICH JOURNAL: November 30th 1771

On Thursday evening the Colchester Stage Coach was robb'd by three highwaymen opposite to the four mile stone by Stratford, who took from the passengers a considerable booty. One of the villains was remarkably impudent, and tarried some time behind his companions, to re-search every body. They afterwards rode on towards Ilford, robbing several persons they met on the road.
IPSWICH JOURNAL:
October 29th 1743

It was reported later in the same paper, that the three men had been taken in Kent and were being held in Maidstone Gaol. A week later, the information was that two of the three had escaped, but one still being held was a butcher from Essex. [shades of Richard Turpin] The two escapees were at it again in December, robbing travellers at Epping. One particularly bold highwayman robbed the same Colchester Stage Coach twice in a fortnight that December. Travelling Essex roads in the 1740s could be perilous. Travellers didn't

even know who to trust. In September 1736, a Quaker from Saffron Walden, Zachariah Whyat met another dressed as he was on the road to Sturbridge Fair. He told the other Quaker he had a purse with fifty guineas. At that, the man threatened him, so Whyat threw the purse into the undergrowth and while the thief ran to find it, Whyat dismounted his own sorry excuse for a horse and rode off with the robber's much finer one. (IPSWICH JOURNAL: September 18th 1736)

If you were prepare to be bold and take the risk, the returns could be quite substantial. Three brothers reported as being arrested at *'a genteel house at Epping Forest'* in March 1784 were apparently doing very nicely for themselves, having among their possessions, *'complete sets of most kinds of tools'* and *'a private stable'* for their fine horses, which were described as *'remarkable for their spirit and speed.'*
One of the brothers, Charles Dunsdon was hanged at Chelmsford later that month. The others were returned to Oxford to face similar charges there. (CHELMSFORD CHRONICLE: March 26th 1784)

Robberies on the highway were plentiful throughout the eighteenth century. Those who travelled tended to carry money and valuables with them and the Essex roads made for relatively easy pickings. Even female highway robbers appeared from time to time. The Chelmsford Gazette for March 7th 1823 described a Norfolk robbery by an 18 year-old woman [other accounts say she was 23] called Durrant. She had robbed a girl at Haddiscoe of a purse containing £28 as well as a bundle of lace and expected to get well away from the area by catching the Yarmouth Coach. However, the coachman, Mr. Hatch had been warned to be on the lookout for her, and when she boarded the coach, he made sure she ended up in the hands of the Mayor's officers in Yarmouth. At the following Assize, she received a death sentence, but was reprieved on account of her youth, and transported to Australia.

Rewards offered for the apprehension of such felons meant that almost anyone might try his hand at criminal-catching. These robberies were all reported in a single issue of the Ipswich Journal in 1774...

CHELMSFORD - *Last Tuesday morning, about eleven o'clock, as Mr. Brickwood of Malden was going to Terling in a one-horse chaise, in company with another gentleman, they were stopped by a single* *highwayman in the lane leading to that place, who robbed them of half a guinea and about a guinea's worth of silver. Information was immediately given of the robbery, with the following very remarkable description of the highwayman, viz. That he was a well-dressed man in dark cloaths, with a round hat, of a ruddy complexion, low in stature, and that he was mounted upon a little bald-faced chestnut horse which trotted very wide behind. With this intelligence, several people went in pursuit of him. A servant belonging to John Strutt Esq. took the great road and came to this place, and, upon enquiry, he was informed that a person exactly answering the above description was seen to go into Mr. Baker's at the Ship; to this house the servant followed, and after surveying the man and horse, he thought they agreed with the particulars he had had from Mr. Brickwood and the other gentleman, sufficient to justify his ordering the man into custody, and went to Terling for the witnesses, but neither of the gentlemen, upon their arrival, would swear to his person. Having been seen that very morning on the Braintree Road by the passengers in the Bury machine and giving a satisfactory acount of himself, he was discharged.*

Friday evening last, a young woman who keeps this market, being on her return home, was stopped by a single footpad, about two miles from Gt. Waltham, who dragged her off her horse and robbed her of 4 pounds, which was all the money she had, and otherwise ill used her.

Monday afternoon, about five o'clock, Mr. John Greenwood and his wife at Halsted were stopped between Bocking and High Garrett by a single highwayman who presented a pistol and threatened to fire upon the least resistance. He took from them what silver they had and a watch from Mrs. Greenwood with a gilt chain and gold seal, maker's name 'Hedge, Colchester.' The highwayman was mounted upon a little bald-faced chestnut horse, was dressed in dark cloaths, low, with a round bound hat, and it is generally supposed, had this information arrived sooner, suspicion would have run higher against the man who was detained at the Ship in this town on Tuesday last, for the robbery in the lane to Terling.   IPSWICH JOURNAL: October 29th 1774

Job Boreham and his wife, accused of murdering their daughter at Stansfield in Suffolk in 1765 must have felt they were at a safe distance when they decamped to join harvesters at Heybridge near Maldon in Essex, but a girl who had read the 'Wanted' notice in the Ipswich Journal recognised them from the description and they were arrested and taken back for trial (where they were acquitted).

The most notorious criminals of their day could become celebrities. Dick Turpin was a name rarely out of the papers during the 1730s. Therefore, it is no surprise that he is well remembered today.

'Turpin the butcher' from the Newgate Calendar

On Thursday morning last between Nine and Ten o'clock, one Farmer Forde, coming from Hertford to London was attacked on Northaw Common by Turpin the Butcher, with whom the Farmer had been formerly acquainted, and making some slight resistance, Turpin pull'd off his Hat, as a Signal to another of his Gang, supposed to be Rowden, who was about 200 Yards off upon the scout, to join him, when they dismounted the Farmer, and robb'd him of £4 3s. and some halfpence, and turn'd his Horse loose; after which they were going to bind him, but two Gentlemen on horseback appearing, they left the Farmer and gave them the meeting, and robb'd them of their Money and a Silver Watch; Turpin chang'd his Hat with one of the Gentlemen, and afterwards obliged them to dismount, pull'd their Saddles and Bridles off, and turn'd their horses loose; They made off towards Enfield Chace, were both well mounted and dress'd and us'd the Gentlemen with good Language and Civility. IPSWICH JOURNAL: October 11th 1735

Not all contemporary accounts of Turpin paint quite so romantic a picture. Soon, he was on the run for murder.

On Tuesday last Turpin and Rowden, two of Gregory's gang, had the insolence to ride through the City at noon day, and in Watling Street they were known by two or three porters who ply'd there, but had not the courage to attack them. They were but indifferently mounted, and went towards the Bridge; so that 'tis thought they are gone upon the Tunbridge Road. IPSWICH JOURNAL: October 18th 1735

It was rumoured that when things became too hot for Turpin in England, he had taken himself abroad for his own safety.

We hear that Turpin has been in Holland, from whence he returned about six Weeks ago in the Ostend Packet-boat. It is said that Daniel Malden knew him there, and that Turpin endeavoured to prevail with Malden to go into Foreign Service and see England no more.
IPSWICH JOURNAL: September 24th 1736

Daniel Malden, as famous as Turpin in his day, is now sadly forgotten. As I recount in my book of his life *'Daniel Malden'*, he was born in Ipswich but, like Turpin, gravitated to the East end of London. Malden escaped from Newgate Gaol twice, once over the rooftops; the other time through the sewers with a hundredweight of chains still attached to him. For many years after his death, anyone escaping from any gaol was referred to as having *'done a Daniel Malden.'* One Essex paper followed the story in this way…

Last Tuesday, a chimney sweeper, by way of experiment, went down into the common sewer through which D. Malden lately made his escape out of Newgate and in about two hours came out at the gully hole at Black Fryars. 'Tis certain that all the means possible have been employ'd to trace Malden, but as yet to no purpose.
PILBOROUGH'S COLCHESTER JOURNAL: July 3rd 1736

The poor often identified with the highwaymen; after all, it did tend to be the wealthy who suffered at their hands.

When a letter came down from York in 1739, claiming that a man in custody was none other than the famous Turpin, Pilborough's Colchester Journal described how, even though he was still to be formally identified, he was attracting a good deal of attention... *"he has been seen by abundance of gentlemen as well as many of the inferior sort this afternoon..."* (March 3rd 1739) *"...a great concourse of people daily flock to see him, and they all give him money..."* (March 17th 1739) *"...Since he was suspected to be Turpin, the whole Country have flock'd here to see him, and have been very liberal to him, insomuch that he has had wine constantly before him till his trial, and 'tis said the Gaoler has made 100£ by selling liquors to him and his visitors. Tho' the fellow has made a great noise in the world, he'll now die like a Dog. A vast number of wagers have been lost on this account."* (IPSWICH JOURNAL: April 1739)
Then, after his trial and execution...

They write from York, that an attempt was made by the surgeons of that place to have got the body of Turpin, but the mob hearing that it was dug up, and being inform'd where it was, went and rescu'd it, and re-inter-r'd it, having strew'd it over with lime to prevent its being anatomiz'd.
IPSWICH JOURNAL: April 1739

People liked to believe highwaymen to be romantic figures, well dressed, well mounted and above all, well-mannered. The *'Gentleman of the Road'* title, often applied to a highwayman, was never more appropriate than here...

Wednesday evening, between 8 and 9 o'clock, a gentleman in his carriage was stopped on the Romford Road by a single highwayman who put a pistol into the carriage, telling the gentleman he would not detain him half a minute but must beg a favour of his watch, money &c. which was accordingly delivered him, when he wished the gentleman a good evening and ordered the coachman to drive on. He was well mounted upon a brown horse and he appeared to have an accomplice as a person was observed to stand a little distance from the carriage during the time the robbery was committing and seemed to be mounted on a dun or white horse. CHELMSFORD CHRONICLE: September 10th 1779

COLCHESTER - On Wednesday morning, the stage coach belonging to this town was stopt between Mile-End and Stratford on its return from London by a single highwayman who, putting his hat into the coach, desired the passengers to put their money therein, which being done, he took leave in a very complaisant manner and rode off. His booty was but small.   PILBOROUGH'S COLCHESTER JOURNAL: September 29th 1739

The roads would not be the only dangerous place for the unwary traveller. When railways were built, not enough thought had been given to how they should be policed. Now we have a designated transport police force. It was not always so...

In May last the plaintiff [Mr. Cobb] *was travelling... between Shrewsbury and Birmingham and when the train stopped at Wellington station, a gang of men, sixteen in number entered the carriage and robbed him of* [£89]... *The plaintiff at once got out and complained to the station master and asked him to detain the train until* [he] *could get some policemen who were on the platform to search the men and take them into custody. The station master refused to do so and the train went on and the plaintiff lost his money.*   WEST HAM HERALD: February 11th 1893

Mr. Cobb had been attempting to sue the Great Western Railway Company for the lost sum. Extraordinary though it may seem, he lost his case. The judge said that there was no negligence on the part of the company and there was no obligation on their part to hold up other passengers while he sorted out his problem. It was suggested that if he had arrested the sixteen men and given them into custody, the station-master might have had to behave in a different manner. Theft and robbery on the railways was rife. Though railway companies paid towards local constables policing their stations, the GWR would not create its own police force until after 1918.

Another frequently reported piece of illegality was smuggling…

SMUGGLING EXTRAORDINARY - On Friday last, a Dagenham constable named Page passed a horse and cart on the road near the marshes, and observing the vehicle was covered over with tarpauling and that three men were attending upon it whose appearance was of a very questionable description, he applied to Aris, the police horse patrol of the district for assistance, and communicated to him his suspicions that the chaise-cart contained stolen sheep. The officers mounted two good steeds and went in pursuit of the party. On passing a stackyard near Barking, they saw certain appearances which left no doubt on their minds that a cart had been backed towards the field; but on questioning some labourers who were cutting hay, they denied all knowledge of any horse and cart having passed in that direction. The constable and patrol, however, being certain that they were on the right scent, left a trustworthy person in the stack-yard and continued the pursuit. They eventually came up with the horse and cart near the Duke's Head at Ilford. The cart was empty and the parties met with in the first instance by the Dagenham constable had made their escape on the approach of Aris and Page. After securing the horse and cart, the officers returned to the stack-yard in which they found 30 tubs of brandy with slings attached for more easy removal on men's backs. The tubs were immediately put on seizure and on Saturday were removed to the Queen's warehouse at the Customs House. The brandy is the best Cognac, 50 above proof, and valued at upwards of £200.

On the cart was a board on which was painted "Messrs Boorman & Co., market gardeners and fruiterers, Middlesex." No such persons as "Messrs. Boorman & Co." can be found and the horse and cart have been condemned by the customs, disposed of for the benefit of the crown.

ESSEX STANDARD: March 16th 1838

One particularly remarkable story about smuggling involves one Richard (or Robert) Chaplin. On December 3rd 1779, the Chelmsford Chronicle reported...

Wednesday, a cause was tried before the Lord Chief Baron in Westminster Hall, wherein the King was plaintiff and Robert Chaplin of Ardleigh in Essex, victualler, defendant. The action was brought for running of goods to the amount of 26 thousand, one hundred pounds. The evidence on behalf of the Crown were William Salmon and John Butler, husbandmen of the parish of Thorpe le Soken in Essex. Salmon swore that the defendant on the 8th of May 1777 at ten o'clock in the evening

at Holland Lough assisted in loading 120 tubs of gin and 1600 lb. weight of tea; on the 4th of October following, at the same place, 4,000 lb. weight of tea; and in February 1778, at the same place, 200 tubs and 2,000 lb. weight of tea. No evidence appeared on behalf of the defendant, but the evidence for the Crown was set aside by cross-examination by the defendant's counsel and a verdict was given in favour of the defendant and he is ordered to be immediately discharged from prison.

We have good reason for believing that six years later, Chaplin had moved to Sudbourne in Suffolk where he had pledged himself to 'go straight.' But he couldn't resist sticking two fingers up at those who had tried to see him punished for his midnight excursions. So, in July 1785, this advertisement appeared in the Ipswich Journal...

RICHARD CHAPLIN, Sudbourn, Suffolk, near Orford, begs leave to acquaint his friends and the public in general, That he has, some time back, declined the branch of Smuggling, and returns thanks for all their past favours.—Also, To be SOLD, on MONDAY, August 8, 1785, at the dwelling-house of SAMUEL BATHERS, Sudbourn, the property of Richard Chaplin aforesaid, A very useful CART, fit for a maltster, ashman, or a smuggler—it will carry 80 half-ankers, or tubs; one small ditto that will carry 40 tubs; also two very good loaden Saddles, three Pads, Straps, Bridles, Girths, Horse-cloth, Corn-bin, very good Vault, and many articles that are very useful to a smuggler.

Probably more than with any other form of criminal, smugglers tended to have aliases or nicknames. The Ipswich Journal for June 4th 1748, mentions Samuel *(Bully)* Chapman, James Watling alias *Tom Tit* and Samuel Costins alias *Slip Gibbet*. In 1747, we find Thomas Puryour alias *Blacktooth* and in 1749, John Mills alias *Smoaker*. Again 1n 1748, the same paper gives us a real insight into the confusing world of a smuggler's life when we read about the trial of William Jeffery alias *Jefferson*, alias *Billy Luke*. It was a dangerous business being in opposition to the smugglers, who often greatly outnumbered the Revenue men charged with defending the Essex coast.

On Monday last, a gang of about 20 smugglers, well-mounted and armed, were seen at five o'clock in the evening about Low Layton in Essex with about 18 horses laded with goods and making towards the water-side. IPSWICH JOURNAL: October 8th 1736

The smugglers on our coast are growing ever more numerous and desperate. The Revenue Officers of Burnham, lately returning with some seized goods, were assaulted by the crews of five free-trading cutters that lay in the river... (CHELMSFORD CHRONICLE: February 20th 1784) This account describes Customs Officers being violently attacked and *'nearly murdered.'*

John Felton aged 15 was charged with shooting at another boy, Robert Pilgrim, at Belchamp Walter with a pistol loaded with stones. It appears that the boy Felton was entrusted with the pistol to frighten birds on Mr Rayner's farm. The chairman remarked that he would be glad to see something done about naughty boys but it was contrary to the laws of the country to shoot them. 10s with 10s 6d costs.
SUDBURY POST: July 21st 1859

It appears from the auditing of accounts of the Maldon Association for Prosecuting Felons that the gross charges amounted only to 13s 6d. This speaks volumes in favour of the honesty of the neighbourhood.
ESSEX STANDARD: January 28th 1831

Halſted Aſſociation,

For the more speedy Detection and Punishment of Highwaymen, House-breakers, Sheep-stealers, Receivers of stolen Goods, and of such as are guilty of petty Thefts, and other Offences, by unlawfully breaking down Hedges, lopping of Trees, carrying away or breaking down Gates, Stiles, Posts, Rails, Iron-work, or setting fire to Premises, or Stacks of any Description, stealing Poultry, Corn, Turnips, Potatoes, or other Roots and Vegetables, Shop-lifting, robbing of Orchards, Fish-ponds, stealing Implements of Husbandry, or being accessary to any Theft or Fraud, by Servants, Workmen or others.

Breaking Into The Head Constable's House

It is well known that thieves are not, as a rule, respecters of persons, and we have occasionally heard of burglaries and robberies at the residences of Magistrates, and of the pockets of lawyers, barristers, and so on, being picked within the precincts of a Court; but we cannot recollect ever hearing of the case of a thief as daring as to break into the dwelling house of the Head Constable of a town.

A case of this kind, however, has occurred in Colchester within the past week. On Sunday evening Head Constable Downes, who resides in Church Street North, left home a few minutes before seven o'clock, accompanied by his wife, to attend Church. No person was left in charge of the house, but the doors and windows were all securely fastened, and on returning home after Church everything appeared still to be all right. On the following day Mrs. Downes missed from a purse in the downstairs keeping-room, ten shillings in silver, which had been seen safe just before leaving for Church on the Sunday evening.

This induced her to examine another purse which she kept upstairs, and on doing so she discovered that £6 in gold had been taken from it; and also a silver watch and gold guard, two lockets, two gold keys, two gold broaches, two gold finger rings, &c., from her box in the same room. The rooms did not appear in any way disturbed, and the premises presented no traces of an entry; and there is very little doubt that the thief, who must have been a practised hand, let himself in at the front door by means of a skeleton key, and having succeeded in obtaining possession of the money and other articles, went out again, re-locking the door after him. No clue to the thief has as yet been obtained, but the robbery is supposed to have been committed by a suspicious looking man whom Mr. Downes, as he was going into Church, noticed loitering about the Churchyard.

ESSEX STANDARD: 10th March 1871

Often, punishment was encouraged at grass roots level, as a deterrent to further misdemeanour...

William Curtis aged 9 years of Acton was charged with breaking into a house of a woman named Duce and stealing a half-penny from a missionary box. After careful consideration the bench suggested to

the father that the boy should have his back well dressed by the police with a birch rod. The father agreed and after the boy had a good flogging he was released with a caution.
SUDBURY POST: August 26th 1858

But there was nothing like a good murder to sell papers. In July 1888, the local press went to town on the story of George Sargeant, who had brutally murdered his wife Annie. At this time, newspapers were far less careful about what they printed before and during a trial, and reports such as these must have been prejudicial...

A shocking wife-murder was perpetrated at Wakes Colne on Tuesday... The victim, whose maiden name was Annie Punt... was only twenty one years old... bore an excellent character and was of spotless reputation. George Sargeant, [pictured here] who is a native of Bury St. Edmunds, is a strong stalwart fellow... and is decidedly good looking... but is of a doubtful reputation and... one labourer at Wakes Colne described him as being 'sly and cunning as a fox.' Sargeant was discharged from his employment on the Great Eastern Railway for miscon-duct, and then he led her a terrible life. Always drunken and idle he used to come home and let the burden of his black humour fall upon his wife.

ESSEX NEWSMAN: July 21st 1888

Remember, at this point, Sargeant had only been committed for trial at the forthcoming County Assize. And when it came to reporting the murder itself, the paper left nothing to the imagination...

About three weeks ago, he [Sargeant] went home drunk, smashed the furniture and ill-treated Mrs. Sargeant. This was the crowning point of months of unhappiness and like most women would act in a similar case, flew with her six-months old baby to her parents for protection and a

THE HOUSE WHERE THE MURDER WAS COMMITTED.

The door and window of the kitchen, situated on the right-hand side of the main building, are not shown in the above sketch. The first window on the right is that of the room where the prisoner first stabbed his victim. The second window opens into the room where the murder was completed.

home... Sargeant, who had been frequently heard to threaten to 'pay his wife out' for her desertion was seen loitering about Chappel and Wakes Colne... He called at the Swan Inn... the Railway Tavern... and a beerhouse... evidently drinking to screw up his courage for a deed he had premeditated... Finally he visited Lane Farm to see his wife... Mrs. Punt and her other daughter Emily were at the back of the house when they were alarmed by loud screaming, and rushing into the room... they found that Sargeant had dealt his wife a terrible stab behind and below the right ear with a clasp knife. With the lioness courage of a mother, Mrs. Punt seized the dastardly assassin and attempted to drag him away. Her strength was not equal to his. He pushed her into a corner of the room, and while he was doing this, the unhappy victim ran into an adjoining parlour. He followed her and then ensued a scene so diabolical, so full of bestial rage, that it makes one's blood run cold to think of it. The murderer threw his wife on the floor and kneeling upon her body, slashed at her throat with his knife, the blood running down her poor body and splashing onto his own clothes. With such fury did he attack her that he nearly severed her head from her body, and then kicking her several *times on the head, ran from the room, leaving her dying, with the blood flowing from her in ghastly torrents.* ESSEX NEWSMAN: July 21st 1888

Suffice it to say, George Sargeant pleaded guilty at his trial later that month. The papers gave fascinating descriptions of all the characters involved. *"The father is a sturdy yeoman, clean shaven, with a fringe of grey whiskers round his honest-looking face... The prisoner... did not by any sign betray fear of the consequences of his horrible deed... his face seemed to have lost the slightly haggard appearance which it bore when he was brought before the magistrates at Colchester."*
ESSEX STANDARD: July 28th 1888

Even the hangman, Mr. Berry, at Sargeant's execution received the following attention...
Berry is a fairly well built man, a little below the average height inclining slightly to stoutness and is apparently between thirty and forty years of age. A very marked scar near his right eye is the only thing about his appearance that could be called sinister. He wore a check suit with a black tie with a gilt horseshoe pin and was apparently a good deal displeased at the number of reporters present [8]. He speaks with a strong North country accent and is a rather smart man with 'his wits about him.'
ESSEX STANDARD: August 18th 1888

According to the Essex Newsman of the same date, this was the 290th execution to be carried out in Chelmsford in a little over a century. Whereas most of them had been before an audience of thousands, this and the previous five had been in private, within the gaol. [In 1868, an ammendment to the Execution Act had put an end to public hangings.]

Murder sold papers. The more graphic the details, the better nineteenth century readers seem to have liked it. When illustrations became readily available, they could be horrifically explicit. The Illustrated Police Gazette in September 1896 had just the kind of story they specialised in. At Pebmarsh near Halstead lived a farmer named Samuel Collis. He had recently been declared bankrupt and had spent some time in an asylum. Taking a gun, he had broken windows on his mother's farm and shot a number of chickens. Then he had turned his attention to John Cockerill, his mother's bailiff, shooting him, then decapitating him with a carving knife, before offering the head in a tin can to the horrified local police officer, Constable Cook.

SHOCKING TRAGEDY IN ESSEX
A Mad Farmer Shoots and Beheads a Man.

This was a case that would never come to trial. Within a week, Collis had been certified and sent to Broadmoor; therefore *'Mr. F.H. Bright, solicitor of Maldon, who had been instructed by the Treasury to prosecute, was spared an arduous duty.'* (ESSEX NEWSMAN September 19th 1896)

A number of violent Essex crimes found their way into the Illustrated Police News, such as the 1893 story pictured here.

In April 1893, the body of Acting-Sergeant Adam Eves was found in a ditch in the parish of Hazeleigh near Maldon. He had been battered to death and had his throat cut. Although several suspects were arrested quite quickly, it would take some months for the full story to emerge. Not until November would John and Richard Davis and James Ramsey be tried for murder. For many the verdict would be not be a very satisfactory conclusion to the case. Sergeant Eves had been a big and strong man. It was unlikely that any of the three suspects could have done the deed alone. Yet John Davis alone would hang for the murder. His brother would face life imprisonment and Ramsey would go free. However, this had been a robbery that had gone wrong, and in a subsequent trial Ramsey faced for the theft of thirteen bushels of corn, he would be sentenced to 14 years in gaol. They couldn't try him again for the murder, but the judge was determined to get the most out of that 'guilty to robbery' verdict.

There was certainly a fascination with death in the eighteenth and nineteenth centuries. Almost anything could be regarded as life-threatening, and stories about **death** would be a significant feature of old local papers...

Chapter 7 - Death

I remember, when writing my book, *'I read it in the Local Rag'*, I found the most fruitful topic for newspaper stories in Norfolk and Suffolk was the subject of 'Death'. Newspapers seemed to be full of amusing, entertaining, sometimes gory tales about graveyards, coffins and funerals. Essex papers have proved to be much the same...

IPSWICH - On Friday last, the remains of Mrs. Joslin, an elderly woman who died at Harwich were interred in the churchyard of Belstead near this town. On Tuesday evening, a young man passing through the churchyard observed the ground where the body had been laid to be disturbed, and gave information to the son of the deceased who resided in Belstead, and also the Parish Clerk. On the following morning, the grave was opened and we are concerned to state that the apprehensions of the grave having been violated was found to be true; only a portion of the hair and part of the shroud of the deceased having been found in the coffin.

ESSEX STANDARD: October 8th 1831

Resurrection Men *- On Friday night last, some of these wretches made a daring attempt at Wanstead church-yard in this county and in part succeeded. They first got up the body of a child recently interred, and afterwards the body of a female, which they placed on the edge of the grave. The then commenced on the grave of the Parish Beadle and had made some progress when they were fortunately disturbed, and made their escape with the child only. These fellows are supposed to belong to the same gang that last year*

105

opened a grave in Chingford church-yard, from which they took a patent iron coffin, broke it to pieces and carried away its unconscious tenant.
COLCHESTER GAZETTE: November 6th 1824

In the same edition of the Essex Herald that was recounting the trial of the infamous body-snatchers, Burke & Hare, this bizarre article appeared...

DISTURBERS OF THE DEAD - *Since the burial of Oades, Cashon and Brien, who were executed here* [Chelmsford] *pursuant to their sentences at the lst Assizes, this neighbourhood has been visited by those unfeeling wretches now commonly designated body-snatchers. In the night of the 1st inst. several men were seen near Springfield Church, who, it was suspected, intended to obtain the bodies of the malefactors, but they were disturbed by the servants of a gentleman residing near, and in their retreat, as proof of their calling, left upon a grave a new shovel. Last Monday night, an attempt was made to disinter a body in Broomfield Churchyard, but here these nocturnal visitors were again repulsed. On Wednesday night however, they appear to have been more successful in a second visit to Springfield. Although it has not been ascertained, it is surmised that the body of one of the Irishmen was obtained. Not being acquainted with the circumstance that the two were buried in the same grave, a second was opened which proved to be that of Williams who was executed here for horse-stealing, and whose remains had lain in the ground since August. Finding the body so much decomposed, these wretches determined to have some part, actually twisted the head from the trunk, carrying away the former, which no doubt will prove acceptable to the Phrenological Society, who, we understand, are endeavouring to procure a collection of the heads of malefactors...*
ESSEX HERALD: January 13th 1829

It is a fact, not generally known, that the sheet which received the head of Charles the First after his decapitation at Whitehall is carefully preserved along with the communion plate in the church at Ashburnham, Suffolk: the blood with which it has almost entirely covered now appears nearly black. - The watch of the unfortunate monarch is also deposited with the linen, the movements of which are still perfect. These relics came into the possession of an ancestor of the present Lord Ashburnham immediately after the death of the King. [There is no place in Suffolk called Ashburnham. It is actually in Sussex, though the Earl of Ashburnham had much land around Needham Market in Suffolk]

COLCHESTER GAZETTE: December 3rd 1814

REMARKABLE OCCURRENCE - On the 6th January, William Turnstall, the walking postman from Billericay to Ramsden was found dead on his route. On Sunday morning, Henry Henniker, 47 years of age, who was appointed his successor, whilst engaged in the duties of his office in delivering the town letters, fell in a fit and remained speechless till the next morning, when he expired.

ESSEX & SUFFOLK TIMES: March 9th 1839

FATAL EFFECTS OF EXCESSIVE JOY

On Wednesday se'nnight, died at Billericay in Essex, Mr. John Burles, shoemaker of Chatham, aged 45. This gentleman had just recovered a considerable estate that he had been deprived of more than twenty years, and such was his ecstasy on receiving possession and his first rents, that he was seized with a fever, that terminated his existence in a few hours.

SUFFOLK CHRONICLE: October 20th 1810

The week before last, a maiden lady, residing at Borham, Sussex, aged 80 was in the morning supposed to be dead and the usual preparations were made for the melancholy occasion; but at four o'clock to the great surprise of her relatives, she revived and is now in perfect health.

ESSEX COUNTY STANDARD: April 15th 1831

Last Saturday, an inquisition [Inquest] *was taken at Prittlewell before William Reynolds esq. on the body of James Nunn, a child about two years of age, who unfortunately drank about a tea spoonful of laudanum which had been inadvertantly left in his way by his grandmother, who had been nursing her daughter, then lying dead.*

CHELMSFORD CHRONICLE: January 10th 1783

Laudaunum and other powerful drugs were easily obtainable and small quantities were often fed to babies to keep them quiet. As this cartoon from Punch (*'The poor child's nurse'*) shows, opiates were regarded in some households as the ideal alternative to a baby-sitter.

Reading through nineteenth century papers, you can't help but be surprised by the number of fatal road accidents. Traffic, after all, moved extremely slowly. But the two main reasons for most of these accidents are made clear here...

A servant of Mr. Bale of Tibenham Old Hall, Norfolk lost his life last week, by the wheels of his master's waggon going over his legs which turned to a mortification and ultimately caused his death - The fatal accident was occasioned by a custom prevalent among farmers' servants when on a journey; first to get drunk, and then attempt to ride on the shafts of the waggon.
                    ESSEX COUNTY CHRONICLE: April 7th 1812

Hence, dangerous practices were outlawed...

George Chinnery horseman to Mrs Ewer of Foxearth was charged with riding on the shafts of a waggon in Melford. Rev John Foster sent a letter of good character and long service. Fined 1s 6d with costs.
                    SUDBURY POST: August 12th 1856

On Sunday noon, The Phenomena Norwich Coach on its way to London met the coach from London near St. Peter's Church in Sudbury, the most difficult and dangerous part of the road between Norwich and London.

In endeavouring to make room for each other, the former coach overset, by which accident one man had his arm broken, a woman an arm broken and a child much hurt in the head, but who is now in a fair way of recovery. We are happy to find that not the smallest blame attaches to either of the coachmen, who are both considered skilful and careful men, nor was the coach over-loaded, having four passengers less than the Act allows, and no luggage upon the roof. A sailor who was supposed to have been much hurt and to have broken some of his ribs, by the whimsicality of  *his conduct, raised a smile even in his fellow sufferers and by the help of a few glasses of grog was enabled to pursue his journey. Mr. Crawcour of Norwich, who recently lost his leg from an accident in a gig was among the passengers.* COLCHESTER GAZETTE: June 29th 1822

However, there could be a lighter side, even to road accidents...

An amusing accident occurred on Lombardy Street on Thursday... The Yarmouth coach was leaving town, laden in an extraordinary manner with every kind of Christmas present in baskets and hampers and barrels of all sizes and shapes... [here the paper really goes to town over the way the coach was loaded] *when the springs gave way under the unusual weight of the load... The wonder did not seem to be that the coach had broken down, but that anyone could suppose it could move without doing so.* CHELMSFORD CHRONICLE: December 31st 1841

Among the various clubs existing in the large and populous parish of West Ham, Essex, we may mention a "Coffin Club." The members pay a weekly contribution, and when it amounts to a stipulated sum, they are entitled to what they term their last suit. One member, whose habits were rather eccentric was measured for one, had it home, and occasionally used to sleep in it, but recently, for want of employment, he was compelled to dispose of it to a neighbouring undertaker, and expressed his deep regret that his circumstances were so adverse as to compel him to sell his long-stored valued treasure.

ILLUSTRATED LONDON NEWS: December 1845

A number of such clubs went so far as to offer a bonus payment to the member surviving the longest. A similar club in the north-east of the county was criticised as a *"Licence to murder"* during the Essex Poisoning Trials, later that decade.

Life was precarious, and almost any accident had to be considered as life-threatening. The Essex Telegraph of October 6th 1863 described how a Mr. Gibbons, whilst reading the newspaper to his invalid wife was disturbed by a gnat on the window pane. In swatting at it, he cut the back of his hand. The wound became inflamed and in less than a week, he was dead. As if to reassure us, the newspaper reported that fortunately he had the foresight *'to insure his life with the Railway Passengers Assurance Company, and his wife received £1,000 by way of compensation.* [Sometimes with old newspapers it is hard to distinguish the genuine stories from the adverts].

This story, however, had a happier ending...

An accident of an alarming nature took place at Boreham House, Essex, the seat of Sir John Tyrell, Bart., on Tuesday night week. Mr Ormsby Gore, who with his lady, was on a visit to the mansion, on leaving his dressing room, overlooked several steps to the staircase, and, losing his balance, was precipitated over the balusters. Mr G., in his alarming descent, grasped the handrail of the next flight, but it gave way, and he fell with considerable violence upon the stairs below - severely, though not seriously - injuring his side and one of his feet. His watch, which was in his hand at the time, was dashed to pieces.

ILLUSTRATED LONDON NEWS: September 20th 1845

Not only death, but the manner by which it might be attained held a fascination for the readers of 18th and 19th century papers, and the publishers certainly didn't hold back when it came to a gory tale.

A sad accident happened at Lamarsh a few days ago. A child aged 8 months and belonging to a poor farm labourer was left by its mother in bed in charge of her aged parent for a little while, on returning she discovered to her great horror that a ferret belonging to her husband and had escaped from its box was attacking the child, the poor infant's nose being entirely eaten off. The screams of the child were not heard by the aged woman who is very deaf. The child is recovering, but of course will be disfigured.
SOUTH SUFFOLK & NORTH ESSEX FREE PRESS: April 16th 1868

There was an inquest at the Cock Inn, Clare, on the body of Thomas Hickford aged 62 who fell in a tub of hot liquor while brewing. John Mansfield a labourer, said, 'I was helping remove the wort, deceased fell backwards into the liquor, I pulled him out, he did not appear drunk.' Accidental death.
SOUTH SUFFOLK & NORTH ESSEX FREE PRESS: April 16th 1868

We have an account from Carlstadt in Transylvania of a most shocking transaction which passed at Carnor, about two leagues from that town. A man who had been a few months married to a young woman of eighteen of whom he was exceeding jealous, having taken some exceptions to her conduct, locked himself up one evening with her and her mother. He stripped his wife and having fastened her to the wall with wooden pegs, he cut off her ears, nose and two breasts and drove a stake into her belly. He then cut open her side with a knife and, not finding her heart, which he wanted, he opened the other side, from which he took it out. He then loosened the poor wretch, laid her on the ground, to which he fastened her with three pegs; after which he laid himself down by the dead body, and as if satiated with barbarity had produced the same effects as drunkenness, he fell into so profound a sleep that his mother-in-law, who expected the same fate, easily opened the doors and escaped into the neighbourhood where she gave an account of the shocking scene she had been witness to. Proper persons were dispatched who seized this furious savage while still asleep. The punishment inflicted on him corresponds with the manners of the ancient Scythians and is proportioned to so unheard-of a crime. The wretch was conducted on foot to the gallows where he was stript, after which his nose, ears and the flesh of his breast were torn off with hot pincers. He was to have had his eyes plucked out, but this was omitted because from a Schismatic, he became a Catholic. They then fastened his feet to the tail of his own horse and dragged him three times round the gallows; after which they cut off his two hands, one after the other, by slow and deliberate strokes. They then cleaved his head, opened his breast, took out his heart, which was cut in several pieces. At last, his limbs were nailed to the gallows so low that dogs and wild animals might reach them; and they were in fact devoured before night. This wretch bore these severe torments with incredible firmness and resolution.

CHELMSFORD CHRONICLE: April 19th 1765

...and even that seems almost humane compared to what the Russian Tsar's judiciary passed by way of punishment on conspirators in [St] Petersbourg according to the Ipswich Journal in October 1743. Other deaths by comparison seem almost comical...

In the evening of Thursday se'nnight, a melancholy accident occurred between Walton Ferry and Landguard Fort. A soldier... set out on his return to the garrison, on the way to which there are three small creeks to pass, the first of which, his friends put hin across and left him. On endeavouring to cross the second, he unfortunately missed the direct way and got into the mud. Incapable of extricating himself... he remained in that awful state of suspense till the tide which was then coming in flowed over him and he was drowned. The next morning, he was found standing upright, fast in the mud.

ESSEX UNION: September 1st 1809

A man hung by a corpse - *The Cincinnati Gazette says that on Saturday night last, a body snatcher who had stolen a corpse from a graveyard in the neighbourhood of that city, which he had placed in a bag, was hung while endeavouring to get over a high fence, the corpse falling on one* *side and the body snatcher on the other, he having placed around his shoulders the cord by which the bag was shut, and the cord slipping about the neck, choking him to death.*

STRATFORD TIMES: March 25th 1859

A very novel species of duel has lately taken place at Paris, M. Granpree and M. Le Pique having quarrelled about Mademoiselle Tirevit, a celebrated opera dancer, who was kept by the former but had been discovered in an intrigue with the latter, a challenge ensued. Being both men of elevated mind, they agreed to fight in balloons, and in order to give time for the preparation, it was determined that the duel should take place on that day month. Accordingly, on the 3rd of May, the parties met at a field adjoining the Tuilleries where their respective balloons were ready to receive them. Each attended by his second ascended his car loaded with blunderbusses, as pistols could not be expected to be efficient in their probable situations. A multitude attended, hearing of the balloons, but little dreaming of the purpose; the Parisians merely looked for the novelty of a balloon race. At nine

o'clock the cords were cut and the balloons ascended majestically amidst the shouts of the spectators. The wind was moderate, blowing from the NNW and they kept, as far as can be judged within about 80 yards of each other. When they had mounted to the height of about 900 yards, M. Le Pique fired his piece ineffectually; almost immediately after, the fire was returned by M. Granpree and penetrated his adversary's balloon; the consequence of which was its rapid descent and M. Le Pique and his second were both dashed to pieces on a house top over which the balloon fell. The victorious Granpree then

mounted aloft in the grandest style and descended safe with his second, about seven leagues from the spot of ascension.
IPSWICH JOURNAL: April 23rd 1808

An altogether more local duel was fought at Danbury in 1808, when two young officers who should have been more interested in killing French soldiers ended up facing up to one another.

Sunday morning, a duel was fought on Danbury Common between Lieuts. O____e and M____n,  *both of the 43rd Foot, which was attended with fatal consequences to the former, who received a ball through the body on the first fire and expired on the spot. This melancholy circumstance originated in a trifling dispute at the mess on the preceding evening. Lieut. M. and the seconds have absconded.*
NORFOLK CHRONICLE February 13th 1808

[The illustration used here is not of this duel, but one where the Duke of Wellington fought the Earl of Winchilsea at Battersea in 1829]

Though the surviving participants had absconded, the law would soon catch up with them. This, as the Judge at the County Assize warned Lieut. R.P. Murchison and the two seconds, Lieuts. Hopkins & Dundas, was murder. Duelling was not legal and the death of Lieut. Ogilvie was an unlawful killing. The jury had it explained to them that should they be certain the men before them had been responsible for Lieut Ogilvie's death, there could be only one result.
Surprise, surprise, *'The Jury, after some hesitation, acquitted all the prisoners.'* (KENTISH GAZETTE: March 15th 1808)

There is a certain elegance with which these early journalists could describe unfortunate events...

DISTRESSING ACCIDENT - *A few days since, as Mr. John Hearn, late of the King's Head, Pebmarsh* [pictured below] *and Mr. C. Humphreys of the Angel Inn, Bures were returning from Boxford in a gig, the horse when within a short distance of Bures, suddenly started at something in the road, by which means both the above named gentlemen*

*were thrown from the vehicle and, we regret to state, Mr. Hearn was so seriously injured that he survived the fall only a short period. Mr. Humphreys was also so much hurt as to prevent his attending to business for the present; but we learn that nothing serious is apprehended in his case. Mr. Simonds, the surgeon of Bures was instantly in attendance, and used every effort to relieve the sufferings under which Mr. Hearn was at that time labouring, but without effect. The deceased was one who was greatly respected by all who knew him, and has left a widow and a large circle of friends to lament their loss. A coroner's jury was held on the body, when a verdict of Accidental Death was returned, with a **Deodand** of one shilling on the horse.*

COLCHESTER GAZETTE & ESSEX INDEPENDENT: January 2nd 1836

[The English common law of **Deodands** traces back to the 11th century and was applied, on and off, until Parliament finally abolished it in 1846. Under the law, personal property, such as a horse was considered a deodand whenever a coroner's jury decided that it had caused the death of a human being. Deodands were forfeit to the crown, which was supposed to sell the item and then apply the profits to some pious use. In reality, the juries who decided that a particular animal or object was a deodand also appraised its value and the owners were expected to pay a fine equal to that value]

Sometimes, however, the callousness sometimes used by local paper journalists could be quite shocking...

MELANCHOLY DEATH OF CAPTAIN NISBETT - Last Friday, as Captain Nisbett of Brettenham Hall, late of the Guards, was trying a horse in harness down the North Hill at Colchester, the animal set off at full speed, and the reins breaking, Captain N. in attempting to get out, was thrown down and severely injured. His face and head were cut and he was a good deal bruised; but the injury inflicted on the knee-pan was the ultimate cause of his death - which was so dreadfully shattered that mortification ensued, and he died on Friday last, just three weeks after this accident occurred

He was in the habit of driving at a furious rate, and it is almost a matter of surprise that no accident sooner occurred... He was but 21 years of age and his widow is barely yet 19.

SUFFOLK HERALD: September 1831

These were harsh times and almost anything could be life-threatening. The following story appeared in the South West Suffolk Echo on February 8th 1890.

WHY WASN'T HE IN SCHOOL? On Thursday, while John Walls, employed by Mrs Raincock of 'Waltons' [Ashdon, near Saffron Walden, Essex] was helping to cut chaff, his right hand came in contact with the cogs of the wheel of the machine and the end of the middle finger was crushed. Dr. Watson of Linton attended to the little fellow.

So far, so good. But a fortnight later, the same paper reported the inquest on Johnny Walls. He had died of *'lock-jaw.'* As the Coroner said, *"He got his hand in the chaff machine and it was nobody's fault but his own."* He was ten years old.

Respect was not always afforded to those who had fought and died for their country. An Essex Standard article from August 1834 reported...

Manure - Between 200 and 300 tons of the bones of horses and men which were lost in Napoleon's retreat from Moscow have arrived... at Grimsby.

Believe it or not, they were to be ground up to make manure. This is borne out by a Suffolk Herald report of November 1829 which

informed readers that... *"A ship laden with bones has arrived at Lossiemouth... the bones were collected from the plains and marshes around Leipzig and are part of the remains of thousands of French soldiers who fought there with Napoleon in 1813."*
The Essex Standard wryly concluded...
"This is a literal realisation of the giant's threat as set forth in the nursery tales - "I'll grind his bones to make my bread."

But few stories on the subject of Death can cap this one. It was part of a long ongoing story...

SURREPTITIOUS REMOVAL OF A CORPSE FROM FOXEARTH CHURCHYARD

A great amount of excitement throughout the parish of Foxearth, near Sudbury, and the adjoining locality, by widespread rumour propagated on Thursday last - and which proved correct - to the effect that the remains of the late Samuel Vial, Esq. had been removed from the church-yard under circumstances of a most extraordinary nature. It appears that about six o'clock on Thursday morning a labourer named Ward, in the employ of the Rev. J. Foster, was passing through the churchyard when he found the tombstone had, by some means or other, had been removed during the night, and the ground rifled of its contents, the earth still remained as it was thrown out, and the grave-stone was broken in two or three pieces. A piece of candle, which evidently had been used to light the men in their operations, was left on the mutilated tomb. Mr. Vial had been buried in a brick grave, which had been covered in the same way with a large slab, the full size; this had been drawn or taken out and placed by the side, but as the grave had not been entirely uncovered at one end of the coffin had been tilted up then lifted to the surface.From thence it was carried to the gate, and placed in a vechicle of some description; the tracks across the meadow clearly showed the marks of a vechicle leading to the Sudbury road. Rev. Foster had been absent for several days. Nothing was heard in the night, either of the men who did the work, or the waggon brought to convey the body away, but certain labourers, in the parish of Otten Belchamp, who were going to their morning's employment, aver that they met a yellow painted vehicle, driving at a moderate pace, towards Belchamp, on which were riding five or six men, but they were so disguised as not to be recognizeable by any of them. The man who first discovered the empty grave was in the gas house, seeing to the works, at two o'clock in the morning, but heard nothing; this might be accountable for, as a strong wind was blowing from the buildings, and the night was dark one.

It will no doubt be fresh in the minds of our readers that the sons of the deceased were anxious to disinter the remains and bury them alongside his wife, who is interred in Otten Belchamp churchyard .

On the same morning, between seven and eight o'clock as the sexton at Otten Belchamp was walking through the churchyard, he noticed a plank lying against the wall, and noticed it was partly encrusted with dirt, and appeared as it had been for some time imbedded in the earth. On making further investigations it was discovered that the grave in which Mrs. Vial had been buried had been opened during the night; not however as in olden days, by body snatchers, who rifled the corpses for plunder, or carried them away in sacks to dispose of them for remuneration as 'subjects' for the dissecting room, but that another corpse might be interred in the same grave. The earth had been shovelled in carefully, and pressed down well, and the turf (which had been cut artistically from the mound) was replaced exactly, apparently by practical and professional hands. All marks of the nocturnal visit and disturbance had been obliterated as far as possible, and a casual glance at the spot would not have detected any recent displacement of soil. But a little 'slip' as often is the case, had occurred, which led to the discovery of the open grate. It appears that when Mrs. Vial was interred, for some reason or other, three planks were left in the ground, laid over the coffin; perhaps in preparation for the other coffin, which might be placed above. On Wednesday night the men who had been employed to disinter the body of Mr. Viall in Foxearth churchyard, had not stayed to obliterate traces of their midnight work, but evidently proceeded immediately to Otten Belchamp, and opened the grave where the wife had been buried, and placed the corpse of her husband there, but in the necessary burying, they had inadvertently left out one of the planks and, finding out too late their mistake, had thrown it against the wall, not deeming it advisable to carry with them any criminatory

118

Foxearth Church today

evidence. It was the plank that led to the discovery of the opening of the grave.

Of course the Foxearth authorities were angry at what had been done, and every effort is being made to discover the parties engaged in the removal of the corpse; it is rumoured that a London detective is likely to be brought down, and by whose skill the midnight depredators brought to justice. Great excitement has been caused locally, (and as is generally the case in parochial disputes and feuds, some persons sympathise with the Rector and are very irate at the 'sacrilege'; while others feel that the Vials were very much injured and aggrieved, and that the secret way the body was removed was cleverly planned, and neatly carried out. As journalists we cannot side with one or the other. Yet we trust that for the peace, and to avoid other scandals which might hurt religion, social rites, and *even trade and business, and that the authorities, be that Foxearth and Belchamp, will now let the dead rest in peace, and abstain from quarrelling with the living. It was a natural feeling that survivors should should wish both parents to rest together in consecrated ground, and there could could be no valid objection to the removal of either body to the other churchyard.*

SOUTH SUFFOLK & NORTH ESSEX FREE PRESS: October 7th 1864

A fortnight later, this advert appeared...

20 POUNDS REWARD - SACRILEDGE AND BODY STEALING
ON WEDNESDAY NIGHT OF THE 19TH INSTANT, THE CHURCH-YARD OF THE PARISH OF FOXEARTH WAS VIOLENTLY ENTERED, AND THE BODY OF LATE SAMUEL VIAL WAS DISINTERRED AND TAKEN AWAY. THE ABOVE REWARD WILL BE PAYED TO ANY PERSON WHO WILL GIVE INFORMATION AS SHALL LEAD TO THE CONVICTION OF THE PERSON OR PERSONS, CONCERNED IN AFORESAID SCANDALOUS IRRELIGIOUS OUTRAGE.
SIGNED RICHARD ALDHAM & HENRY COKER,
CHURCHWARDENS.

So, why bother with burial at all? Cremation was far from a new idea. Our distant ancestors had used it, so maybe it was time to reintroduce the practice...

The Halstead Times of May 23rd 1874 described the formation of a New York Cremation Club, estimating the cost of a body being burnt as 5 - 8 dollars...

"They intend to lease a piece of land in New York and erect thereon buildings and furnaces. A great deal of interest in this subject is being developed in this country."

The British public required a bit more convincing. It would be another ten years before, under much protest, the first cremations would be carried out; another thirty years before crematoriums would start to be set up across the country.

In a more humourous vein...

Among the numerous patents, we observe one lately granted to John Hughes of Barking in this county, for certain means of securing the bodies of the dead in coffins. This intention consists in the use or application of an extra or additional bottom to the coffin and fastening thereto the body by means of plates, chains, bars, springs or straps of cast or wrought iron.

COLCHESTER GAZETTE: April 10th 1824

As was shown in the previous chapter, violent death was always newsworthy. Graphic accounts and even pictures appeared in a variety of publications. One week in June 1893 saw two Essex murders filling the columns of the papers.

When Emma Hunt was murdered at Rochford, suspicion fell on Alfred Hazell (17). Following an inquest that seemed to point the finger at him, Hazell was sent for trial at the Summer Essex Assize, but the evidence was thin in the extreme and he walked free from the court. A public subscription was raised to build a memorial to Mrs. Hunt at Rochford.

In a remarkably similar

THE ROCHFORD MURDER.

A monument has been erected by public subscription over the grave of the late Mrs. Emma Hunt in Rochford Churchyard. The surplus money will be utilised for the benefit of the deceased's son.

case, Johanna O'Driscoll, an itinerant pea-picker was found in a ditch with her throat cut at Aveley near Thurrock. Though descriptions were published of wanted men and arrests were made, again nobody was ever tried for the killing and as with Emma Hunt, her death was brought about by *'person or persons unknown.'* (Essex Newsman)

Whilst those responsible for death were publicly reviled, there were those causers of death who achieved an almost legendary status. The celebrity surrounding Essex man William Calcraft will be described in chapter 8. He was, for much of the nineteenth century, presider over a succession of public hangings that drew enormous crowds. Detailed reports of these executions would appear in local papers. If there were none from one's own county to describe, those from other parts of the country would be published. This article, relating to two Essex murderers in 1851 appeared in a number of papers. I chose to take selections from this lengthy account from the Kentish Gazette.

THE CHELMSFORD EXECUTIONS

On Tuesday morning, the perpetrators of two horrible and barbarous murders expiated their crimes by an ignominious death in front of the county gaol at Springfield near Chelmsford...

Thomas Drory was convicted upon the clearest evidence of having under circumstances of peculiar treachery and brutality, strangled a poor girl, [Jael Denny] *the daughter-in-law of an old servant of his father... He said on one occasion that he carried the rope with which he committed the murder for several days in his bosom... he said that he and Jael Denny talked and walked about, after which, at her suggestion, they sat down on the bank. She had come to urge him to marry her. He passed the rope gently round her as they were sitting and had got the end into the loop before she had perceived it... he pulled hard and she fell without a struggle. He then left her in the field and went to Brentwood.*

Turning to the case of Sarah Chesham, we find in her a criminal of even deeper dye than the young man who perished on the same scaffold. She was 42 years of age and the general repute of the county had raised her poisoning arts to the consequence of a professional murderess. Twice she had stood the peril of a trial for her life, and as often, though her guilt was said to be clear, had she escaped from justice... Among the crimes with which she was charged were the poisoning of her own children, and now, as if to crown the enormities of her career, and to show that no perils could turn her from her guilty purposes, she has been tried and found guilty of having taken away her husband's life by small doses of arsenic. [By 1851, forensic testing for arsenic poisoning had been introduced.]

...And now it is requisite to give some account of the manner in which these guilty wretches bore the last trying and awful moments of their fate. Drory slept until half past four o'clock, after which he rose and prepared himself by devotional exercises for the execution of his sentence. Chesham passed such a night as the guilty who are about to die inpenitent might be expected to endure. Her mental sufferings were extreme. She never closed her eyes in sleep, and could taste no food...

Drory appeared first on the platform and as soon as he presented himself, with drooping head and pinioned arms and faint and trembling limbs, the vast crowd of spectators assembled below were hushed into solemn and affecting silence. To the number of 6,000 or 7,000 they had been slowly gathering there from six o'clock in the morning: their behaviour throughout, very orderly and sedate, though the shrill voices of boys at play and the calls of orange vendors might be heard at intervals. From all parts of the surrounding country the assemblage had come. It consisted principally of smock-frocked labourers... There were hardly any repectable people observable in the crowd, but a most disgusting number of women. Some of these had gay flowers in their bonnets, and evidently set up for rustic belles; others were mothers giving suck to infants, whom they carried in their arms; others were elderly matrons presiding at the head of their families, and from the elevation of the domestic spring-cart, pointing out to their young daughters how they could best see the execution...

After a delay of several minutes, during which many began to fear there was something wrong, Sarah Chesham was with difficulty placed under the fatal beam, supported, like the other prisoner by two attendants. Without an instant's delay, Calcraft completed his simple but dreadful preparations; and then while with bated breath the thousands of spectators below looked on, the bolt was drawn. A faint murmur of horror spread among the crowd as they saw the sentence of the law carried into effect, which was prolonged as the conclusive struggles of the dying man and woman were painfully visible. In Drory, all sign of animation was extinct in four or five minutes, but Chesham struggled for six or seven. They were both light figures and they 'died hard.'

...In little more than an hour after the bodies were cut down, that of Drory was buried within the precincts of the gaol. The body of Sarah Chesham was not buried within the precincts of the gaol, having been claimed by a relative. It appears that having been indicted for poisoning, and not expressly for murder, the statute was not considered binding in her case.

KENTISH GAZETTE: April 1st 1851

By 1851 hangings were much reduced by comparison with a hundred years earlier. In October 1749, the Ipswich Journal had reported the hanging of 15 felons at one public execution at Tyburn. Several were highway robbers. One was a woman named Mary Dimer, who had robbed Captain Harris of his watch and peruke [wig]. Around the same time, Amy Hutchinson of Whittlesea was tried at Ely for poisoning her husband with arsenic. This was considered to be even worse than murder and was described as *'Petit Treason'*. Amy Hutchinson, aged just 17, was dragged to her place of execution on a sledge and burned alive.

Some hangings were followed by gibetting; hanging the body in chains or encased in a metal cage. In January 1749, according to the Grays & Tilbury Gazette of 1884, in a jolly little article entitled *'Gallows reminiscences,'* a man named Jackson at Chichester had *'died from the shock of being measured for his irons.'* According to the Ipswich Journal of January 28th 1749, he had been one of a gang of seven murderers. The rest survived to hang. However, the odd manner of Jackson's death appeared in the

Scots Magazine earlier that month but was not mentioned in other reports. As he had died of 'natural causes,' it was then felt inappropriate to gibbet Jackson, but he was placed in a grave beneath the scaffold where a pyramid was erected with a plaque recounting his crimes.

In a remarkable story from Cork in Ireland, the Chelmsford Gazette of October 4th 1822 reported the execution of two highwaymen, James Corbett and Patrick Bourke. It appears that a last minute reprieve was issued, but such was the feeling locally against the men that soldiers from the nearby barracks blocked the road and would not let the King's messenger through until after the men had been hanged.

But not everyone was happy with these 'exhibitions of legalised brutalty.' Though it would be many years before capital punishment would be abandoned in this country, there had been a strong drive for its removal since the 1830s. This leader from the Essex & Suffolk Mercury is typical of what a number of newspapers were saying by the middle of the nineteenth century...

THE APPROACHING EXECUTIONS FOR MURDER

The result of the recent trials for murder at the Essex Assizes necessarily forces upon our attention, the question of Capital Punishment. We have on several occasions expressed our opinion as to the uselessness of the sanguinary exhibitions of the scaffold as regards example, and of the indirect injury which they are calculated to produce on society, by the encouragement of that ignorance which is the fruitful parent of vice and of crime. We have not a single word to utter in defence of the criminals under sentence of death in the Essex County Gaol. Their guilt has been established beyond a doubt... The convict Drory was justly found guilty of one of the most diabolical and cowardly murders that ever disgraced humanity; Mrs. Chesham stands attainted with the horrible crime of poisoning her husband - only one, it is feared - of a long catalogue of similar murderous outrages which her hand has perpetrated... the question arises whether the interests of society require that the penalty of death should be inflicted. We think not... Capital punishment does not repress crime by the force of example... What deterring example can there be in human executions when they are accompanied by grotesque ribaldry or by the excitement of a theatrical entertainment?... The history of our country within the last few years shows that murders have not diminished either in numbers or atrocity. And yet the scaffold has been employed for the extermination of the offenders... The penalty of death, moreover, provides impunity for the guilty by indisposing juries to convict. It is said that when Mrs. Chesham was tried three or four years ago for the murder by poison of two of her children, the jury would have returned a verdict of guilty, had not the penalty annexed to the offence been death. But notwithstanding they had no real doubt as to her guilt... overwhelmed by the thought that their remorse would be insupportable if by their verdict, they sacrificed the innocent, acquitted the accused, and thus a professional poisoner was let loose upon society to pursue her infernal practices... We feel assured... the entire abolition of the punishment of death is justified at once... by expediency, by humanity and by the enlightened spirit of the age.

ESSEX & SUFFOLK MERCURY: March 18th 1851

Sometimes unlikely characters became the celebrities of their day: criminals, hangmen, performers, inventors, soldiers and, of course, a Royal or two. So it is, we now turn to the **important figures of their day**...

Chapter 8
Important figures of their day

Inevitably, Queen Victoria gets more than a few mentions. Anyone who has watched the film *'Young Victoria'* will be aware of her closeness to the Liberal politician, Lord Melbourne, especially early in her reign. In February 1838, the Essex, Herts & Kent Mercury commented...

Lord Melbourne had "better mind what he is about." The Tory journals are evidently furious at his dining so often with Her Majesty and 'ere long, he may possibly be called upon to render a due account of his "conversations and behaviour" at the Palace. We wish him well out of the scrape. We all along suspected that his good fortune in making himself so agreeable to her Majesty would provoke the envy and uncharitableness of rival politicians and now the thing has come to pass. We hope, since the Tories have mooted the matter, that his lordship will turn it over in his mind and seriously reflect whether he is the fittest companion for a youthful Queen. The Times says he is not, from which it must be inferred that it thinks that he would be less dangerous in the company of old women. We dare say, however, that his lordship can lay his hand on his heart and declare himself perfectly harmless - at least we hope so. And if, from the daily invitations to the Palace, he can save the expense of a cook, we know not why any body shall grudge him that retrenchment.

All of which again goes to show that many of our major local papers were politically aligned. The Tory press were incandescent over this matter. Liberal papers such as this could see the funny side of it. During the 'Victoria and Albert years', all kinds of royal stories were immensely popular.

It appears that His Royal Highness [Prince Albert] *was walking in the Royal Gardens in the company of her Majesty, the only attendant present being the Hon. Miss Murray, one of the Queen's maids of Honour in waiting upon the Queen... After walking for a short time with the Queen on the margin of the lake, His Royal Highness put on his skates and left her Majesty, who remained watching the movements of the Prince from the gardens. He had not been on the ice more than three or four minutes when, as he was proceeding at a rapid rate towards where the Queen was standing, and had reached within about three or four feet of the water's edge, the ice suddenly broke and instantaneously he was immersed over head and ears in the water. His Royal Highness immediately rose to the surface, when her Majesty, with great presence of mind, joined her hand to that of the Hon. Miss Murray (telling her to stand firm and betray no fear), and extending her right hand to the Prince, dragged him to the shore. Her Majesty manifested the greatest courage upon the occasion and acted with the most intrepid coolness. As soon as the Prince was safe on dry ground, the Queen gave way to the natural emotions of joy and thankfulness at his providential escape. The Prince then lost no time in proceeding to the Palace, where a warm bath was immediately prepared, and his Royal Highness was sufficiently well to receive the King of the Belgians upon his Majesty's arrival from Claremont.*

HERTFORD MERCURY & REFORMER: February 13th 1841

Victoria & Albert

Queen Victoria would live to see her Golden and Diamond Jubilees celebrated, though somewhat differently in different towns and villages. The Chelmsford Chronicle described in detail in June 1897 how Boreham made a real day of it in the *'picturesque grounds of Boreham House, kindly lent for the occasion by Col. Tufnell-Tyrell.'* The event included rural sports, a great feast with meat and beer among other treats, and fairground entertainments. The house was lit with fairy lamps and Jubilee mugs given to each child in the village, as well as a 6d copy of *'The Life of the Queen.'*

However, in contrast, at a public meeting held earlier in Blackmore near Ongar, not everyone was convinced they needed to go to such lengths. There was talk of decorating the village green and lighting the village with lamps, but Mr. Fletcher, the Baptist minister *'did not think it was advisable to give a feast as that was only an hour's amusement and he did not believe in feasting.'* (Chelmsford Chronicle: April 30th 1897)

Some people became well-known in their day by virtue of their notoriety. Dick Turpin's story has already been covered in Chapter 6, but he was not the only notorious Essex criminal to attract a great deal of public attention. **Frederick Von K. Browne**, an artist from Ashingdon near Rochford was rarely out of the news in the late 1890s. Though local papers like the Chelmsford Chronicle reported regularly on his pechant for *'sending obscene and offensive postcards through the post,'* the papers are rather less specific about precisely what he had written. His common defence was that everything on the postcards coulds be found in the Bible or the plays of Shakespeare. However, it was felt that *'lady clerks in the post-office might be scandalised,'* and he was given six months hard labour. In the end, his lack of co-operation led to him being removed to Brentwood Asylum (described in the Chelmsford Chronicle as a *'hell on earth with 2,000 prisoners'*). It didn't cure him of the habit and in October 1898, *'Browne the anarchist'* was back in court at the Essex Quarter Session accused of *'offending the Queen's dignity by sending yet more obscene and offensive postcards.'* Ironically, one of his main contentions this time was that the Bible was an obscene book that should not be taught to children. He was found guilty and sent back to gaol for nine months. In April 1900, the Essex Newsman would report his escape from Warley Asylum... *"He got the putty out of the window and painted it over and then at a favourable opportunity one night, took out the pane, climbed down the pipe and went home"* [to his family]. As few people really doubted his sanity, it was difficult to re-admit him and it was felt safer to leave him alone, but he would continue to re-emerge in the papers from time to time.

When **Richard Perry** was finally caught in 1765 after a long life of crime; also having deserted thirty-seven times from different army regiments; everyone wanted to read his story. A book was published detailing his life, priced 6d. Though the account published in the Chelmsford Chronicle in May that year is long, as an example of its kind, I think it is worth including in its entirety...

The account and exploits of RICHARD PERRY, who was tried for receiving stolen goods at the last Lent Assizes held at Chemsford before Mr. Baron Smythe and sentenced to be transported for 7 years. He was born in the year 1738 at Theydon Garnon in this county. At the age of 17, he left his father's house and went to live at Chipping Ongar where he fell in love with the maid-servant, but his friends disappointed the match. Being now unsettled, he entered in Mordannt's Dragoons, but soon deserted. He returned to his regiment, and deserted a second time; was taken by a party, and entered into the Fifth Regiment of Foot.

Being now reduced, he determined on the road to supply his extravagancies and stopt a person between St. Albans and Barmet and robbed him of £11 and his watch. Soon after the above robbery, he went to an aunt of his in London and from thence set out on horseback for York, and between Doncaster and Ferrybridge, robbed a gentleman of £15 and his watch. He then proceeded to York, from thence to Cambridge, sold his horse and stole another from a Gentleman's park; went to Royston Fair and cheated a gentleman of £24.

From thence, he returned to London and was apprehended as a deserter, and was sent to Maidstone to the first troop he enlisted in and was soon after draughted into the Heavy Horse and sent to Germany, where he remained two years and a half: and in company with one of his comrades, robbed a jew of £52 in money and goods. He then deserted, and getting on board a Sunderland hoy, landed at Burlington in Yorkshire. From thence, he went to Beverley, Horncastle, Peterborough, London, Winchester, Portsmouth, Turnbridge-Wells, Feversham and Chatham: at all places he enlisted and received the bounty money. He then entered into The Essex Militia at Chelmsford; made his escape; went to Bishop's Stortford and again enlisted. He went to Hertford, St. Albans, Uxbridge, Hitchin, Luton, Wallington, Buckinghan, Newport Pagnell and Northampton and enlisted into the different parties quartered in those towns. He then came to London and staid five weeks.

From London, he went to Barking; from thence he proceeded to Romford where he enlisted, but being apprehended as a deserter, was committed to gaol, from which he made his escape and took the road to Maldon.

On his journey, he robbed Mr. Long, a farmer of Southminster of £1 and a watch, and taking his horse, returned to London. He then went to St. Albans, from thence to Epping Forest and waited till four o'clock in the morning for Mr. B____ of L____, without sucess. Returning to St. Albans, he was stopped by a warrener enquiring his business, whom he robbed of four pounds. A day or two after, he went to L____ fair, and getting acquainted with Mrs. B____'s servant, received information what time her master returned from London and where he put his money. On this, he again took his stand in the forest and meeting Mr. B____ at Buckets Hill, demanded his money: the gentleman told him he had none, but Perry cut his boot and robbed him of £35 12s. Upon his return to St. Albans, he stopt two butchers: one escaped, but the other he robbed of £22 17s, but returned the 17s back again.

His next robbery was between Aylesbury and Buckingham where he took from a gentleman £17, his watch and a diamond ring, but returned the latter. He also robbed the Rev. Mr. Hatfield, a Justice of the Peace, of £42 and his watch and then made the rest of his way to Annick in Westmoreland where he staid four days. After this adventure, he went to Scotland and from thence to Peterborough races where, laying bets and unable to pay, was obliged to decamp, and overtaking a gentleman between Cambridge and Huntingdon, robbed him of £113. So after this he set out for his native place and having staid one day, went to Winchester. Within seven miles of that city, he robbed Capt. Pollard of the Black Musketeers of £34, his watch and a ring.

Soon after this meeting the Bishop's Stortford stage on Epping Forest, he stopped it and on opening the coach door, one of the passengers fired a pistol which narrowly missed him, but did not prevent his robbing the passengers of £32, two watches, two rings and one pistol. He returned one of the rings and retired into Lancashire.

Soon after this, he came to London and became acquainted with a young woman who had been seduced from her father's house by a soldier and went with her in a post-chaise to her father's; when the unsuspecting father gave him twenty guineas, with which, and his daughter, he proceeded immediately to London.

After this, he came to the house of James Smith of Doddinghurst near Braintree and the people being at church, he broke into the house and took away in money and goods the amount of £30. He sold the goods in Billericay, in which town he staid four days; then he went to Romford. Between this place and Hornchurch, he robbed Mr. Baxter, farmer of Kelvedon of nine pounds which he returned as he knew that person and could not think of distressing him.

Perry had been hitherto without accomplices in the robberies he had committed in England, but having returned to his old station at St. Albans, he went on foot with two young men and robbed a gentleman of seven pounds fourteen shillings but one of his companions ran away. He went next to Newport Pagnell in Buckinghamshire and being discovered to be a deserter and being suspected to be the Flying Highwayman, he was committed to the town Bridewell, from where he attempted to escape; but, being stopped, he was removed to Buckingham Gaol where, his friends providing some implements, he made his escape.

Being advertised, he thought it prudent to retreat into Kent and between Maidstone and Cranbrook, robbed a person in a chaise of six pounds and a watch. After the commission of this, he was apprehended and conducted to Maidstone Gaol, and lay till within four days of the sessions when he broke out with four sailors, one of whom was afterwards retaken.

He now retreated into Hertfordshire, and between Walford and St. Albans he accidentally met with I____ B____, a sergeant of the 66th regiment of foot, who had deserted with the regiment's money. They soon formed a scheme to turn the beating order to their advantage. Accordingly, they went to Bedford, Cambridge, Lincoln and Northampton and collected large sums of money, but being advertised they were apprehended and sent to gaol, where they lay three weeks, and being sent to join their regiments, made their escape and soon after met again at St. Albans. They afterward separated and he went to Dundee, surrendered himself to his own regiment and after laying nine months, was discharged at the late reduction of the army.

Being now free from being apprehended for a deserter, he revisited Theydon Garnon, his native place, and finding the York innkeeper's daughter was dead, he yielded to the persuasion of his friends and married a widow. He then settled at Theydon Garnon as a dealer and chapman; but his wife dying about five months afterwards, he once more betook himself to the highway. Riding between Gravesend and Chatham, he robbed Mr. White of Feversham of eleven pounds and his watch. After this, near Ongar he was informed that Mr. P____l and his gang had declared they would take him dead or alive. Accordingly, they met him and knew him immediately. He fled and they pursued him, but Mr. P____l only was able to keep up with him. Perry rode on until Mr. P____l was at a sufficient distance from his companions, when he suddenly stopped and presented his pistol, robbed his pursuer of his money and watch. He was then apprehended at the Three Pigeons in Stratford for buying stolen goods: these consisted of some wearing apparel which he had bought for nineteen shillings and sixpence of J____ G____ whom he had accidentally met near Chadwell. The owner, Mr. Nicholas Boreham, discovering them on his back, and having *carried him before Charles Smith Esq., that Magistrate committed him to Chelmsford Gaol. Having been so successful in his attempts to escape, he formed a design in conjunction with some of his fellow prisoners to break out of this prison. They actually proceeded so far as to make a breach in a chimney and intended to burn their way through one of the wards, having secreted their allowance of fewel for that purpose, but their design was frustrated by the vigilance of the turnkey, and they were chained by the neck in couples. At the last Assizes for Essex, he was tried and sentenced to be transported for seven years.*

It seems remarkable, if they knew all this, how Perry received such a light sentence. However, on this occasion, he was being tried for a somewhat lesser crime of receiving. He may well have been passed on to another court to be prosecuted for his more serious crimes. It seems a strange coincidence that a criminal of the same name was, in February that year, tried at the Old Bailey and later hanged at Tyburn. But that Richard Perry claimed he had been born in Staffordshire.

People well known in their time are not always remembered today as some of the previous names show. One such character was **Edith O'Gorman**, known in the 1890s as *'The Escaped Nun.'* Her lectures drew large crowds. Having 'escaped' from an American

convent, she was full of contempt for the Catholic church; a view that carried a good deal of support in protestant Essex. Her talks could clearly be very entertaining. At Brentwood in November 1890, she said that...

...Upon entering a convent, a nun must bring plenty of money, especially in the United States... After speaking of the blind obedience required of the nuns, she said she once knew six nuns in love with one priest at the same time, and he was the ugliest man she ever saw (laughter). (At this stage, some ladies left)...

CHELMSFORD CHRONICLE:
November 7th 1890

Sometimes it takes the death of someone to wake people up to their very existence. Such a case was that of **Fiddler Ben**...

Boreham Red Lion

The well-known face of Benjamin Bacon, or as he was commonly called, 'Fiddler Ben' will no more be seen in Boreham, for he died on Christmas day. During about 20 years he had lived the life of a hermit in a cottage near the Red Lion Inn... poor old Ben was found in a very weak condition, quite naked, lying on an old bundle of dirty rags...

Benjamin, whose father was at one time post-master of Chelmsford, years ago conducted a barber's business in Moulsham Street. It is said he fell in love with a young woman who, however, married a soldier. Since then it seems that Ben has not been the same man and has lived like a recluse. He was the possessor of a violin, said to be a very old and valuable one, and with this he used to frequent public houses in the villages around Chelmsford to earn a crust. For the past two or three years, he has been in failing health and has spent the greater part of his time in seclusion, his only companions being his cat and a novel, for he was very fond of reading and was well educated. Rumour has it that he has titled relations.

Some of the inhabitants of Boreham think it scandalous that a person in a Christian land should 'die like he has, worse than a beast.'

ESSEX NEWSMAN: January 7th 1899

But of course, many of the names on people's lips a century or more ago are still renowned today. The travels of **Dr. Livingstone** for example, were widely reported. Even four-page weekly papers like the Halstead Gazette, in 1857, were prepared to give a lot of column space to a subject that had very much grabbed the public's attention. Late that year, Essex newspapers were regularly reporting on lectures being given on Livingstone's travels in Africa. The Rev. C. Gill of Sudbury spoke at the Public Hall Colchester in December 1857. Collections were made for his work in Africa. When in 1872, nothing had been heard of him for a considerable time, speculation was rife as to his whereabouts. Stanley's venture to find Doctor Livingstone became the story of its day and in August that year, when the Chelmsford Gazette was able to report on the meeting of the men, it was as if every reader had been a part of that search and its ultimate success...

The lost is found. Doctor Livingstone, so long unheard of and lost sight of amid those mysterious and unknown wilds of central Africa, whose exploration has been the one absorbing ambition of his life, that even his most sanguine friends had almost relinquished their last hope of his existence and safety, is once again heard of and is found not only in health and safety, but in positively high spirits and unabated enthusiasm for the gigantic task to which he has devoted himself... He is still as resolute, as indomitable and as hopeful as he was when in his prime... Let us not be niggard then of praise for the man who brings us good tidings of our long-lost countryman. He may be American by birth or by adoption, but his pluck no less than his name proclaim him of English blood. In truth, his heroic tenacity of purpose was all British. The seeker and the sought were worthy of each other.

CHELMSFORD GAZETTE: August 9th 1872

This was a story that would run and run. At least, where Livingstone was concerned, his reputation held up well throughout his lifetime. Not all high-flyers of their day were able to avoid their share of criticism and mockery. **Isambard Kingdom Brunel** epitomised Victorian invention and creativity. However, when, in 1857, his great iron steam yacht, the Leviathan was completed, it began a long-running saga. Tickets were sold and thousands turned up to see a ship that failed to launch. Again and again attempts were made to free the grounded giant. According to the Halstead Gazette of Dec 17th 1857, it had already cost more to launch the ship than it had to build it. 'Mechanics Monthly' for December 1857, of course, was full of all the ways Brunel had gone wrong and how it could all be put to rights.

Eventually, about a fortnight later, it would be afloat, but it would always be a bit of a white elephant, and trouble would follow it throughout its life. Renamed the 'Great Eastern,' to try to enable the ship to forget its ignominious beginnings, even its maiden voyage was beset by problems. The Herts Guardian in late September 1859, put Brunel's early death at fifty-four down to *'a paralysis induced by over-anxiety.'* His obituaries written for a host of papers focused on his many successes, but there were always severe reservations...

...Unlike Stephenson who made everything pay, Brunel made nothing pay. As an engineer, he raised the mightiest works and ruined the richest men... The same splendour and evil waited on the last large enterprise of his life, the Great Eastern. The engineers won renown and the shareholders lost their money.

ESSEX STANDARD: September 30th 1859

A name that crops up time and time again in the newspapers of the nineteenth century is that of **George Wombwell**. He has already had quite a mention in chapter 4 of this book, but as he was hardly ever out of the newspapers during his lifetime, there is a lot more to tell. Born at Duddenhoe End near Saffron Walden in 1777, he began his working life in London as an apprentice shoemaker before going on to become the country's leading menagerie owner. Wombwell's travelling zoo took animals the length and breadth of the country, adverts and reports of his shows regularly appearing in East Anglian papers. This account from the Essex & Suffolk Times for September 22nd 1838 explains how he got started...

WOMBWELL'S MENAGERIE - On Saturday evening last, Mr. Wombwell gave the inhabitants of this town a treat by exhibiting his menagerie on his return from Maldon Fair. We are always very glad when it suits him to bring his broad-wheeled wagons to Chelmsford... His collections surpass any thing of the kind to be met with in the kingdom and even when divided are well worthy of the attention of all who love the study of animals. Since he was last here, he has added to the menagerie a rhinoceros and four young lions together with several smaller animals.

Mr. Wombwell, when a boy, was a bird fancier and beyond this had no intention of becoming a caravan keeper, and in fact was made one by the force of accident rather than of circumstances.

138

At the London Docks, he saw the first boas imported into Britain. Most persons were afraid of and ignorant of managing them; prices from this cause gave way a little and our friend at last ventured to offer £75 for a pair. He got them and in the course of three weeks cleared more than the sum he advanced, a circumstance which he confesses makes him partial to serpents up to this hour as the first thing that gave him a lift in his profession. Mr. Wombwell, from the first, was attached to his trade and when ships arrived from India containing rare animals, parted so freely with his money that he sometimes got so bare that he hardly knew how to find his way through a toll of a morning; and this too when he was surprisingly rich in a species of stock which might supply the marts of all Europe... Mr. Wombwell's largest stud consists of 42 horses, some of which would bring very heavy prices... His band, which is a fine one, costs him about £1200 yearly and the expenses of the establishment are calculated at £35 per day or £12,000 in the year. Fairs he must study as carefully as the Jews do the stocks, and manage matters so as to be present at all the best.

Wombwell was renowned as an expert in the breeding of and husbandry of all manner of animals and started to breed his own lions in England as early as 1820. Following his death in 1850, the menagerie continued to tour until as late as 1930.

One renowned Essex man was closely associated with Wombwell's Menagerie. This was **George Newcomb**.

DEATH OF A LION TAMER
The death has just occurred in Chelmsford of Mr. George Newcomb, known as the Chelmsford lion tamer. The deceased, who was 54 years of age had had a very adventurous life. When about 17 years old, he joined Smith's Circus from Drury Lane which was visiting Chelmsford and at Ramsgate he got an engagement as bottom den's man at Wombwell's No. 2 Menagerie. From this position, he rose to be a lion tamer. In 1874, he had a terrible encounter with five African lions at Swindon, where he received nine severe wounds on the right arm in addition to other injuries. Three of the lions died in the struggle. Previously, he had had his left eye torn out by a leopard.
WHITSTABLE TIMES & HERNE BAY HERALD: January 18th 1890

Over the last three hundred years, certain people have achieved legendary status. There is something rather exciting about reading the stuff of legend in your own local papers. Here are a few...

The famous Miss Flora Macdonald... was last week very particularly examined as to her conduct in relation to her harbouring and secreting the young Pretender after the Battle of Culloden and re-committed into the custody of a messenger, and affects great humanity and benevolence, has certainly a good share of sense, and her deportment very modest and reserv'd.

IPSWICH JOURNAL: January 3rd 1747

The Victory of 160 guns, Capt. Hardy, with the body of the late Lord Nelson came to an anchor on Tuesday afternoon at two o'clock at St. Helen's, the tide not serving to proceed to Spithead. His Lordship's flag was hoisted half mast high on the fore as was also the ensign on the staff. The body of Lord Nelson was put in spirits the day after the action, in which state it will be brought to Greenwich, where it is to be shifted into the shell coffin made out of the main-mast of the French flag-ship L'Orient; the shell is lined with white satin and the outside covered with black cloth; over this is placed the brass plate on which is inscribed Capt. R. Holloway's certificate of the coffin being made of the wood of the said French mast, picked up at sea after the Battle of the Nile.

IPSWICH JOURNAL: December 7th 1805

GRIMALDI - *That clown of clowns and the most classic clown that ever raised a laugh in this care-corroded world has bid farewell to the stage for ever and for aye. He quietly resigned his theatrical life at twelve o'clock on Monday night; in the 49th year of his age, surrounded by a host of friends at the Sadler's Wells Theatre... at the end, he came on the stage dressed in black, with white waistcoat and gloves , and advancing to the footlights, whilst the crowd of performers arranged themselves around him, he addressed the audience with much feeling... amidst long continued applause.*

ESSEX HERALD: March 25th 1828

Though Joseph Grimaldi had been a legendary performer, he had virtually retired five years earlier. A depressed alcoholic, his health was deteriorating, and he died in poverty in 1837. By that time, the world's greatest acrobat and tightrope walker, **Charles Blondin** was already beginning to establish himself.

...A still more extraordinary feat, in the acrobatic line, has been performed at Niagara Falls; one that fits the performer for the highest place in the lunatic asylum. A.M. Blondin [initials as printed] *has actually walked across the seething abyss upon a slack rope, stopping in the middle to lower a bottle for water. When you reflect that the distance is so great that, with all care, the slack at the rope made a descent of 60 feet to the centre, and that a single false step must have plunged him to certain death in the current that runs with a rapidity which defies the sounding lead, you can have some idea of the difficulties and dangers, and can appreciate the foolhardiness of the man who did such a feat.*

ESSEX STANDARD: July 20 1859

Victorian England loved its heroes and heroines. In the early hours of September 7th 1838, **Grace Darling** and her father, William, keeper of the Longstone Lighthouse in the Farne Islands, were looking out from an upstairs window of Lighthouse on the Farne Islands when they spotted the wreck and survivors of the *'Forfarshire'* on a nearby low rocky island. The Forfarshire had foundered on the rocks and broken in two; one of the halves had already sunk during the night. In spite of tempestuous waves and gale force winds, they successfully attempted an amazing rescue of the survivors. The nation took Grace to their hearts and a national subscription raised £700. She would become a reluctant celebrity, with poems written in praise of her courage, and paintings produced of the rescue itself. But as this story shows, it was to be short-lived...

DEATH OF GRACE DARLING - *Grace Darling, the heroine of the Longstone Lighthouse, died on Thursday se'nnight at Bamburgh at the early age of 25... For the last few months, symptoms of a decline have been manifest in her constitution* [Tuberculosis] *and notwithstanding every care and attention that change of residence and medical skill could effect, she has ceased to be. Not so her fame - this we may safely predict will be as lasting as the rock, the scene of her noble exploit. She expired without any apparent pain at the house of her sister at Bamburgh, her mother and sister alone being present...* [Ironically] *a severe gale from the N.N.E. prevented her three brothers from being present at the last mournful tribute of affection to their dear sister.*

Yet this was a story that, as predicted, would continue to be remembered: every female act of heroism for the next fifty years would be compared with that of Grace Darling...

A deed of timely daring, somewhat of the Grace Darling character was done by a young woman at Southend on Saturday last, which excited much admiration in all who witnessed it and is likely to render the heroine an object of interest to the visitors of that watering place... An elderly gentleman had engaged a bathing machine on the beach and boldly plunged into the refreshing waves, he swam out about a hundred yards from the machine when he was seized, it appears, with cramp, and finding he could not touch the bottom, he uttered a cry of "Save me, save me!" and throwing up his arms, went down. George Ingram, the son of the owner of the machine, struck off to his assistance, but on reaching him, the drowning man clung to him with such tenacity, that he pulled him down twice, and both appeared on the point of perishing. Miss Emma Ingram, who was in the warm Bath House, seeing the peril of her brother and the stranger was in an instant on the beach and plunging into the water with all her clothes on, swam to the drowning men whom she supported until another brother arrived with a boat and to whom she triumphantly exclaimed, "Never mind me - save them." The heroine assisted in getting both into the boat, the old gentleman being quite insensible, and her brother much exhausted... The ladies who were present stated to her that it was the act of a Grace Darling... The matter

142

has been laid before the Royal Humane Society and we hope to hear she has been decorated with an honorary medal.

CHELMSFORD CHRONICLE: September 12th 1856

One of the most romantic and mysterious Essex figures to assume almost legendary status was **Catherine Gough**, otherwise known as **Kitty Canham**. Though truly contemporary accounts have

proved hard to find, various versions of this story have appeared through the years in East Anglian papers and magazines. One of the most complete accounts appeared in the Essex Review of 1903 and was written by Miss E. Vaughan. She quotes from the General Evening Post of 1752, but I have been unable to find any reference to the existence of this paper before 1800.

The burial register for Thorpe-le-Soken in Essex contains an entry for July 9th 1752 listing a burial for Catherine Gough. What also mentions is that she was the wife of the vicar, Henry Gough. But there appears to be much more to the story than that. In July 1880, The Bury Post reviewed a newly published account of this remarkable tale, by then over a century old...

The story is told by her great great niece of the unsuitableness of the wayward beauty [Catherine 'Kitty' Canham] *to the quietude of the country parsonage, and how in an evil hour, she set forth from home alone, leaving no clue behind by which her destination could be traced... preserving her secret, she was introduced to and shortly afterwards married John Viscount Dalrie* [most other accounts call him Lord Dalmeny] *the heir to an Earldom... During the next four years, they travelled over the greater part of Europe and lord Dalrie's confidence in her merit and truth was never clouded by suspicion of doubt. But the keeping of her guilty secret consumed her spirits and strength and at last... though unable to speak, she could yet make signs for paper and ink and wrote these sentences: 'I am the wife of Rev. Alexander Henry Gough, vicar of Thorpe-le-Soken in Essex. My maiden name was Catherine Canham. My last request is to be buried at Thorpe.' Before Lord Dalrie had gathered the astounding meaning of these lines, she was dead. Her last request was carried out with much difficulty: a pompous funeral was arranged and Mr. Gough and Lord Dalrie stood together at the grave.*

BURY POST: July 13th 1880

This account tells far from the whole story. According to a version in the Essex County Standard in 1927, in July 1752...

...a sailing vessel bound for Harwich was driven by evil weather into Brightlingsea harbour. Those were bad smuggling days and the Customs officers were ever on the look-out. They boarded this vessel and they found on it a large chest, stated to belong to one of the passengers, Mr. Williams, merchant of Hamburg. The officers suspected that it might contain contraband. Mr. Williams protested that it contained nothing of the sort, but would not give a satisfactory account of its contents. He had other smaller chests. These were opened and were found to contain, amongst other things, many articles of rich female attire and some costly jewellery. Mr. Williams explained that these belonged to his wife, who was dead. Finally the officers opened the great chest... it was found to contain a coffin... and on opening the coffin, the officers found the well-preserved body of a beautiful young woman. The body had been embalmed.

ESSEX COUNTY CHRONICLE: September 10th 1927

The story continues with 'Mr. Williams' revealing that he was really *'Lord Dalmeny, eldest son of the second Earl of Rosebery.'* Admitting that he had married the girl who had called herself Kitty Canham, he described the details of her last request. According to most versions of the story, the two husbands attended her funeral at Thorpe, side by side.

The Bury Post account says, *"Kitty's monument has been removed by the vicar and a flat stone put down over her remains to make the floor of the vestry. So there she is, shut up out of sight and mind along with the parish registers and every Sunday, the officiating parson and clerk tramp solemnly over the author of a scandal too great and romantic to be quite forgotten even in the third or fourth generation."*

Both of these versions have Kitty's lover dying three years later, though other accounts say he lived long and married twice more. Some say when the boat first came with her body to either Hythe or Brightlingsea, the man later to be identified as Lord Dalmeny appeared not to speak any English. Like so many of our best stories, it doesn't take long for time and the telling to change them. All agree however that the Rev. Alexander Henry Gough lived the remainder of his days at Thorpe-le-Soken, dying in 1774 when... (as Miss Vaughan describes) *his simpler funeral went the way that Kitty's had gone, up the village street to the old church where all that was mortal of her faithful husband and the erring beauty now rest in hope.* (Essex Review Vol. X1X)

We have already mentioned **William Calcraft** of Little Baddow. For half of the nineteenth century he would become one of the most surprising celebrities of his day, as this short obituary shows...

DEATH OF CALCRAFT - *On Saturday evening, John* [William] *Calcraft... who for a great many years officiated as the executioner at Newgate and Horsemonger Lane Gaols and also at Springfield* [Chelmsford] *and all the principal prisons throughout the country, died at his residence at Hoxton. Calcraft received his official appointment as executioner to the Corporation of London in connection with the gaol of Newgate in the year 1828 and he had a standing salary of one guinea per week, being allowed when his services were not required at Newgate, to officiate at any other gaol where the capital sentence was to be carried out. In 1874, in consequence of his advanced age, it was notified to him that it would be better for him to resign, and he accordingly did so after 46 years of service. During the time he was in office, he had to execute some of the most extraordinary criminals... Calcraft was very retired in his manner and habits, and he was very*

averse to giving any information with regard to the number of criminals who had passed through his hands during his long career.
CHELMSFORD CHRONICLE: December 19th 1879

Calcraft [pictured right], a shoemaker by trade, favoured the 'short drop', which meant his victims rarely died instantly, though he resented newspapers reporting on prisoners' lengthy death struggles and resented even more being made to retire when he considered he was still fit to continue. Quiet though he may have been, he seems to have enjoyed being cheered through the towns he visited, and being recognised the length and breadth of the country.

Amongst the other great names of their day have been writers and artists and musicians...

Mr. CHARLES DICKENS
WILL READ AT THE
CORN EXCHANGE, IPSWICH,
On Monday Evening, Oct. 10, 1859,
At EIGHT o'clock, his
CHRISTMAS CAROL,
AND
TRIAL FROM PICKWICK.
——— (5802
PLACES for the Reading (numbered and reserved) 4s.; Second Seats, 2s.; Back Seats, 1s. Tickets to be obtained at Haddock's Library, where the PLAN OF RESERVED SEATS IS NOW READY.

Also, there were scientists and inventors whose ideas would prove increasingly exciting as time went on. By the end of the nineteenth century some local papers even carried a regular science column.

All forms of **invention and discovery** were becoming ever more newsworthy...

Chapter 9
Science & Medicine;
Invention & Discovery

In 1739, when quack doctor, Joanna Stephens came up with 'a cure for the stone', the Exchequer paid her £5,000. According to Colchester newspapers of the time, this cure was composed of pills made from 'calcined snail and egg shells' and a powder to accompany them composed of soap, honey and herbs.

As medical science progressed, all manner of bizarre remedies were reported…

On Wednesday, the 19th inst., a little boy of the name of Jackson, playing on Manwood Bridge imprudently attempted to walk along the brick-work. He missed his footing and, falling down into the river below, was unfortunately drowned. Another child who had been his companion gave the alarm and after a search of six hours his body was discovered in the deepest part of the stream not far from where the melancholy accident occurred. Life of course was extinct. Doctor Buchan mentions the restoration of a body after six hours immersion by the method of burying it in a hot dunghill.
ESSEX STANDARD: October 29th 1831

Two medical gentlemen in St. Petersburg have discovered that common kitchen salt is an effective cure for cholera. An old woman was brought to the hospital in a dying state. She refused every medicine but kept eating as much as she could get down of salt herrings, a cure which had been recommended by other common people, and to the astonishment of the doctors, she recovered. One of them gave two table spoonfuls of salt to two men who were apparently dying, and repeated the dose at intervals; and both of them recovered. The same remedy was tried upon

thirteen other patients, eleven of whom recovered.
ESSEX STANDARD: November 12th 1831

Another remedy suggested at the time included a combination of nitrous acid, peppermint water, camphor mixture and tincture of opium.
From time to time tales appeared of people who seemed to be able to defy the accepted medical understanding of the day...

Colcheſter, March 2. We have the following odd Story from Leaden-Wrothing near Ongar in this County, viz. That a Girl about 12 Years of Age, belonging to that Town, had lived 13 Weeks without eating or drinking, or any Think thing paſſing through her, of which her Mother had voluntarily taken an Oath before a juſtice of Peace. Two Women were by the Officers of the Pariſh appointed to watch the Girl, which they did four Nights and three Days, and have likewiſe ſince made Oath, that during that Time ſhe took no Nouriſhment, nor had any Diſchaige. She pretends to be ſupported in a miraculous Way; but there is great Reaſon to believe ſhe will in the End prove an Impoſtor.

IPSWICH JOURNAL: March 1734

Even though the Bubonic Plague had ceased to be a problem in this country by the time local papers appeared, epidemics of other killer diseases were the plagues of their day, especially Smallpox and Cholera.

Notice has been given of the postponement of Sudbury market till Friday in consequence of the day of thanksgiving for the removal of Cholera from this district.
The thanksgiving is fixed for Thursday next, there will be full services in the churches and a collection for the poor and thanks be to God for the removal of Cholera from this district.
This town has been mercifully preserved from the epidemic which has been raging around us, it is hoped every employer will allow his workmen the privilege of acknowledging the goodness of the Lord without abatement of wages.
SUDBURY POST: November 15th 1849

Alarming spread of smallpox - *There have been 11 deaths and 34 cases at Brentwood Asylum... and over 40 cases in a week at West Ham.*
SOUTHEND-ON-SEA OBSERVER: March 15th 1894

Typhus Fever still prevails in Lt. Clacton and upwards of 70 cases have occurred, 13 of which have proved fatal.
IPSWICH & COLCHESTER TIMES: November 19th 1858

BRENTWOOD - *Dyphtheria continues its deadly ravages in various parts of the kingdom. We have heard of a painful case... where Mr. Carter, son of Mr. Carter of Brentwood, his wife and child all now lie dead from this disease.*
IPSWICH & COLCHESTER TIMES: December 3rd 1858

During the winter of 1863, Essex papers reported large numbers of deaths (nearly all children) from Scarlatina. The Essex Standard and Essex & W. Suffolk Gazette published mortality figures for a number of Essex towns. In November that year, Colchester, Witham, Halstead, Hedingham and West Ham published up to half of their deaths being due to the disease. In giving similar results for Chemsford, one paper reported, *"I cannot refrain from attributing the disease in a great measure to the water in the wells which are polluted by the drainage from the churchyard."* Poignantly, among the deaths for December 11th 1863 are listed Edward aged 4 , Henry (9) and Eliza (7), children of P. Stevenson, bootmaker of Balkerne Lane, Colchester, all from Scarlatina.

With so much disease about, medical advances were what people really wanted to read about. That, and how to live more healthily...

As the season of the year is now fast approaching when the amusement of bathing is resorted to by the young as well as the aged, the following hints may not be unworthy of attention. The head should first come into contact with the water by diving head foremost. As the immersion will be less felt when it is effected suddenly: and as it is of consequence that the first impression should be uniform over the body, we must not enter the bath slowly or timorously, but with a degree of boldness. A contrary method would be dangerous as it might repel the blood from the lower to the upper parts of the body and thus occasion a fit of apoplexy. The morning is the most proper time for using the cold bath, unless it be in a river, in which case the afternoon or from one to two hours before sunset will be more eligible; as the water has then acquired additional warmth from the rays of the sun and the immersion will not interfere with digestion: on the whole, one hour after a light breakfast - or two hours before, or four hours after dinner are the best periods of the day for this purpose.

Where the bather is in the water, he should not remain inactive, but apply brisk general friction to promote the circulation of the fluids from the heart to the extremities. Immediately after the person leaves the water, it is necessary to use the utmost dispatch in drying the body in a coarse cloth. He should not afterwards sit inactive, unless warmly clothed and wearing flannel next the skin: it will be highly beneficial to take general exercise till the equilibrium of the circulation be restored and the vessels as well as the muscles have acquired a due degree of reaction...

CHELMSFORD CHRONICLE: May 22nd 1801

Successful transfusion of blood

Elizabeth Evans... in consequence of a miscarriage, the poor woman had from a violent hemorrhage become quite exhausted, her pulse imperceptible for about an hour and a half, her extremities cold and perspiration clammy; added to which symptoms, her stomach was so irritable as to reject every nourishment. At this critical moment, it occurred to Mr. W.J. Clement, the surgical gentleman called in, that the only chance was to attempt the above operation. And having procured a stout healthy gentleman who was willing to aid the operation by allowing the requisite amount of blood to be taken from him, Mr. C. opened a vein in the arm of each and by means of Weiss's patent syringe and tubes, injected about 15 ounces of blood with complete success.

KENT & ESSEX MERCURY: February 5th 1828

Adverts like this and those on the following page appeared in most local papers from their earliest days. These are all from the Ipswich Journal 1763, 1839, & 1774. Daffy's Elixir was advertised from about 1730 onwards. The Chelmsford Chronicle was still singing its praises as late as 1890.

I N O C U L A T I O N.
MR. MUSGRAVE, Surgeon, at Colchester, continues to inoculate by his easy and successful Method at his House at MILE-END, near Colchester, on his usual Terms ; where Patients may be assured of the greatest Care to their Welfare, by constant Attendance & genteel Accommodation, having within these last nine Years inoculated 3000 Persons of all Ages, from six Weeks old to 70 Years of age, without the Loss of a single Patient, or any alarming Symptom.--- All those Patients that chuse may come to his House, where he has the Opportunity of attending them every Day. He requires no Preparation previous to Inoculation. Parties inoculated at their own Houses on reasonable Terms.

150

SCROFULA, OR KING'S EVIL,
CANCERS, SCURVY,
LEPROSY, WHITE SWELLINGS, &C.
CURED BY

MR. M SMITH,

Of Providence Place, Diss, Norfolk.

Another Proof of the extraordinary and superior Efficacy of

Smith's Botanical Medicines.

The Cure of Benjamin Bennett, of Swainthorpe, near Norwich, Shoemaker, aged 26 years—one of the most extraordinary that M. Smith has ever met with.

THIS patient was afflicted with the Scrofula during the space of eleven months, fourteen weeks of which he was in the Norfolk and Norwich Hospital, from which he was at length discharged incurable. He first applied to Mr. Smith on the 26th of August, 1827. He was then afflicted with several wounds on the left breast, and one in particular of great magnitude under the left arm. Indeed his case appeared so hopeless of relief, that it was only through the persuasions of his family, and in commiseration of his sufferings, that M. Smith was induced to take him in hand, the seat of his complaint being so near the springs of life, that there was the greatest danger in attempting to do anything towards eradicating the disease or effecting a cure, as the patient appeared sinking under his sufferings, and fast approaching to a termination of his life; but after the application of these medicines, M. Smith had the satisfaction of beholding the most beneficial results, and seeing him in the course of two or three weeks so much amended, as to afford the most promising expectation of a perfect cure, which was fully completed within the space of four months, having the use of his arm, which he never expected to have had, and to be in the full enjoyment of perfect health, and in which he still continues, with full ability of following his business, and performing every part of the same, as well as he ever had done in his life before.
Attested and signed by us, the 16th day of April, 1828.

GEORGE GEORGE,
EGESTER WICKHAM, } Churchwardens.
WILLIAM SCALES,
JOHN GOOCH, } Gentlemen
T. S. GOOCH, } of the
R. BRANSFORD, Innkeeper. } Parish.

N.B. He, after leaving the Hospital, was under the care of two celebrated Professors of Scrofulous Medicine, in the county of Suffolk, without experiencing the least benefit.
M. Smith saw Mr. Bennet on Sunday, Jan. 13th, 1839, and can assure the public that he is still living in the above parish, following his business, and is as well in every respect as any man in the kingdom.

M. SMITH

May be consulted at the GEORGE INN, HIGH STREET, COLCHESTER, on Tuesday, February the 19th, 1839, and following day.

PURGING SUGAR-PLUMBS,
For WORMS in Men, Women, and Children,
[Price 1 s. each Box, with a Bill of Directions]

WHICH will infallibly destroy all Kinds of WORMS, and cure all those Diseases which are occasioned by them.
It is a safe and pleasant Medicine, may be taken at all Times without Danger, and may be given to the tenderest Constitution.
These Plumbs are also a certain Cure for the Rheumatism, the Third Ague, and the Cold Scurvy.
They will keep in a dry Place many Years without losing their Virtue, and may be carried into any Climate.
Sold wholesale and retail by J. SHAVE, Bookseller, in Ipswich;
Sold likewise, by Appointment of the Proprietor, by

Mr.Keymer, Colchester.	Walford, Woodbridge.	Ormes, Walton.
Keymer, Hadleigh.	Miller, Bungay.	Sell, Little Thurlow.
Eaton, Yarmouth.	Woodward, Wickham	Andrews, Maldenhall.
Cronse, Norwich.	Morling, Debenham.	Bigsby, Clare.
Steel & Rogers, Bury.	Baker, Saxmundham.	Moore, Melford.
Whittingham, Lynn.	Abbot, Needham.	Studd, Lavenham.
Tost, Chelmsford.	Pettit, Stowmarket.	Robjent, Sudbury.
Miller, Halesworth.	Jarrold, Manningtree.	Ware & Taylor, at
Gibbs, Witham.	Curtis, Dedham.	Boxford.
Keer, Framlingham.	Enefer, Harwich.	Thorp, Newmarket.
Davie, Southwold.	Brunwin, Neyland.	Gudgeon, Eye.
Tine, St. Osyth.	Munsey, Wivenhoe.	Raton, Bumstow.
Hill, Thorp.	White, Ongar.	Winstanley, Walden.
Gray, Billericay.	King, Epping.	Samford, Coggeshall.
Asplin, Rochford.	Emery, Hatfield B. O.	Livermere, Braintree.
Atkinson, Southminst.	Holland, Wabham A.	Hewitt, Ingatstone.
Pattison, Co. Maldon	Hayward, Haverhill.	Saward, Thaxted.
Sach, Tillsbury.	Totman, Halsted.	Allen, Long-Stratton.
Mrs. M. King, Raleigh.		

** They are a most useful Family Purge, particularly after the Small-Pox or Measles.
N. B. Of J Shave, and of most of the above-mentioned may be had an incomparable POWDER for cleaning the TEETH and preserving the Gums. It will prevent Teeth already decayed from being the least offensive, and gives a pleasant Fragrancy to the Breath. It cures the Tooth-Ach, if applied according to the printed Direction to be had with each BOX, Price 6d.

Truly Prepared,
At the Original Warehouse in LONDON, and sold Wholesale and Retail, by
J. PILBOROUGH, Printer in Colchester;
S. WATSON, Bookseller in Bury; and
W. CRAIGHTON, in Ipswich;

Dr. DAFFY's
Right and Never-failing Cordial Drink.

UNiversally allowed to be the most beneficial Cordial in the World, and a Sovereign Remedy in most Distempers incident to Mankind: 'Tis no trifling Thing to allure the Publick withal, but a real and well experienc'd Medicine, and was approv'd of and recommended by several of the most eminent of the College of Physicians in London, who declared it was the best Medicine ever exposed to Sale. For more than Eighty Years past, this Noble Elixir hath had wonderful Success in curing and relieving Persons of all Ages, afflicted with the Cholick, Gout, Rheumatism, Stone and Gravel, Worms, Scurvy, Dropsy, Black and Yellow Jaundice, Surfeits, Gripes or Piles: And in all other Distempers where Purging is required, this Cordial affists Nature in the most agreeable Manner, as appears by the Number of Cures it has performed. Sold also by Retail, by Mr. William Goodchild, and Mr. Samuel Stead, in Ipswich; Mr. Walford in Woodridge, Mr. Stebbing in Diss; Mr. Ray in Saxmundham, Mr. Nichols in Yoxford, Mr. Robinson in Leiston, Mrs. Harper in Southwold, Mr. Stebbing in Framingham, Mr. Hall in Debenham, Mr. Chisnall in Hadlam near Stratford, Mr. Goldsmith in Stonham, Stow-Market, Mr. Biggen in Needham, Mr. Keymer in Hadleigh, Mrs. Stannard at the Queen's-Head in Haughley; Mr. Benjamin Ham in Ixworth; and by the Men that sell this News Paper.
Price One Shilling a BOTTLE.

HOW IT FEELS TO TAKE CHLOROFORM - *The circumstance which led to my having to take chloroform was, says a writer, an accident to my leg that necessitated its amputation... I found myself in* *the midst of a party of five or six doctors who proceeded to business by arranging their various implements in order. The effect of the razor-like instruments exposed to view would not be very pleasant to weak nerves, but the business-like way in which the doctors go about their work and the tone of their conversation generally help to dispel or alleviate any feelings of horror... Following their advice, I took a good sniff from a towel that was placed over my face; the towel being saturated with the chloroform, when instantly, the world and every recollection of it vanished from my mind. For a few seconds I felt as if I was suspended in a horizontal position somewhere in space... I fancied I could hear some kind of inward beating, but was powerless to move. The feeling was not one of pain but somewhat the reverse... my brain for the time being felt as if a quantity of needles and pins were pressing upon it and bobbing up and down. These sensations only last for a few seconds, then all is chaos until the action of the chloroform is spent; and so far as my experience goes, I felt not the slightest indication of actual pain until*

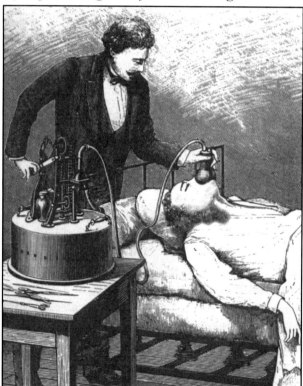

I came to my senses... about four hours afterwards. I saw then that I was a one-legged man but I felt so stupefied that I fell into a natural slumber.

ESSEX STANDARD:
January 26th 1889

Anaesthetics would prove a great relief, but although this was far from new technology in 1889, it was still experimental and there were far more reports of deaths under its use than positive reports like the one above.

152

However, not all old surgeons were idiots, and anecdotes like this amuse us as much now as they did when they first appeared...

Sir Richard Jebb [a celebrated 18th century physician born at Stratford, Essex] *...being called to see a patient who fancied himself very ill, told him ingenuously what he thought, and declined prescribing, thinking it unnecessary.*
"Now you are here," said the patient, "I shall be obliged to you, Sir Richard if you will tell me how I must live, what I may eat and what not."
"My directions as to that point," replied Sir Richard, "will be few and simple. You must not eat the poker, shovel or tongs for they are hard of digestion: nor the bellows because they are windy; but anything else you please."

CAMBRIDGE CHRONICLE & JOURNAL: March 23rd 1827

The inventiveness of the Victorians is legendary. Our local papers took a delight in reporting innovations, not merely from this country...

NEW BEE HIVE: *An inhabitant of Connecticut, Mr. Judd, has invented a contrivance by means of which bees are made to build their cells and deposit their honey in the chamber of a dwelling house in neat little drawers from which it may be taken fresh by the owner without killing the insect.*

COLCHESTER & CHELMSFORD GAZETTE: March 18th 1837

A WONDERFUL BED - *A Parisian millionaire has recently had made for him a wonderful bed which is certainly one of the most luxurious pieces of furniture yet heard of. If only it could become universal, what a boon it would be to early risers. The description makes one envy the fortunate possessor. The bed itself is a model of comfort, and the following devices have been adopted to render rising from it as little unpleasant as possible. When it is time to get up, a chime of bells rings. The occupant continues to sleep. Suddenly a candle is lit by a mechanical arrangement. The sleeper rubs his eyes and an invisible hand proceeds to divest him of his nightcap. By means of electricity, a spirit lamp with coffee-roasting apparatus affixed next begins to burn.*

The water soon boils and the smell of coffee fills the room with a delicious fragrance. Luxuriously revelling a crown of agreeable sensations, the occupant now just beginning to awake is soothed by sounds proceeding from a costly musical-box. At length, the bells ring out another merry peal, and at the foot of the bed, a card with 'Levez-vous' (Get up) inscribed on it appears. If this invitation is without effect, a more powerful mechanism lifts the occupant bodily from his bed and deposits him on the floor.

SUFFOLK & ESSEX FREE PRESS: March 10th 1886

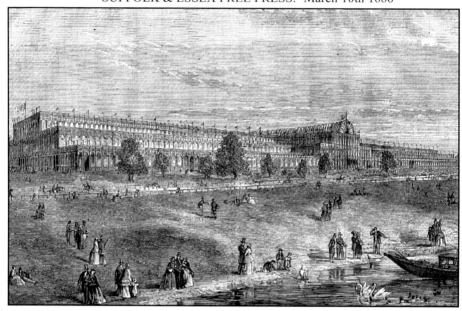

In 1851, the Great Exhibition at the Crystal Palace in London [pictured above] was the major event of the year, if not the decade. It became a show-place for manufacturers throughout the world and drew crowds of many thousands every day. You just had to be there if you were seriously intending to exhibit, to buy or merely to view Victorian creativity and invention. In May that year, in describing the official opening, the Chelmsford Chronicle gave full details of the contribution by Essex companies. These included...

Mr. Bentall of Heybridge Iron Foundry, Maldon with his patent broadshare and subsoil plough, patent mangel or ridge hoe, round hogs' trough, patent double-Tom, and patent dynamometer [which apparently measured the depth of implements such as ploughs in uneven ground].

Mr. R. Coleman's implement manufactory with their drag harrow or scarifier and expanding lever harrow (prizes have been awarded for this invention from the Royal & Highland Society).

Mr. Blowers of Maldon, who... *exhibits specimens of approved farming horse harness, which, though not altogether of a novel character, are examples of good workmanship.*

Mr. F. Chancellor of Chemsford with his working model of the perfect farm, complete with tramways between the animal compartments, enabling the feeding of sheep and pigs without any labourers needing to enter the yards.

Mr. George Henry Aggio with his elegant cottage piano forte, exhibited in a glass case. The *'stool ottoman'* that appeared with it was worked in an antique style in imitation of gold lace, *'the design and execution of Miss C. Aggio.'*

Mr. William Doe of Long Wyre St., Colchester with his exhibition composed of two enormous pairs of Navvys' shoes.

Mr. Faiers of Colchester with his 'Elysian Balsamic Hair Cream, guaranteed to restore hair, complete with the written testimonials of seven medical men of the county as to the product's efficacy.'

Mr. J. Tabor and his *'improved application of the whistle to Locomotive Steam Engines, ingeniously explained by diagrams.'*

Mr. Fitch of Chelmsford with his patent oven for *'economising and facilitating the baking of bread, pastry &c.'* He claimed to be able to cook *'one bushel of bread and forty pounds of meat at the cost of one penny for fuel.'*

The Chronicle went on to describe other astonishing items including the great Koh-i-noor diamond, protected, courtesy of Mr. Chubb, by an *'ingenious piece of machinery by which the diamond is raised so as to be visible to the visitors during the day, and lowered at night into an impenetrable strong-box.'*

COLCHESTER CHRONICLE: May 2nd 1851

Vegetarian Boots - *On Saturday evening last, we visited the Trades Exhibition at the Thames Ironworks...* [One] *thing that attracted our attention was the exhibition of the new vegetarian boots. These boots are made entirely from vegetable matter and present a superficial appearance that compares favourably with leather. Whether they will be a success, time and the weather alone will prove.*

WOODFORD MAIL: November 6th 1897

[At this time, Woodford had a Vegetarian Society]

But it would be changes to the ways in which people travelled about that would have the greatest impact on people's lives...

Mr Hills, silversmith of Friars Street, Sudbury, can claim the honour of introducing the first two wheeled velocipede to Sudbury, his riding through the streets of Sudbury on a singular looking conveyance now so much the fashion in France and America has quite excited the wonder of the crowds of persons although we understand it is not all that difficult and with a little practice it appears that 8 miles per hour can easily be done by an expert.

S. SUFFOLK & N. ESSEX FREE PRESS: April 8th 1869

AEROSTATION - *On the 15th inst., Mr. Green Jun. made his second aerial ascent at Cambridge. He was accompanied by Dr. Woodhouse of Caius College and James Ackers and F.W. Beaumont Esqs. of Trinity College... When at a height of about 1800 feet, Mr. Green dropped a parachute, to which was attached a basket containing a live dog. The parachute almost immediately expanded and gently descended into the river near Chesterton, from which the dog was rescued without injury.*

ESSEX HERALD: May 25th 1828

COLCHESTER: *There is every reason to believe that the borough will soon be in possession of a steam fire engine, the Corporation having sanctioned the head constable canvassing for subscriptions* [which have] *up to the present time had very encouraging results.*

EAST ANGLIAN DAILY TIMES: January 28th 1880

A passenger in a Greenwich railway carriage on Monday last says that in one of the experimental trips the train of 6 carriages was conveyed at the rate of a mile per minute, at 60 miles per hour. He adds that the sensation experienced was that of flying rather than that which is felt in the most rapid of the ordinary modes of travelling. There were two numerous parties of ladies in the carriages, who seemed highly delighted.

COLCHESTER GAZETTE & ESSEX INDEPENDENT: January 31st 1836

The coming of the railways was a mixed blessing. Huge numbers were killed in the second half of the nineteenth century in railway accidents of various kinds. From its opening in June 1839, the Eastern Counties Railway was the scene of a succession of serious crashes. In August 1840, the driver, Mr. Eastman, and a number of passengers died in a horrific accident...

When descending the inclined plane which approaches Brentwood Hill, the engine driver neglected to shut off the steam... the train descended at a rate of 60 or 70 miles an hour [and] *...finally ran off the rails dragging three of the carriages with it down the embankment.*

CHELMSFORD CHRONICLE: August 21st 1840

One of the survivors, a guard named Collier, had been fortunate not to be killed in another similar accident at Stratford earlier in the year. Less than a month later, the Chelmsford Chronicle would be describing another high speed collision near Stratford where two of the passengers had been none other than the great railway engineers, John Braithwaite and George Stephenson. The Bury and Norwich Post in reporting the inquest on the dead driver claimed that there had been at least a dozen fatal accidents on the line between Brentwood and Romford. In a letter to the paper in September that year, the manager of Eastern Counties Railway, Mr. Richard Hall categorically denied this.

The Essex Standard reported in April 1848 that in the latter half of 1847, 110 people had been killed and 74 injured on the railways of Great Britain. As the network grew, the numbers rose. A typical week is demonstrated in the Essex County Chronicle for January 8th 1892, where a detailed account of the suicide of C.C. Lewis of Saffron Walden (decapitated) appears beside that of Sarah Beard of Colne Engaine, *'cut to pieces at Langley Mill'*. It was stated that she *'did not see it and was very close when she opened the crossing gate.'* She was near-sighted and deaf. The train was travelling at the terrifying speed of 35 miles per hour.

The Halstead Gazette in June 1876 quoted an article from the British Medical gazette warning of *'the danger incurred by persons of advanced age hastening to catch trains.'*

Other later inventions could also be responsible for large numbers of accidents. The bicycle had much to answer for. Under the headline *'Alleged scorching at West Hanningfield,'* the following article appeared in 1900...

At Chelmsford on Friday, Ernest Smee, groom and gardener to the Rev. W. Wace, West Hanningfield was summoned for furiously cycling at West Hanningfield. Mr. F.P. Sutthery defended. P.C. Jacobs said as he was returning from church on Sunday evening, he saw people in the road in all directions. Defendent, who was on a bicycle, 'went by like a flash of light- ning.' He just touched witness's wife and knocked down a Mrs. Mott, who was a few yards distant, the force of the impact sending the woman three or four feet

across the road. When picked up, she was so dazed she could not stand without assistance. Defendant came off his machine but he remounted and rode away, although he was ordered by witness to stop.

SOUTHEND-ON-SEA ADVERTISER: May 24th 1900

Other witnesses described Smee's cycling as exemplary and gave evidence to suggest it was just an unfortunate accident. His employer, Rev. Wace described him as the best servant he had found in those parts. The result of this was that the magistrates could not agree and Smee was acquitted. However, plenty of other cases led to fines and even imprisonment. It was not uncommon in the 1890s to read in a single issue of a number of broken bones sustained as a result of cycling accidents.

We have already heard several reliable stories about cyclists losing control of their machines and dashing through plate glass windows. In the South of London there is a hill from the top of which there seems no outlet, but only a dead obstacle in the form of a confectioner's. Into this shop, several cyclists have precipitated through losing control of their machines.

ILFORD GUARDIAN: August 27th 1898

Without doubt, whilst land-based transport carried its dangers, taking to the water was far more problematic. In June 1893, the sinking of the Flagship Victoria (The picture on the right is from Illustrated London News) in calm seas would be reported in the Essex Standard in some detail. It was one disaster of many. In a report in the Essex & West Suffolk Gazette for October 2nd

159

1863, the readers were informed that in the previous year, 455 British ships had been lost and a further 695 seriously damaged. Over the previous ten years, 800 sailors a year had lost their lives at sea. Each year one in two hundred of our ships would not return.

But these were also remarkable times. People were encouraged to believe that science and technology would find answers to everything. Invention was bringing exciting changes. The papers were full of them.

GRAYS - *The works of Messrs. Brooks, Shoebridge & Co are to be lit by electricity.*
ESSEX COUNTY CHRONICLE: April 12th 1889

But even when power was available, it had to be used sparingly...
Instructions were ordered to be issued to the Manager of the [Maldon] *Gas Works, that the town lamps should be lighted at his discretion on such nights as they should be obscured during the period of the full moon.*
ESSEX WEEKLY NEWS: January 20th 1888

On Tuesday for the second time, electricity was used in America as a means of executing criminals and in all four cases was a complete success... A New York correspondent states that the men died painlessly and instantaneously and that no doubt now remains that the new method is a great improvement on death by hanging.
SOUTH WEST SUFFOLK ECHO: July 11th 1891

TELEGRAM FROM THE PLANET MARS - *It is the belief of an Italian astronomer that the people in the planet Mars are endeavouring to make electric communication with the people of this country. This is an interesting statement in which we place the utmost reliance, and we hope that some gentleman in the M.P. line will immediately bring it before the notice of the Government. Signor Pemignani of Teramo in the Abruzzi has ascertained the presence on the face of the planet Mars, of several luminous points of exceeding brilliancy, which shift from place to place with methodical regularity as if they were controlled by some intelligent action. The observer has therefore concluded that the sparks*

are telegraphic signals sent on speculation by the inhabitants of Mars to their neighbours on the Earth. Up to the present, the meaning of the signals has not been interpreted, but those interested in the discovery, do not despair of finding their signification and are now engaged in attempting to answer the astral messages.
SUFFOLK & ESSEX FREE PRESS: March 17th 1886

TENTH WONDER OF THE WORLD - A lieutenant of the Royal Navy has invented a new kind of paddle wheel for steam vessels which he says are to propel them at the rate of 30, 40, 50 or even 100 miles an hour!!! We shall therefore soon be able to cross from Dover to Calais in ten or twelve minutes. From London to Lisbon will not occupy a day! And our cockney citizens, instead of making Margate the ne plus ultra *of their Summer excursions, will very shortly be enabled to embark at Tower Stairs, breakfast at Madeira, dine upon Buonaparte's tomb at St. Helena, sup and sleep at the Brazils.*
ESSEX HERALD: March 25th 1828

The East Essex & Halstead Times of March 10th 1877 described a talk that had been given earlier that year by Professor A. Graham Bell, *'the inventor of that wonderful instrument, the telephone.'* The lecture was one of a course organised by the Essex Institute and about 500 people attended. He had demonstrated how, with his associate Mr. Thos. A. Watson of Boston, sounds, music and finally voices had been transmitted over a distance of twenty miles.

These were times when all manner of dangerous items were available over the counter, sometimes with tragic results...

Explosion of detonating silver - On Tuesday last, whilst Mrs. H. Cutts of South Ockendon was in the set of mixing in a tea-cup with a table knife a composition in which detonating silver was an ingredient for making crackers and balls to amuse her children, the friction caused an explosion. The knife was forced back into her hand, from which it completely severed two of her fingers, cut a deep gash in the arm of one of the children and was subsequently found sticking in the ceiling of the room. Mrs. C. was at the time deprived of her sight by the effects of the

161

explosion, but it is hoped that this lamentable deprivation will be but temporary. Fifteen panes of glass were forced out of the window and a large quantity of soot was, by the concussion, brought down the chimney.

ESSEX STANDARD: March 1st 1834

Throughout much of the 19th century, arsenic was readily available to be purchased in most village shops as a killer of vermin. Accidents whereby it contaminated foodstuffs or was mistaken for something less harmful were not uncommon.

THE GT. BROMLEY POISONING CASE

Examination of the Prisoners.

The Magistrates of the Tendring Hundred Bench held a special sitting at the Police-Court, Mistley, on Thursday for the purpose of commencing an investigation into the charge preferred against *William Kittel* and *Ellen Kittel* (his wife) of poisoning a former wife of the first-named prisoner, at Great Bromley, in October last.

In this case (April 1872), there was measure of doubt involved as to whether the Kittels had deliberately killed Elizabeth Kittel and they were both acquitted. The locals were not convinced and there were reports of attempts by them to make life for William Kittel as difficult as they could. Twenty-four years earlier, a poisoning at the nearby village of Wix in Essex had led to a series of trials and accusations involving arsenic. As the Essex Standard for August 18th 1848 shows, this time it had resulted in a guilty verdict.

THE WIX MURDER.—EXECUTION OF THE CULPRIT.

On Monday morning *Mary May*, who was found guilty at the last assizes of poisoning her brother, William Constable, *alias* Watts, at the parish of Wix, in this county, expiated her heinous crime (as far as human laws and institutions are concerned) upon the scaffold.

As already mentioned on page 109 of this book, 'Death clubs' had been set up whereby the longest living member stood to gain a bumper pay-out. Further accusations and trials would follow Mary May's trial, with exhumations and suspicion that there had been, in that part of Essex, just too many 'accidental deaths' from swallowing arsenic.

As knowledge and understanding of the world became more accessible to a wider reading public, changes in attitude became more evident. Resistance to change was often mocked by a reformist press and through our local papers it is possible to chart **attitudes and change**...

Chapter 10
Attitudes and change

We often complain about modern health and safety regulations, but you only have to look back to a time when there were none, to see why we now need them...

AT HARWICH, a seaman called Robert Cook, engaged in unloading a steamer, caught his fingers in the cogs of a crane leading to their amputation. This was the 17th similar accident with this crane, and surely the cogs could be cased.
  FRAMLINGHAM WEEKLY
      NEWS: June 1877

This was a minor problem compared with what seemed to be going on in Tilbury. The Grays & Tilbury Gazette at the end of the nineteenth century was reporting about a death a week by way of *'accidents'* at Tilbury Docks.

A little girl between 5 and 6 years of age has died at Poplar, London from the effects of poison administered in mistake. The child was unwell and its mother bought a powder at a chemist's shop. The chemist was out and had left the place in charge of a lad who served the woman with morphia instead of a composition for children's powders.
      EAST ANGLIAN DAILY TIMES: January 5th 1880

...On Tuesday, the corning house number 4 at Faversham [in Kent] blew up with a most tremendous explosion. Of the six men employed in the building at the time, four were blown to pieces and their bodies and

163

limbs were scattered to a distance upwards of a hundred yards from the site of the building. One of the arms was found on the top of a high elm tree. A fifth man was taken up alive, but no hopes of his recovery are entertained. The sixth man, Geo. Holmes, the foreman of the work, singular to relate, was found alive also, sitting in the midst of the smoking ruins with his clothes burning, but he was otherwise not much injured and is likely to do well. At the door of the corning house was standing a tumbril... with two horses and a driver. The wagon was blown to pieces and the driver and horses were killed. [According to the Kentish Gazette of January 19th that year, this explosion could be heard 14 miles away]*

...The scattered remains of two of the men were collected on Wednesday evening for interment; the remains of the other three had not been found. No circumstances have transpired from which an opinion can be formed with respect to the cause of the accident: it is the third of the kind that has happened at these mills within these seven years.

ESSEX UNION: January 23rd 1810

Under the headlines, *EXPLOSION AT WALTHAM ABBEY* and *THE DANGER INSPECTOR NEARLY KILLED*, the Woodford Mail in October 1797 began one of a number of such articles...

"The season of explosions has again commenced at Waltham Abbey." They manufactured *'a special kind of black powder which is prepared principally for rockets.'*

Where lives might be at risk, certain safety measures could always be employed, or, on the other hand, prove to be a good selling point...

It is proposed that each man-of-war shall be fitted with at least one lifeboat.

ESSEX STANDARD: Dec. 11th 1863

[advert on the right is taken from Chemsford Chronicle: February 1891]

THE ESSEX COUNTY CYCLE MANUFACTORY, MARKET-PLACE, ROMFORD, ESSEX.

Largest Stock in Essex of **SAFETY & OTHER BICYCLES, TRICYCLES, AND TANDEMS,** New and Second Hand.

ALL kinds of Cycle Accessories in Stock. Bells, Lamps, Wrenches, Valises, Oilcans, &c., &c. Safeties a speciality, built to order or supplied from stock at prices from £5 to £15. Send for Quotations. Repairs, Enamelling, and Plating at lowest trade prices. Easy payments taken.

Another significant difference between now and times past was what constituted a reasonable form of entertainment...

A child was exhibited at Salisbury last week with two faces, four eyes, two mouths, two noses and two chins, all in perfect nature.
KENT & ESSEX MERCURY: June 10th 1828

As can be seen from above, *'freak shows'* of many kinds were quite acceptable throughout most of the eighteen and nineteenth centuries. *'Human oddities'* carried a certain fascination. Some *'stars'* in this way achieved celebrity status. One such was Daniel Lambert, the Leicester giant, whose death in 1809, shortly after he had appeared in Chelmsford, caused a bit of a problem...

Mr. D. Lambert, so celebrated for his corpulence, died without any previous illness on Wednesday morning last at Stamford, whither he had gone with an intent to exhibit himself during the races. He was in his 40th year and upon being placed in the famous Caledonian balance within a few days of his death was found to weigh 52 stone 11 lbs, which is 10 stone 11 lbs more than the famous Mr. Bright of Essex ever weighed. His coffin... consists of 12 superficial feet of elm, is built upon 2 axle trees and 4 clog wheels and upon these the poor man will be rolled into the grave... The window and wall of the room in which he lies must be taken down to allow the removal of the corpse.
ESSEX UNION: June 27th 1809

*A **modern Daniel Lambert** - Upper Norwood boasts at the present time of a most wonderful specimen of humanity in the person of a boy aged 7 who weighs 13 stone.*
WALTHAM ABBEY & CHESHUNT WEEKLY
TELEGRAPH: March 2nd 1872

Early in the twentieth century, Frederick Kempster from Landermere in Essex [pictured here] would become quite a celebrity.

On Friday last, a woman at Coggeshall was delivered of a child without arms, and in the place thereof were two thumbs, having nails thereon: it had no neck, the head leaning against the breast-bone.

PILBOROUGH'S COLCHESTER JOURNAL: May 26th 1739

On Friday died about two o'clock in the afternoon, at Charing Cross, Mademoiselle Chimpanzee, a native of Africa, and one greatly admir'd by all who have seen her. It is said that she died of a kind of intermitting fever, seem'd to be very sensible that she should die, and to the surprise of those present, behaved in a great measure like a Negro in the like circumstances. The owner's loss by her death is very considerable, as she was a kind of estate to him.

PILBOROUGH'S COLCHESTER JOURNAL: March 3rd 1739

Cruel sports were the order of the day in past centuries, though they would gradually become less acceptable...

To all Gentlemen and Others

That at J. HOGG'S COCK-
PIT at the KING'S HEAD at GAL-
LARD COMMON, within two miles of
CHELMSFORD, ESSEX; there is a COCK
Match to be fought on Tuesday the 17th of
February, between some Gentlemen of
BRENTWOOD and J. Hogg, Master of
the said Pitt, for 4 Guineas a Battle, and 10 guineas
the Odd Battle; and the first
Pair of COCKS to be on the Pit by Eleven a-
clock in the Morning, exactly.
N.B. The COCKS are to be weigh'd and
match'd the Monday, by Ten a clock, be
fore Fighting; on which Day there will be
several bye Battles

PILBOROUGH'S COLCHESTER JOURNAL: January 31st 1736

As can be seen from the following announcement from 1764, there were limits to what could be regarded as sporting...

E S S E X.

MOOT-HALL } *To wit.* *At the General Quarter-Seffion of* in COLCHESTER. } *the Peace of our Sovereign Lord the King, holden for the faid Town and Borough of* Colchefter, *on* Monday *next after the* Epiphany, *(to wit) the* Ninth Day *of* January, *in the Fourth Year of the Reign of our Sovereign Lord* GEORGE *the Third, now King of* Great Britain, *&c and in the Year of our Lord one thoufand feven hundred and fixty-four, before* Thomas Clamtree, *Efq;* Mayor, Wm. Mayhew, *the younger,* Efq; Deputy-Recorder, *and Alderman* William Mayhew, *Juftices of our faid Lord the King, affigned to keep the Peace of the faid Lord the King, and to hear and determine divers Felonies, Trefpaffes, and other Mifdemeanors committed in the faid Borough and Liberties thereof, &c*

THIS Court taking into Confideration the many Riots, Mifchiefs, and other Diforders committed by Perfons following the cruel Practice of THROWING AT COCKS, and being defirous to difcountenance fuch Cuftoms for the future, doth hereby charge and command all Chief Conftables and Petty Conftables within the feveral Wards of the faid Borough, to ufe their utmoft Endeavours to fupprefs and prevent all fuch unlawful and diforderly Meetings and Practices; and if they fhall find any Perfons throwing at Cocks within any of their faid Wards, that they do immediately take fuch Perfons into Cuftody and carry them before the Mayor, or fome other Juftice of the Peace for the Borough aforefaid, to be further dealt with, and punifhed according to Law.

By the Court, ENNEW, Town-Clerk.

The Monthly magazine in 1801 described a particularly brutal piece of bull-baiting at Bury St. Edmunds in Suffolk where the beast was tethered, goaded and gored by dogs. Even then, this was deplored. However, when it came to attempts to ban cruel sports such as bear and badger baiting, parliamentary opponents described it as *'a very objectionable way to take away any sports which formed the relaxation of the lower classes after the labour of the day was over.'* (Norfolk Chronicle: March 6th 1824)

However, just eleven years later an all-embracing *'Cruelty to Animals Act'* would put an end to many of these 'sports' of the past. Abuses did continue, and from time to time, reports appeared in local papers such as the bull-baiting at Lavenham in Suffolk in 1842, (Chelmsford Chronicle & Ipswich Journal: Nov. 18th & 19th 1842) whereby a dozen men from towns nearby were fined or imprisoned for their part in *'these cruel and disgraceful practices.'*

William Mattham landlord of Lavenham Black Lion, Noah Must a horse dealer of Sudbury, John Chinney, Martin Stearn and William Gurling all butchers of Lavenham, Isaac Scarfe, Fred Stock, William Snell and William Duce all of Lavenham were summoned to answer a charge by Henry Thomas, secretary of the Society for the Prevention of Cruelty to Animals, charging them with on November 5th at Washmere Green, Lavenham, that they did use a certain ground for bull baiting.

John Smith said he went to Washmere Green at 12 o'clock on November 5th where a great many people were assembled. At between 3 and 4 a bull was brought from the direction of Lavenham and several persons fixed a rope to its horns They then led it to a stake fixed in the ground where a collar was put round its neck and the rope taken from its horns, then by noise and other means the bull was irritated to make it wild, Carter being the most active in this, he also collected money from the spectators.

Stearn had a dog which he set on the bull which it bit and several times, the dog was tossed in the air and severely injured. Gurling, Chinney and Ransom had dogs which they also set on the bull, Natham was on horse back and appeared to direct the proceedings. The bull was baited for about an hour and was torn about the face and nose, several of the dogs were much injured and bled a great deal.

There were about 200 people present during the baiting with great uproar and filthy language being used. Matham, Must, Ransom, Chinney and Carter were fined £5 each. Gurling 20s. Hughes, Snell, Stock, Scarfe and Duce were fined 10s. Matham, Must, Stearn, Gurling and Duce paid their fines, the rest were committed to prison for 2 months hard labour, the prosecution gave the fines to Lavenham National school. SUDBURY POST: November 23rd 1842

This is to acquaint the Public that there will be a BULL BAIT on IPSWICH RACE GROUND on MONDAY next Nov. 1 - The first two dogs are to run the best of ten puts for Ten Guineas; and the next best dog will be intitled to a collar of 5s value. [IPSWICH JOURNAL: Oct 30th 1784]

As in all ages, the late Victorian period had its scandals. One of these was the practice of baby farming. What had begun as wet-nursing and baby care had slowly deteriorated to the point where, for a set fee, women would fill their homes with unwanted infants and were often impervious to the suffering and neglect imposed on these children. It was only when a string of inquests on dead infants exposed what was happening, that new laws of child protection were hastily passed. But it did not put an end to stories of ill-treatment and abuse; even manslaughter and murder. Essex newspapers chronicled a host of these.

Baby Farming

Abi Joan Barton of Epping was charged with having neglected the eighteen children in her care… aged between three and thirteen, all were found to be in a very dirty and neglected condition… she had advertised in the 'People' newspaper, offering a 'happy home for children'… she described how one gentleman had offered her £30 to take a child and he didn't expect to see it again.

SUFFOLK & ESSEX FREE PRESS: February 4th 1891

After four deaths of babies in the charge of Miss Wills at Green's Farm, Magdalen Laver, near Epping, it emerged that thirty babies were being kept there in insanitary conditions. Closing down her operation hardly improved matters as the children were distributed around the homes of Miss Wills' friends and relations, many of which were already overcrowded (Essex Newsman: November 7th 1908)

...and it wasn't only babies being abused. This dramatic and disturbing case received the full treatment in the Illustrated Police News for April 8th 1893. Here the *National Society for the Prevention of Cruelty to Children'* would attempt to prosecute Selina Bickmore of Chelmsford for ill-treating her fifteen year-old servant, Hattie Alderton.

A catalogue of cruelty and abuse would emerge, but this was all too much for Essex. To avoid the rowdy scenes that had been experienced at the preliminary hearings, the case was moved to the Old Bailey, where Mrs Bickmore would be found guilty and subsequently spend two years in Holloway.

Links between the water supply, sewage and bad health were recognised early in the nineteenth century, but it took a while for the message to get across. In 1866, Essex papers were reporting how handles were being removed from water pumps in areas of London where the water was believed to be contaminated. As a result numbers of deaths from cholera fell, in spite of the protests. In August 1895, when a new well was proposed at Basildon on the old Rectory ground, there were objections from those who were being compelled to pay for it as... *"it would be of no benefit to anyone in the parish except the inhabitants of 5 or 6 newly built houses situated in the locality... Remarks were made as to the condition of the water in the well, the oldest inhabitants stating that the water was never fit for drinking purposes, while one person said a cow was buried in the well."*

CHELMSFORD CHRONICLE: August 2nd 1895

However, in those parts of Essex that were rapidly being absorbed by an expanding London, the state of the tributaries of the Thames like the Lea and the the Roding was a major concern. The Walthamstow Times of August 18th 1882 described thousands of dead fish floating on the surface of the River Lea... *"Many persons have carried away baskets full of these poisoned fish and it is feared have sold or otherwise used them."* The Ilford Guardian in September 1898 described their concern over the River Roding, which was *'polluted all along the line'* and warned against eating water cress found growing along its banks.

Those who could afford to were already starting to move out of the East end, as a series of Chelmsford Chronicle articles showed in the closing years of the nineteenth century. Under the heading *'COLONY OF ISRAELITES AT SOUTH BENFLEET,'* plots of building land, once belonging to the Thundersley Manor estate, were being snapped up by Jews who had originally come to this country from Poland and Russia. The sales were heavily over- subscribed and numbers of bidders had to be limited on each occasion. *"If train, tent and provisions had been adequate, there would have been 1,000 to 2,000 Jews down for the sale, and most of them intending buyers."* Those choosing to settle in the South Benfleet area were described as *"entering into possession of the promised land."* This would lead to a boom in the building of houses and factories. The Chelmsford Chronicle of September 3rd 1897 closed by

commenting, *"The English language was conspicuous by its absence."*

Rapid growth of an area often fails to be matched by the services demanded from an expanding population. In South Benfleet, there was little room left in the churchyard to bury people and the rise in the price of land made it difficult to purchase more. Hence, by the end of 1898, old graves were being excavated to make more room for more burials. In the same year, the shortage of water would also become an issue. Within five years, an elegant new water-tower (pictured left) would be built.

Editors today are expected to be fairly cautious in the way they report what may be criminal acts for fear of prejudicing any further prosecutions. This was not always so. As late as January 28th 1817, the Essex Herald reported the murder of a bastard child at Little Baddow by the sister of the mother. *...this inhuman woman, it appears, after having tied the legs and hands of the innocent victim, threw him into a large pond near Grace's Farm, and being observed by a person who most humanely used his utmost endeavours to rescue the orphan babe, she took the opportunity to run off...*

Unfortunately, a fortnight later, the Herald would have to revise its report of the story. *...The accounts hitherto published... are erroneous and might tend to the prejudice of the unfortunate girl in the minds of the public... we find that Ann Campion, under whose care the illegitimate child of her sister was placed... nursed the poor infant with the most affectionate regard, even as though it had been her own.*

All of this would not prevent Ann Campion being tried a month later for murder. Circumstantial evidence pointed to it having been anything but an accident. The Essex Herald, in reporting the trial, portrayed Ann Campion as a disturbed soul. However, witnesses testified to her care for her sister's child and as there was no clear motive, it took the jury just five minutes to find her 'Not Guilty.'

In a bizarre follow-up to this story, in May that year, the same paper would describe how Ann Campion had sworn an affidavit accusing her own father of the child's murder, an accusation she would later retract. *...The sanity of the young woman... may be doubted; although her manners and appearance in other respects do not favour so charitable a conclusion.* (Essex Herald: May 13th 1917)

Perhaps not surprisingly, no-one was ever successfully prosecuted for the child's murder.

A topic that really enables us to see how attitudes changed is that of slavery. We can trace the progress of slavery and people's changing views as the years passed...

Yesterday, a very respectable meeting of the West Indies Planters & Merchants trading to the West India Islands was held at the London Tavern for the purpose of preparing a memorial to be presented to Lord Grenville requesting that a sufficient force may be immediately sent to the West India Islands in order to keep the negroes in subjection.
CHELMSFORD CHRONICLE: March 5th 1791

SALE OF SLAVES BY AUCTION IN LONDON - *On Wednesday, an extraordinary sale... took place at the Auction Mart which excited considerable interest. The property consisted of two sugar plantations in St. Kitts, containing 400 acres of land with dwelling houses and all necessary buildings, and live stock, consisting of 107 negro men and boys, 94 women and girls and 69 children, all stated to be in good condition; one bull and 43 oxen, 24 cows, 25 calves, 4 horses, seven mules and six asses... It was knocked down at £16, 250.*
THE SICKLE: September 25th 1828

NEGRO SLAVERY - *On Tuesday evening, a numerous meeting was held in the Meeting House of the Society of Friends at Chelmsford to consider the propriety of petitioning Parliament for the abolition of the apprenticeship system, under the Slave-Emancipation Act.*
His Majesty's sloop of war Buzzard captured on the 27th November off Bonny River after a long chase and a hard fight, a slaver with 280 slaves on board.
ESSEX STANDARD: March 18th 1836

By the1830s, we were well on the way to having nothing more to do with slavery (and feeling suitably self-righteous about it).

SLAVERY IN AMERICA - *The Attorney-General of Virginia has commenced proceedings against two Quakers, for circulating an address on the subject of slavery, adopted at a meeting of Quakers in Philadelphia. The Act under which the prosecution is authorised was passed last year (during the anti-slavery agitation), and makes it a felony for any person "to promote by writing or speaking the abolition of slavery or to deny the right of property of the master in the slave." Virginia is the most civilized and enlightened of the Slave States.*
[Irony proving an important journalist's tool, even then]
ESSEX & SUFFOLK TIMES: December 1st 1837

For the British, being kicked out of America in the 1770s had been hard to bear. As the article above shows, our newspapers took every opportunity to demonstrate how our former colony was populated by savages. On the same page as the previous story is one describing a treacherous meeting between two American Generals, Jessup and Powell and a group of 'native Indians.'

"The warriors attended, not suspecting any trap: in the midst of the council however, they were surrounded by a strong body of troops and taken prisoners."

The Essex & Suffolk Times goes on to comment, *"This infamous proceeding is consistent with the uniform policy of the Americans in their transactions with the poor Indians."*

In December 1868, the Essex Weekly News described how public whippings were still the order of the day in the state of Delaware. They continued... *"It was only in 1855 that some ray of civilisation, some glimmer of decency shone in upon the dull brains of the legislators and woman-whipping was abolished. We can thank God and take hope from that forward stride."* ...all a bit sanctimonious considering it was little more than a decade since Charles Finch, the Rivenhall murderer had been publicly executed ouside Chelmsford gaol before a crowd of thousands.

These rather different articles betray other prevalent attitudes of their time..

On May 13th 1859, a story appeared in the Stratford Times telling of a female Robinson Crusoe. Miss Richardson of Cleveland had been cast away on an island in Lake Superior where she had survived for 3 years before being discovered and rescued by some Indians. It was said she had recovered from the wreck some animal skins, matches and a case of sardines which had kept her alive whilst she taught herself to fish. It was described as a *'rather doubtful story.'* Presumably as no-one could imagine a woman surviving that long without a man to take care of her.

In early December 1897, the Woodford Mail, told the story of Frederick Martin, who was tried for stealing 12lbs of walnuts and 56 lbs of chestnuts. He had claimed, *'they were lying there and he had taken them just to keep wicked people from stealing them.'* He also claimed that drink was the cause of his longing for a vegetarian diet...

"The prisoner had been in Her Majesty's service before and he will continue this loyal occupation at Pentonville for 3 months. They will also allow him to do a little hard labour, just to keep his liver in order."
[It was widely believed that vegetarians suffered from liver damage as a reesult of their restricted diet.]

The 1830s were great times of social change in this country. There was a strong drive to go much further. What had been acceptable a few years earlier was no longer considered 'right.'

Chimney Sweeps - The practice of employing children to sweep chimnies is a disgrace to a civilised country. It is a matter of astonishment that any person with the common feelings of humanity should permit the practice in his own dwelling. When machinery can be employed as effectually, why expose a fellow creature to the miseries of a climbing boy's life. It is our imperative duty to use all our influence to put a stop to this barbarous custom.

ESSEX & SUFFOLK TIMES: January 5th 1838

Many people disapproved of capital punishment, especially as it extended to women and sometimes children. Plenty believed, even then, that education rather than punishment was the answer to the county's social problems.

It is not six months since a boy at the tender age of fourteen was hanged for murder in England. [In August that year, the Standard had reported the execution of a 13 year-old at Maidstone in Kent. Following the hanging, his body had been given to surgeons at Rochester to dissect.] *He could neither read nor write and was therefore little removed from the state of a born idiot. It would be well if our reformers could contrive to form a free school in every hamlet, for by means of such institutions the "praise and the glory" of having a well-instructed population might be theirs. This is a "reform" which the land may abide and by which those high in place no less than the lowly will be benefited.*

ESSEX STANDARD: November 5th 1831

However, not all parents were willing to avail themselves of education for their children even when it was on offer. There were countless cases brought before magistrates of parents failing to send their children to school. They could be too useful at home and as the leaving age gradually rose, so did cases of non-attendance. In the year 1898-9, from the village of Ardleigh, William Hettle, William Nichol, Arthur Jarrold, John Butler & William Baker were all fined for this offence. Added to these, Richard Thurman of Ardleigh was fined for employing a boy of under 12 years of age to drive cattle; all a bit embarassing as he was a member of the School Board. (Chelmsford Chronicle)

It would be hard to examine the beliefs and attitudes of the time without giving a glance at fashion. One remarkable new 'fashion' was described here (East Anglian Daily Times: July 3rd 1873) ...

A new and terrible fashion, which may perhaps completely revolutionise the style of feminine dress, has received the stamp of approval of the American girl. This gentle creature, says a correspondent of the *St. James's Gazette*, has resolved to decorate her skin with much the same designs and figures that the materials of her dresses are often decorated with. In other words, plain white skins will soon be fashionable no longer; they will be ornamented like brocaded silks or printed calicoes. Tattooed arms and legs are becoming the latest fad, and all sorts of curious figures and designs indelibly printed in the soft flesh of the Transatlantic beauties will be one of the interesting features of an American ball-room. Probably ere long a young lady's tendencies will be easily discernible by the nature of the ornaments engraved in ink upon her skin. The patriotic girl wears a United States flag between shoulder and elbow; the maiden who has a taste for natural history will carry for ever on her skin the images of her favourite beasts or reptiles; the limbs of the sentimental lass will be adorned with pictures of "just lovely men," while those religiously inclined will have nothing but Biblical pictures or quotations. A widow already has the features of her "first two" side by side on her left arm just below the elbow. It would be interesting to gauge the feelings of her "next" when he contemplates the vacant space on the other arm. Recent developments in electricity have, it is said, rendered the process of tattooing painless and innocuous, and the primitive system of jabbing with needles has become obsolete. India ink and Chinese vermilion are the only ingredients used, neither of them being injurious.

Forms of religious belief proliferated during the nineteenth century. Many of the non-conformist churches we are familiar with today gained much of their momentum during this time. But Essex gave birth to one particular sect that remained largely all its own. **The Peculiar People** were a fundamentalist Wesleyan group that grew out of the preaching of James Banyard of Romford. They gained notoriety through their refusal to seek medical care when sick. Instead, they tended to rely on faith and prayer. When the child of John Benton of Plaistow died in May 1878, the father was heavily criticised by the coroner. Benton's attitude was contemptuous. *"The law was not made for the righteous man, but for the disobedient,"* he said. This was one of a sequence of cases where charges of neglect; even of manslaughter were considered against members of the sect for failing to consult doctors when their children were sick. However, though one or two received short prison sentences, judges were reluctant *'to make martyrs of the prisoners by sending them to gaol.'* (Manchester Evening News: October 29th 1897). The Grays & Tilbury Gazette reported an inquest in May 1884 on 18 month-old Lavinia Dedman of Steeple, near Burnham-on-Crouch, where the Coroner's jury returned a verdict of 'Death by manslaughter' and sent her father for trial. He was a member of the Peculiar People and had resisted all suggestions that his daughter needed medical help. At the Assize in August that year, Dedman was found guilty but his sentence would be just one month without hard labour. The S.P.C.C. (later to be the N.S.P.C.C.) brought a high profile case at Southend in 1895 against William Cable of Rayleigh for *'cruelly ill-using his four children by refusing to send for a doctor'* when they contracted, and subsequently died from, diphtheria. In a long trial that, somewhat surprisingly, had its comical moments (Chelmsford Chronicle: November 15th 1895), William Cable was acquitted, much to the disapproval of a number of local papers, in particular the Essex Newsman (November 23rd 1895).

A not dissimilar story surrounds, Joseph Fenton, a signalman from Ongar, who objected to his child being vaccinated against smallpox. His wife had lost a brother through vaccination, it was said and he claimed *"it gives children bad sores and poisons the blood and in many cases it spoils a child's health for life."* (Essex Newsman/ Chelmsford Chronicle: September 1901) Fenton stuck to his guns and after five applications to magistrates was finally granted an exemption. Two years later, he won a similar battle.

The Salvation Army, founded in 1865 by William Booth brought a new aggressive style of Christianity to the country, a challenge that was sometimes taken too literally. The Essex Times in 1886 reported fights that had occurred between (sometimes well-bevvied) groups of men and Salvation Army parades. People took umbridge over the Sally-Army's tendency to fill a street and force the public into doorways as they passed.

In March 1886, such confrontations happened at Romford, Bishop's Stortford and especially in Colchester, where things had got more than a little fractious. The Essex Times tried to defend the minor scuffles that had taken place at Brentwood, claiming they had been nowhere near as bad as *'the odious savagery of the mob at Colchester.'*

When the law relating to witchcraft was largely removed from the statute book in 1736, it must have been hoped that the superstitious folk of Essex would abandon their old ways, but a change of law does not always mean a change of attitude...

At the Inquest of *'Old Sam Payne'* (64) at Tollesbury in April 1894, who had died from extreme neglect, his sister Eliza Holder was declared to be *'morally responsible'* for his death. Though she claimed she had fed and cared for him, he was found in a thoroughly pitiful state. The local people would be slow to forget it, and had their own way of dealing with such matters, as the following cutting from a little later that month clearly demonstrates. (Chelmsford Chronicle: 20th April 1894).

I have found a number of similar tales from this area. In December 1868, four men from Leyton were fined for burning an effigy of Mr. *('Old Jelly Bean')* Fenton, thus causing a breach of the peace (EssexWeekly News).

MORE DEMONSTRATIONS AT TOLLESBURY.

MRS. HOLDER BURNT IN EFFIGY.

A CURIOUS VERSE.

The demonstrations of feeling against Mrs. Holder continued every evening during last week. A large bonfire was made and another effigy burnt. It is stated that for Saturday evening four effigies had been prepared, and a horse and cart hired, and it was intended to have a procession, but extra police were present, and the proceedings were confined to another fire and the burning of one more effigy. The funeral of the deceased, S. Payne, took place very quietly on Friday afternoon. A wreath was sent which bore the following curious verse :—

Odd I lived; odd I died;
Nobody laughed; nobody cried.

In August 1863, in Sible Hedingham, an old man known locally as *'Dummy'* was accused by a crowd led by beer-house keeper Emma Smith of practising witchcraft. He was dragged to a nearby stream and swum in a way that had been outlawed over a century before. Though he was pulled out before he drowned, a month later he was dead. At the Essex Assize the following Spring, the ringleaders of the lynch mob were tried for manslaughter.

THE WITCHCRAFT CASE AT SIBLE HEDINGHAM

Emma Smith, married woman and James Stammers, both on bail, were charged with the manslaughter of an aged Frenchman known as Dummy at Sible Hedingham on the 3rd August 1863... After a long investigation, the jury returned a verdict of guilty and His Lordship sentenced each to six months hard labour.

ESSEX STANDARD: March 9th 1864

A far more detailed account appeared in the Ipswich Journal...

Emma Smith, the wife of a beer-house keeper at Ridgewell and Saml. Stammers, a carpenter of Sible Hedingham, were charged with causing the death of a man called Dummey under the following peculiar circumstances:- *The poor old man Dummey, who was deaf and dumb and about 80 years of age had lived near the town of Sible Hedingham in a small mud hut for the last eight years and had been known in the neighbourhood and in the county for a period of twenty years; but his name, the place of his birth or his country were never known, though he was generally supposed to be a Frenchman. His habits were peculiar, and his inability to express himself otherwise than by grotesque gestures and being also of a very excitable nature, caused him to be regarded by many as a person possessed of the power of witchcraft. He was in the habit of travelling about to the adjoining villages and no doubt gained his livelihood by telling fortunes, and was generally consulted by the young people of the locality as to their love affairs... He seems to have been a very inoffensive old man and was treated with great kindness by the good families of the neighbourhood, and as a source of merriment and amusement by the youthful and idle.*

Amongst other places, the old man went to the village of Ridgewell, a few miles distant from Hedingham and there made the acquaintance of the prisoner Smith at the beer-house of her husband. It seems that on the occasion of one of these visits to Ridgewell, the poor old man wanted to sleep at the prisoner's house and on her refusing to allow him to do so, he stroked his walking-stick and used other threatening signs to her as signifying his displeasure at her refusal; and although he could neither hear nor speak, he had no difficulty in understanding and being understood and some of these signs accompanied by violent gestures were looked upon with considerable awe. Soon after this expression of the old man's displeasure, Emma Smith became ill and disordered, and was reduced to a low nervous condition and at once expressed her conviction that she had been bewitched by old Dummey and that she would never recover till she had induced him to remove the spell from her and made several applications to him for that purpose, as it would seem without effect.. At last, while labouring under great mental and nervous excitement, she went from her home at Rigewell to Sible Hedingham on the evening of the 3rd August 1863 and met old Dummey at the Swan public house, which is situated about a quarter of a mile from Dummey's hut. They remained there together for some hours, she endeavouring to persuade him to go to

Ridgewell with her and sleep in her house, and offering him three sovereigns to do so. Dummey however, refused to go and drew his fingers across his throat implying that he was afraid of having his throat cut. As soon as it became known in the town that a woman from Ridgewell who had been bewitched by old Dummey was at the Swan, a great number of villagers flocked to see her, and the Swan became a scene of riot and confusion, and the old man was pulled and danced about, falling once or twice violently to the ground.

The prisoner Smith still continued to urge the old man to go home with her, repeating that she would give him three sovereigns and would treat him well and that she had been in a bad state for nine or ten months and that she was bewitched. After the closing of the Swan, the parties adjourned outside and the prisoner Smith was seen standing by the side of Dummey declaring that he should go home with her. She then tore the old man's coat, struck him several times over the arms and shoulders with his stick and kicked him and dragged him down to a little brook

The Swan at Sible Hedingham, recently closed

which runs across the road and down a lane near the Swan and was proved to have said, "You old devil, you served me out and now I'll serve you out!" Smith then shoved him into the brook and when he was getting out the other side, she went round over a little bridge and the *other prisoner Stammers went through the brook and they both pushed him back into the brook. He afterwards succeeded in getting out and went and sat on a stone heap until the two prisoners again dragged him towards the brook and one taking hold of him under the armpits and the other by the legs, they threw him into the brook at a point where the water is dammed up and was of some little depth, where he remained struggling until one of the villagers called out that if someone did not take the old man out, he would die in a minute, when the prisoner Stammers jumped into the water and pulled him out. He lay on the grass for some time in a very exhausted and wet and muddy state, and was ultimately led home to his miserable hut, where he lay in that condition, in his wet clothes all night. The only direct evidence of the throwing into the brook by the two prisoners was that of a little girl named Eva Henrietta Garrad, about ten years of age, who gave her evidence in such a way as to elicit from the learned judge the observation that she was gifted with the most extraordinary power of intellect and clearness of expression he had ever met with, and that he could conceive no possible reason to doubt the truth of her story.*

On the morning of the 4th, the old man was seen in his hut by Mr. Fowke, still in his wet clothes and trembling violently. He was also a good deal bruised and screamed from pain when his things were taken off. He was then under the direction of a surgeon of Hedingham, taken to the Union House at Halsted and placed under the care of Mr. Sinclair the house surgeon, where he remained until his death on the 4th September last. The post-mortem examination showed that the lungs and kidneys were much disorganised, the pericardium adhering to the heart and a suffusion of lymph on the membrane of the brain, indicating recent inflammatory action, and the witness gave it as his opinion that he died from the disease of the kidneys produced by the immersion in the water and the sleeping in his wet clothes, and in this opinion, the witness was corroborated by another medical man who attended the post-mortem examination.

For the defence, it was contended that the evidence of the little girl could not be relied on and without it there was no evidence that either of the prisoners threw the old man into the water; and secondly there was not sufficient evidence that death resulted from the immersion;

that it might have resulted from disease of the lungs or kidneys, or from some injury received by the falls the old man had had in the tap room of the Swan public house.

The learned judge summed up the case with great care and the jury immediately found the prisoners guilty, and they were sentenced to six months' hard labour, the learned judge saying he took into his consideration the circumstance of the mental condition of the female prisoner and the fact that when Stammers found there was really danger, he took the poor old man out of the water.

IPSWICH JOURNAL: March 11th 1864

Essex had been the scene of some of the earliest English witch trials and continued to harbour pockets of superstition. Cunning people like the famed James Murrell of Hadleigh in Essex continued to draw patronage from those who believed he genuinely possessed supernatural powers.

EAST THORPE - WITCHCRAFT IN THE NINETEENTH CENTURY

It is a painful duty to have to narrate in this boasted enlightened age instances of the grossest superstition prevailing in some of our rural parishes of this county, and we are sorry to say, by no means confined to the lower classes.

East Thorpe, on Monday se'nnight, presented probably one of the most disgraceful scenes that ever occurred in North Essex since the days of the famous Matthew Hopkins, the witch finder, of Maningtree. It appears that Emma Brazier, age 22, the daughter of a labourer in the above parish, has lately caused much annoyance by making use of most violent, abusive, and filthy language, under the pretence that she has been bewitched by a neighbour - a Mrs. Mole, 75 years of age, wife of a labourer, who has lived for many years at the Hall Farm, and who, with his wife, is of irreproachable character. The poor old woman has been accused by the Brazier family of working marvellous spells upon their livestock, such as causing one of their pigs to climb a cherry tree and help itself to the fruits from the top boughs!

Recourse was had by the girl's parents to a cunning man, named Burrell, residing at Copford, who has long borne the name of 'The

Wizard of the North:' but her case was of so peculiar a character as to baffle his skill to dissolve the spell. Application was next made to a witch doctor named Murrell, residing at Hadleigh, Essex, who undertook to effect a cure, giving a bottle of medication, for which he did not forget to charge 3s. 6d., and promising to pay a visit on Monday evening to the 'old witch,' Mrs. Mole, and put an end to her subtle arts. Matters had reached this stage during the temporary absence for a few weeks of the rector, who on his return was deeply pained to find that, after years of earnest labour, such gross ignorance should still exist in his parish that the belief in the bewitchment of the girl and the Satanic agency of an inoffensive old woman was all but universal.

Stephen Choppen, once the village blacksmith of Hadleigh in Essex, whose suicide was reported lately, took his life just as he had entered upon a wider notoriety. He was one of the characters in Mr. Arthur Morrison's last book *'Cunning Murrell,'* which was published only a few weeks back... Choppen was a link with a strange survival of superstition. It was he who forged the iron witch bottles with which the wizard Murrell drove out devils...

ALDEBURGH, LEISTON & SAXM'M TIMES: November 10th 1900

Having visited the girl (suspecting from her violent conduct that she was insane) he called in the relieving officer of the district, who concurred in thinking that she was unfit to be at liberty, and recommended her removal to the union-house for examination by the parish surgeon, at the same time giving an order for her admission, but which the overseers refused to act upon, assigning as the reason for such refusal that there was a man coming from Hadleigh who was expected to cure the girl. The rector next sought the advice of the magistrates, and obtained a promise that the police should have an eye upon the neighbourhood.

In the meantime the news of the expected coming of the witchdoctor spread far and wide, and about eight o'clock there could not have been less than 200 people collected near the cottage of Mrs. Mole to witness the supernatural powers of the Hadleigh wizard. Drunkenness and riotous conduct were the characteristics of the meeting; and to protect Mrs. Mole from actual violence the rector was obliged to mount guard at the cottage door: for, although the proceeding took place immediately before the parish constable's windows (and he had known of the intention for some days previously), he never attempted to disperse the crowd, or took any steps to prevent or put a stop to the disgraceful riot. Ultimately two of the police made their appearance, and the crowd dispersed. The young woman has since been apprehended for threatening the life of her neighbour, Mrs. Mole, and bound over to keep the peace; and we sincerely hope that no more will be heard of this disgraceful affair.

ESSEX STANDARD: September 22nd 1858

At James 'Cunning' Murrell's death in 1860, he was described as a 'Quack Doctor.'

Two days after this article appeared in the Essex Standard, a letter from the Rector of Copford, Kennett C. Bayley appeared, forcefully insisting that 'Burrell the cunning of Copford' did not in fact reside in his parish, and this may be a confusion with Murrell himself.

All too often, there was a perfectly logical explanation for apparently inexplicable events. Close to the famously haunted Borley Rectory, this story emerged...

Liston: *During this last fortnight of November the quietitude of the inhabitants of Liston rectory was sadly disturbed by strange unusual knockings which were heard in various parts of the mansion which sometimes appeared to come from the roof and sometimes from different rooms in the house, windows were broken and casements rattled, sometimes the foundations of the house seemed shaken.*

The Rev. Fisher and family were of course annoyed and a watch was set but to no purpose, the sounds continued, at length the nuisance became unbearable and the police constable of Foxearth, P.C. Edwards, was called in, endeavouring to put a stop to it. For several days it baffled the shrewdness of the officer but being no believer in ghost stories he went to work on the convictions that the sounds proceeded from someone who had not yet 'shuffled off this mortal coil'.

186

Liston old rectory

Accordingly he kept a close eye on the domestics, and his suspicions fell upon a girl named Deeks of about 14 years: it was noticed that the sounds generally occurred when she had the occasion to go to some part of the house when she would be alone. She would rush back exclaiming, 'did you hear that noise?' At length, his suspicions were amply verified having observed her going into one of the rooms, he followed her noiselessly and when there was a rapping he saw the shadow of her arm commenced in corresponding motion upon the opposite wall. When she came gliding out of the room he met her: she was pretending to be alarmed and enquired, 'did you hear that?' By reply, he said, 'yes I did and you did it.' It was an accusation she did not long attempt to deny, her master was informed of the discovery and experiments were tried out in other parts of the house and the same effects were produced. The mansion is somewhat antiquated and the divisions of the walls are in places hollow, being composed of wood panelling. The girl had discovered what had escaped general observations, that striking on hollow walls in different parts of the house would have remarkable varied sounds and effects, it is supposed she used to vary her performances occasionally by slyly lifting up the sash of a window and stepping onto the lawn and throw a stone or two through some of the windows. No motive can be ascribed for her pranks; the Rev gentleman and his lady are remarkably kind and indulgent to all about them, the girl was dismissed at once and conveyed home to her parents and the removal of the cause of the rapping had ceased in Liston Rectory and usual quietude is restored.

S. SUFFOLK & N. ESSEX FREE PRESS: December 17th 1857

In the nineteenth century, in particular, attitudes to alcohol abuse varied greatly. The Temperance movement gained momentum as the century grew older, but for many, being drunk was a cause for humour...

On Saturday night, a young blood, in a drunken frolick, made his doxey (a Covent Garden lass) a present of his hat, coat, waistcoat, shoes and stockings and the next morning returned home in triumph, escorted by seven chairmen whom he had retained in his service for the night.

CHELMSFORD CHRONICLE: September 14th 1764

At the Petty Sessions on Friday the 31st, Master Smith, gunmaker of Springfield, with the inward man duly fortified with 'something comfortable,' stalked with rather an irregular motion into Court, and complained that some evil-disposed mortal had disfigured his hair form by blacking his face and cutting off his hair.
Bench - Were you sober?
Smith - Sober! Oh as sober as I am now (catching hold of the bar to support his tottering frame).
(Laughter)
Bench - That is very likely - That is not saying a great deal.
(Laughter)
Smith - If I am to have my face blackened and my hair cut off, they may as well kill me at once. (A laugh) I can tell exactly what I've had today.
Mr. Brooksby - Well, how many glasses have you had?
Smith - Glasses! Oh I never uses glasses: I mugs it!
(Laughter)

188

Mr. Bartlett - I would advise you to go. It may strike some gentlemen
that you are not sober now, and that would be rather
awkward for you.
Smith took the hint, observing, "It is very hard," and in his egress, made
very intimate acquaintance with the door-post.

ESSEX STANDARD: February 8th 1834

Mr. Petitt, overseer of Wormingford, complained of a pauper, Wm. Potter, for getting drunk and for general misconduct in the poor-house. The pauper said he was nearly 80 years of age, and that he could not help getting drunk when people *'put it upon him.'* He was severely reprimanded and told that at his time of life he ought to think of other things than getting drunk. No one would *'put it upon him'* if he did not feel so inclined. (ESSEX STANDARD: August 18th 1837)

According to the Chelmsford Chronicle (March 8th 1901), the Reverend A. Waller of Southend had offered £2 per annum to any local publican prepared to hang over his bar the following cautionary rhyme...

Sowing the seed of a lingering pain,
Sowing the seed of a maddened brain,
Sowing the seed of eternal shame,
Oh, what will the harvest be?

Mr. Alec White of the Cricketers, Southend had been besieged by youngsters who had been promised 2/6d by Reverend Waller if they could persuade a publican to hang his sign. Mr. White was reported as saying he would happily hang it in his bar if he could hang a sign in St. Paul's church reading, *'Good bottled ales and stout, 2s 6d a dozen, to be obtained at the Cricketers Inn.'*

On the other hand, when it was suggested by the Master at a meeting of the Maldon Workhouse Guardians in 1902, that on Coronation Day, the

Signing the pledge

inmates should have just half a pint of beer, Mr. H. Stevens was reported as saying, *"It's insulting for each man to only have half a pint of beer - half a pint makes a fool of a man's mouth."* It was agreed they should receive a pint. (Essex Newsman: June 7th 1902)

COGGESHALL - *James Mays, otherwise Scotchey Mays, the informer of Coggeshall, lately laid an information against a very respectable publican in the town, for drawing beer on the Sunday, out of time. It appears after all that he was ashamed of his conduct. At night, his effigy and his wife's were carried round to all the public houses in the town and then burnt. The publican, who was summoned to Witham, was acquitted, the informer having to pay the cost of the summons.*
IPSWICH & COLCHESTER TIMES: February 4th 1858

On Wednesday, one Green, a journeyman pipe-maker died very suddenly of excessive drinking of Geneva, having drunk half a pint of this pernicious liquor a few minutes before his death.
PILBOROUGH'S COLCHESTER JOURNAL: March 10th 1739

William Jewers and Francis Jewers of Ardleigh, convicted of drunkenness, were ordered to be placed in the stocks for the period of six hours.
ESSEX HERALD: May 25th 1828

Our towns were noisy places in the eighteen and early nineteenth centuries. By 1834, they were about to become a little quieter...

A soot-able penalty - *By the new Chimney-sweeper's Act, which came into operation last week, many person crying 'Sweep!' is liable to a penalty of 40s. Uttering the cry is a breach of the peace, as can be verified by thousands who have been roused by it from their peaceful slumbering.* [Yes, we even had cold-callers then]
ESSEX STANDARD: August 8th 1834

One thing that becomes clear when reading old newspapers is that nothing in this world is new. It has all happened before. Take job-creation schemes, for example...

EPPING - THE LAKE *- The lake, which is being constructed for the purpose of finding work for the unemployed labourers of Epping, Theydon Bois and Coopersale is progressing satisfactorily. In answer to the appeal for funds, about £155 has been raised... and work has been found for an average of 30 men working from 4 to 5 days a week at 2s per day. The lake, which will be of considerable depth at one end, is likely to prove of great benefit to those who are fond of bathing, while the large surface will be much appreciated by lovers of skating. The average depth of this lake is about three feet.*

SOUTHEND-ON-SEA OBSERVER: March 22nd 1894

At the end of the day, local papers tend to report what ordinary people are talking about on the street. And being British, of course we discuss **the weather**...

The great Thames Frost Fair in February 1814 was reported in most local papers of the time, though the best reports are in the Norfolk Chronicle, which reminds us that as well as all the fun and festivities enjoyed, a number of lives were lost.

The Regent's Park skating disaster of January 1867 (pictured left and below) brought home to readers of papers like the Essex Standard just how dangerous ice sports could be.

For all that, as the stories opposite demonstrate, skating would continue to be a favourite Victorian winter pastime, and a danger that Essex people were prepared to face.

Chapter 11
Weather and the environment

Skating by torchlight

The novelty of skating by torchlight was witnessed on Bourne Ponds [Colchester] on Tuesday night. A great many torches obtained from London at the expense of the skating club and officers of the garrison were used for the purpose of carrying on the exciting sport. The torches cast a lurid glare over the ice and lighted up the surrounding neighbourhood. A vast number of persons were present either as sitters and sliders or spectators of the novel evening's amusement.

BRAINTREE & BOCKING ADVERTISER: December 28th 1859

It is many years since those who are fond of skating remember having had such extensive sheets of ice to disport themselves upon as existed last week. The marshes were flooded between Manningtree and Sudbury, a distance of 16 miles and were frozen throughout... At Chelmsford, hundreds of persons of both sexes and all ages enjoyed the pastime, very animated scenes being witnessed... in the Springfield Meads, on the Navigation river near the wharf and at the railway cutting.

MALDON EXPRESS: January 16th 1879

CHELMSFORD *- The inhabitants of this town have raised a large sum by subscription for the relief of the poor at this inclement time. We hear that as 13 boys were sliding last Thursday near a mill dam at Weatherfield in this county, the ice broke by the miller's sudden drawing up the sluices and they were all drowned.*

IPSWICH JOURNAL: January 22nd 1763

The poor were known to suffer greatly in winter time, but help was at hand...

WITHAM SOUP KITCHEN - *During the week, this institution has been re-opened and soup at 1d per quart has found numerous customers.*
MALDON EXPRESS: February 6th 1879

Stratford - *On Monday afternoon, a young man aged 19 an apprentice to a shipwright while engaged in repairing a vessel in the Victoria Docks accidentally fell into the water. Assistance was promptly rendered and the unfortunate youth was taken out about five minutes after. Dr. Banks was speedily in attendance, but after repeated attempts to restore animation, he did not succeed, the vital spark having fled. The quickness with which death ensued is to be attributed doubtless to the poisonous nature of the water.*
BRAINTREE & BOCKING ADVERTISER: August 22nd 1860

As if in support, Punch Magazine at this time, in a separate report, commented... *"The sixth sense is really the scents that arise from the Thames - stronger than the other five senses put together."*

We are assured from Bristol that there was seen in that channel last week a great waterspout hanging in the air, a thing never known before in the British or Irish seas.
PILBOROUGH'S COLCHESTER JOURNAL: April 7th 1739

BOXFORD - *On Sunday morning the mail cart from Colchester to Boxford got fixed in the ice between Horksley and Nayland. It appears that the road near Nayland for two or three hundred yards has been flooded several days. On Sunday morning, water two or three feet deep was frozen over, and after the driver had got about thirty yards into it, it became too deep for the horse to break the ice, and being blocked in by the broken ice at the back, the driver was unable to go either backwards or forwards. In this dilemma, assistance was rendered by several men who with poles tried to break the ice but with dubious results; and at last a horse and tumbril were driven through several times and thus the ice got churned up and the unfortunate mailman was enabled to proceed. Both driver and horse suffered severely from the cold.*
SUFFOLK CHRONICLE: January 11th 1879

194

UNSEASONABLE FACTS - *Last week, a strawberry, full ripe was gathered in the garden of Mr. J. Holmes, Bellevue, West Derby. A gooseberry bush in the garden of Mr. Bothwell, Greenbank* [Aberdeen] *is covered not only with buds, but exhibits some well-formed berries. A robin's nest with four eggs has recently been discovered in a flue in the* [Bedford] *County Lunatic Asylum. The nest with three of the eggs is now to be seen at the Cross Keys Inn. A whinchat's nest with two eggs was found in Carrock Fell on Christmas Day by two boys. Cowslips were last week plucked in the neighbourhood of Norton, Yorkshire, and a fig tree at the Lord Seaham Inn near Hartlepool is now bearing fruit, being the third crop this year. A Salisbury correspondent of a local paper relates that whilst walking in his garden on Christmas Day, he observed a very beautiful yellow butterfly as full of activity as in the month of June.*

ESSEX STANDARD: January 5th 1838

COGGESHALL - *A remarkable instance of the mildness and open character of the present December weather was seen in this town on Wednesday last. A young man named Ruffell, working for Mr. James Johnson of Salmon's Farm, about a mile and a half distant, took from a stack a wren's nest, containing six eggs.*

COLCHESTER CHRONICLE: December 11th 1868

SOUTHEND - *this beautiful and salubrious watering place is beginning to fill for the season. Several of the lodging houses are occupied.* [You heard it here!]

ESSEX STANDARD: June 3rd 1831

THE EARTHQUAKE - GREAT DESTRUCTION OF PROPERTY
Probably the most severe earthquake which has been felt in this country for a century took place on Tuesday morning last, being more or less felt throughout the entire length of the island. But especially in East Anglia, and in its fullest force and destruction at Colchester, where it destroyed property to the value of more than £10,000. Four shocks followed one another. The stone spire of Lion Walk Congregational Church... was broken off and fell with terrific force... smashing the roof of the north aisle. A large number of civic buildings were damaged. At the Essex

THE GRAPHIC

AN ILLUSTRATED WEEKLY NEWSPAPER

No. 753—Vol. XXIX. | ÉDITION DE LUXE | SATURDAY, MAY 3, 1884 | WITH EXTRA SUPPLEMENT | PRICE NINEPENCE By Post Ninepence Halfpenny
Registered as a Newspaper

EXTERIOR OF LANGENHOE CHURCH

INTERIOR OF LANGENHOE CHURCH

CONGREGATIONAL CHURCH, LION WALK, COLCHESTER
(The dotted portion of the Steeple was shaken down)

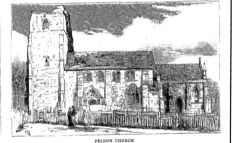

IN THE HYTHE, COLCHESTER : THE RUSH FOR THE GASWORKS

PELDON CHURCH

hall asylum for idiots, the patients were most of them frightened, but through the assiduous endeavours of the attendants, quiet was quickly restored. At North Station, the engine of the up-express from Ipswich which was waiting to leave, visibly oscillated, and the carriages were likewise shaken. At Langen-hoe, the fine old church of St. Andrews was completely destroyed, many other villages in the neighbourhood also reporting sad tales of injury and loss. The shock was felt to a lesser degree throughout Suffolk, but most were unaware of its cause until the East Anglian Daily Times, with praiseworthy enterprise, issued an extra special, which was eagerly purchased by thousands.

HALESWORTH TIMES: April 29th 1884

196

But serious and dramatic natural events gave rise to yet more serious and dramatic reporting. Four headlines led this report.

APPALLING STORM IN ESSEX
HAILSTONES AS BIG AS WALNUTS
FEAR AMONG THE PEOPLE
IMMENSE HAVOC WROUGHT

At three o'clock yesterday afternoon, an appalling storm of thunder and lightning accompanied by an extraordinary deluge of hail and rain broke over Essex. Chelmsford appeared to be about the centre of the tempest... The storm clouds began to gather overhead about two o'clock and the atmosphere was singularly oppressive, the temperature being 88 degrees in the shade. By a quarter to three, darkness prevailed ...Immediately the storm began, a scene was presented that has no parallel in local memory. The sky seemed a mixture of ink and fused copper, belching forth peal after peal of loud thunder and putting all the Jubilee fireworks to shame with vivid tongues of electric flame. ...The hailstones were of an extraordinary size, some being as big as marbles and others the size of walnuts... Some people are said to have believed the end of the world had come, so dreadful were the noise, darkness and destruction. Windows facing the north and north-west were broken by the thousands and... in less than ten minutes... the town of Chelmsford looked for all the world like a place that had been bombarded by a hostile army... Water poured into rooms and down staircases; chimney-pots were hurled from their places, cellars were flooded and streets were turned into rushing and turbid rivers.

At three o'clock the front of the residence of the Mayor of Chelmsford was a blooming garden of geraniums, lobelia and other flowers; at five minutes past, it was a wilderness of stalks and brown pots. Many of the roadways and footpaths were completely submerged... Trees in nearly all the outlying districts were rooted up and lay across the thoroughfares. The same unbroken tale of disaster comes from every quarter.

ESSEX COUNTY CHRONICLE: June 25th 1897

197

The greatest sufferers were farmers and nurserymen who saw crops and glass-houses destroyed. William Newcomb of Kelvedon Hatch, on seeing he was ruined, was so distraught that he had to be removed to the Asylum at Brentwood, where he died soon after. Other local reports included houses struck at Burnham, large numbers of birds killed by hailstones at Danbury, a man at Ingatestone had his face *'torn open by falling ice'* and a woman was killed at Margaretting. And all this amidst a week of great celebration for the Diamond Jubilee of Queen Victoria.

Immediately, a collection was started for the sufferers, which in a month had risen to £33,000. Long lists of the contributors were published. Donations came flooding in from all over the country as reports of the *'Essex tornado'* appeared in just about all regional papers.

> **THE ESSEX STORM.**
>
> In response to an appeal from the Lord-Lieutenant and the Parliamentary representatives of Essex in regard to the devastating storm which caused widespread ruin and misery in that county, the Lord Mayor of London has opened a Mansion-House fund. In a letter from the representatives of that county it is stated that the amount required to relieve the worst cases only is estimated at £100,000. The storm raged over an area exceeding 60 square miles In that area there will be no harvest.
>
> In the House of Commons last night, answering a question regarding "Devastated Essex," Mr Akers Douglas intimated that the damage done was estimated at £200,000, and that many of the farmers and gardeners would be absolutely ruined.

EDINBURGH EXPRESS: July 7th 1897

A black servant of William Stapleton Esq. of Danbury Hall, in attempting to cross the river near Chelmsford on horseback, was carried away by the rapidity of the stream and both the servant and the horse were drowned. IPSWICH JOURNAL: December 10th 1768

A Shower of Hay at Belchamp St. Paul's... *a curious phenomenon was witnessed in this neighbourhood...For some minutes the atmosphere was laden with falling hay... supposed to be the effect of a whirlwind on a distant hay field.* CHELMSFORD CHRONICLE: July 2nd 1797

Laſt Sunday, about 1 o'clock, a remarkable whirl-wind paſſed through the town of Thaxted, in this county, which was attended with the following cir-cumſtances : A dog walking in the town, was raiſed from the ground and carried to the diſtance of ſe-veral rods ; an apple-tree in the garden of Mr. Woolley, was ſhivered in pieces, as though done by lightning ; the corner of a houſe, in the ſame town, was taken off ; a heavy cart which was ſtanding near the market place, was, by the force of the wind, dri-ven a conſiderable number of rods up the ſteep hill, by the church ; and a great number of caſements were ſhattered in its courſe. During the time the hurricane continued, a noiſe was heard, ſimilar to that of thunder, and the atmoſphere was, for the ſpace of a minute, one continued cloud of ſtraw and leaves.

IPSWICH JOURNAL: November 7th 1795

The Stratford Times in early 1859 published death statistics from the previous five years.   These included a total of 103 deaths from lightning strikes. This was well above present-day figures, in spite of the much smaller population.   This was probably because far more people then worked out of doors.

21. We hear from Braintree in Eſſex, that they had a violent Storm of Thunder and Lightning there on Monday laſt, by which Accident the Lightning ſet fire to the Steeple, which entirely conſumed it.   *Lond. Ev. Poſt, &c.*

N. B.   *We hear that Part of the Spire at Danbury in Eſſex was deſtroy'd by Lightning that very Day: But, as our Informa-tion comes from Chelmsford, without the leaſt Mention of any ſuch Accident at Braintree, we hope there is a Miſtake in one of theſe Accounts.*

IPSWICH JOURNAL: February 10th 1750

Fierce and dramatic weather from time to time caused problems for ships along the Essex coast. The locals did not always present themselves in the best possible light.

The following instance of Shore Piracy lately occurred on the Essex Coast- the Dutch ship "Vrow Johanna," Captain Hendrick de Vries, laden with corn and on her voyage from Embden to London, being in great danger of foundering, in a heavy gale of wind, off the Gunfleet Sand, the Captain, Mate and men, took to their boat, to save their lives, and left her with all their property, behind ; but could not prevail upon the cabin-boy to accompany them, who was in bed, nearly frozen to death. The wind shifting, the vessel drove ashore near Bradwell Marshes, without sustaining any material damage. On the instant, however, she was boarded by more than thirty of the Marsh-men, who drank out all the liquor, and then rifled her of every article they could find, not leaving a morsel of food on board; and one of them was brutal enough to threaten to beat the poor cabin-boy's brains out with a bludgeon, because he would not get up to let him have the sheets from under him... One of the ringleaders has been lately apprehended and sent to our Gaol... and from the vigilant pursuit that is made of the others there is great reason to believe that the principal of these inhuman desparadoes will soon be brought to justice.
CHELMSFORD CHRONICLE: March 17th 1803

SATURDAY NIGHT'S GALE - *On Saturday night, a heavy gale passed over this district. At Yeldham, a stack of straw was blown from a field into the road, impeding the progress of the Halstead Mail, and at Mr. Chaplin's of Ridgewell, half of a large straw stack was overturned.*
SOUTH WEST SUFFOLK ECHO: March 15th 1890

Different reporters used different descriptions. In November 1863, the *'Extraordinary Hurricane'* at Coggeshall was a *'severe gale'* at Great Braxted and a *'heavy gale'* at Maldon (but just a gale in Chelmsford).

About half-past eleven on Friday morning, a water-spout burst right over the village of Boxted, deluging the place in an instant to the depth of 2 or 3 inches. Such a phenomenon has hardly ever been seen in the neighbourhood before and Capt. Peel, who was an eye-witness of it and has travelled extensively, states that he has not seen anything like it for many years.

ESSEX TELEGRAPH: July 21st 1888

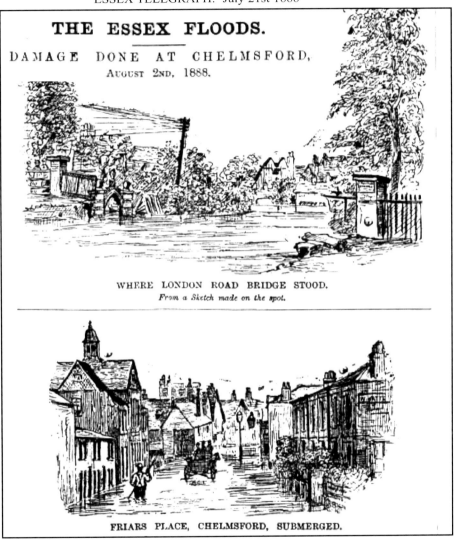

THE ESSEX FLOODS.

DAMAGE DONE AT CHELMSFORD,
Augusт 2nd, 1888.

WHERE LONDON ROAD BRIDGE STOOD.
From a Sketch made on the spot.

FRIARS PLACE, CHELMSFORD, SUBMERGED.

On Sunday the 29th ultimo [the previous month], *the intense power of lightening was evinced on an oak situated near Windmill Hall on Tiptree Heath in the parish of Messing, in a most singular manner. The accompanying storm was completely local, for at the distance of a mile its influence was scarcely felt. The tree was of considerable magnitude, being more than two feet in diameter and nearly 60 feet in height... every branch was torn from the trunk and that also was riven into splinters... the bark was entirely stripped from the tree... and scattered in a circle of between 30 and 40 yards radius of which the tree formed the centre. A portion of the tree remains standing as a memorial and evidence of the destruction and of the immensity of the destroying power... No certain mark is visible of the passage of the electric fluid, but it rather appears to have forced for its outlets a passage through every fibre. It had often been a matter of surprise to us how an entire flock of sheep resting beneath a tree should be immolated by a single flash, but this wide and general dispersion of the electric matter has demonstrated to us the possibility and in some measure seems to point out the modus operandi... no person we are convinced will view this tree without being led thence to contemplate the omnipotence of him who can thus dash into atoms the proudest ornaments of the forest.*

COLCHESTER GAZETTE: July 12th 1823

In a great 'inundation at Maldon in 1736, 5 people would be drowned '*in view of many hundred of people none of whom could afford them any succour.*' IPSWICH JOURNAL: February 28th 1736

Not within the knowledge of even that undeniable authority, 'the oldest inhabitant,' has Rochford and the district been visited with such serious floods as those of Sunday last... The River Roach and other outlets for the water were swollen to such an extent that the roads in the lower parts of the town were entirely submerged and the ground floors and base- ments of the houses filled with water... In one of the houses known as the Barracks, lived a labourer named Turner and his family - the water rose to such a height that the boiler in which the Sunday's dinner was being cooked had to be tied on to the fireplace to prevent it floating away...

The only mishap which threatened to be of a fatal nature happened to a man named Innefer, who had hired a pony and trap of Mr. Goodman of Wakering to fetch his daughter from service at Stowe. He was returning with his daughter by the way of Potash Road where the water was deepest, and in trying to clear the corner near the White Horse, he went onto some brickwork which overturned the pony and cart and pitched Innefer and his daughter into the water. Assistance was promptly rendered by Mr. Sales, Police Sergeant Megran and others and the man and girl were rescued. Innefer however received several kicks from the pony in its attempts to swim. He was taken to the Old Ship, where he received every kindness from Mr. and Mrs. Brown (the landlord & landlady), who had him put to bed between warm blankets.

SOUTHEND OBSERVER: October 15th 1880

The Old Ship is now no longer a pub but, as the small picture shows, a sign on the back wall still displays its former name.

Local papers from past centuries at times seem cruel and unfeeling, but often surprise us with their warmth and sentimentality, as this previous story shows. It would therefore be wrong to assume that these were harsh times and people cared any less than they do at the best of times. Editors knew a long time ago that there was nothing like a good **heart-warming tale** to encourage their readers to keep coming back for more...

The Graphic: October 1883

Chapter 12
Heart-warming Stories

FRUITFUL FAMILY

There is now living at Halstead, Essex, a man of the name of Smith in the 70th year of his age, who is the father of 29 children. The eldest and youngest are now living, the former a son 52 years of age, the latter a daughter, not yet 17 but married and has been a mother about 6 weeks. He also has 54 other grandchildren and 34 great grandchildren and is likely to have an increase.

SUFFOLK CHRONICLE: April 1817

Salubrity of Thorpe [-le-Soken]

Died on January 19th, Frances Lake, widow of William Lake at the advanced age of 94 years. As proof of the great salubrity of the neighbourhood, may be noticed the fact that there are now 40 persons residing in Thorpe whose united ages average upwards of 80 years.

IPSWICH & COLCHESTER TIMES: February 18th 1859

BRAINTREE - A Patriarch - *An inhabitant of this town named Anthony Tyler on Wednesday last completed his 94th year; he has eleven children living... upwards of 100 grandchildren and great-grandchildren and has lived to see his fourth generation. He is able to get about and work a little in his garden.*

IPSWICH & COLCHESTER TIMES: December 31st 1858

A number of accounts appeared of particularly aged Essex inhabitants. Unfortunately, people's claims were not always to be relied on...

Letters to the Editor

I was surprised to read in the Suffolk Free Press the obituary to Mrs Hart at Belchamp Walter aged 106. I examined our Parish register at Great Yeldham and found her baptism recorded, I also called on a

relative of the deceased who is in the possesion of a document written by her father, Mr John Fuller, saying, 'Ann our daughter, born this morning, August 12th 1784 at 1 in the morning.'
Editor's comment: *Mrs Hart's age was furnished us on good authority so there must be a mistake on her age of 106 years.*
S. SUFFOLK & N. ESSEX FREE PRESS: October 22nd 1868

People have written letters to the editor since the earliest publications got underway. Typical was the Ilford Guardian for November 26th 1898 which included 9 such letters, only three of which included the real name of the correspondent. Nom-de-plumes like *'an old bird,'* *'a ratepayer'* or just *'vigilant'* abounded then even more than now. My favourite has to be *'A. Mugwump,'* a regular contributor to the Ilford Guardian on a wide range of subjects. Here, he is amused by the plan to build a public house on a piece of open space in Ilford, right next to the Catholic Church (November 19th 1898)...

Whenever God erects a house of prayer,
The Devil always builds a chapel there;
And 'twill be found upon examination,
The latter has the larger congregation.

Then, as now, there was nothing like a happy ending to make readers of the papers feel better about things...

The following singular circumstance took place a few days ago, at the Royal Navy Asylum, at Greenwich. - A female child, five years of age was sent anonymously to that establishment with an intimation that £50 in bank notes were sewed up in the child's clothes, which were accordingly found. The following account of the birth, parentage and education of the little foundling was also given. The father was described as a seaman on board a British man-of-war, and however unusual it appears, that his wife, from some cause or other was permitted to go to sea with him. The tar was killed in action, and the day after his death, his wife was delivered of a female infant under one of the guns and almost immediately expired. The child was taken care of by the messmates of its deceased parents, and fed with biscuit and water; all of them acting the part of nurses, by turns, and carefully removing it from hammock to hammock when they were called upon duty. On the ship's arrival in port, the £50 above mentioned were collected among the ship's company and the object of their bounty transmitted to the asylum. The child, which is remarkably healthy has been baptized 'Sally Trunnion.'

SUFFOLK CHRONICLE: May 19th 1810

AGED WORKHOUSE COUPLE ARE ANXIOUS TO MARRY

Two of the oldest inmates of Chelmsford Workhouse, a woman of 73 and a man of 65 have fallen in love with each other. Both are anxious to marry, but they cannot do so in the workhouse, and they have no home to go to outside.

The story of their love-making shows how affection triumphs over difficulty. A few years ago, William Chapman, widower and farm labourer, met Lena McCrow, who was then a widow of about 70. Mrs. McCrow consoled Chapman for the loss of his work owing to the death of his employer, and a warm friendship began.

Chapman found it impossible to secure work, and told Mrs. McCrow one eventful evening that he would have to enter the workhouse. Mrs. McCrow, who also had a difficulty, owing to her age, in finding work as a charwoman, said at once that she would go too. The few things that she had collected in her cottage were that night handed over to her sister, and the next morning, two old figures were seen tramping along the road to the grim grey building outside the town.

They parted inside the gate, and for some days they had no opportunity of speaking to each other. Nothing had then been said about marriage, but the forced separation in the workhouse stimulated their affection, and soon, they frankly became lovers. Little subterfuges *were adopted to make meeting possible. Mrs. McCrow had been appointed ward-woman in one of the infirmary rooms on the ground floor. There is a garden outside, and here one morning, Chapman appeared to attend to the flowers... Occasionally she would join him in the garden to water some plants, which had been given to her by the Chaplain.*

As the winter came, however, the meetings in the garden became less frequent and it was necessary to arrange some other trysting place. Fortunately, the lovers had a friend in the town, the widowed sister of Mrs. McCrow, who lives in a small cottage and makes a precarious living by selling sweets. This cottage, with its few peppermints and acid-drops in the window, is now the rendezvous.

Romance is not encouraged in the workhouse, and Chapman and his Lena are not allowed to go out together; but they are equal to the emergency. Mrs. McCrow goes out one day and stays the night with her sister, and the next morning she waits patiently outside the door till the tall bent figure of her lover comes round the corner. Then her face lights up and she goes to meet him, and they spend the day together, sitting by the fire. In the evening, the two walk back, arm in arm, to their only home, and part reluctantly outside the gate.

They are anxious to start, as they put it, a little home somewhere. They could easily be happy, they insist, on seven or eight shillings a week, but they see no chance of leaving the workhouse. The Chaplain however, has offered to marry them for nothing, and it is likely that before long they will be married in the little village church close by the workhouse.

FRAMLINGHAM WEEKLY NEWS: January 18th 1908

Monday se'nnight, a distressing scene occurred at Happisburgh in Norfolk. A north country vessel had driven ashore in the gale which prevailed during that day and the preceding evening, and was lying just beyond the breakers. Five brave fellows of the above place went off in a boat in a most tremendous surf to assist the crew in their endeavours to get the vessel off, she being light. After having cleared the breakers and, as they vainly hoped, surmounted all their difficulties, whilst under the bow of the vessel, a sea heavier than they had before experienced, struck the boat and in an instant, turned her bottom upwards. The spectators on this beach viewed with painful solicitude the fate of the poor sufferers. After watching for a quarter of an hour the progress of every wave, not a man could be seen afloat. The boat, which had been driven by the tide, by this time approached the shore near enough for the persons standing thereon to sieze hold of her: while they were employed in dragging her out of the reach of the breakers, a sea struck her with such violence as to bilge in one of her sides, from whence crept uninjured the five men whose fate they were deploring. They ascribed their truly providential escape to the suddenness with which the boat was capsized, by which means not only themselves were overwhelmed by her, but a quantity of air was included; and, by holding on the seats, they were enabled to keep their heads above water, and by so doing, respiration continued and their lives were preserved

ESSEX COUNTY CHRONICLE: February 25th 1812

COGGESHALL

A BRAVE BOY - An instance of unusual presence of mind in a lad occurred here on Monday last. It appears that a boy named Reeve, about 13 years of age, in the employ of Mr. R. Browning Smith, was sent by his master in the afternoon of that day to fetch up the cows for milking, and while doing so, his attention was arrested by something in the water of what is called the Black Ditch. The lad almost immediately discovered it to be a little girl in the act of sinking for the last time, and with great promptitude jumped in and rescued her from her watery grave, when she was found to be the daughter of a person named Joseph Everett who was staying in the town and who liberally rewarded the gallant boy. We think this a fit subject for representation to the Royal Humane Society.

CHELMSFORD CHRONICLE: October 2nd 1863

Laſt Week, a Labourer cleanſing a Ditch at Seabright, in the Pariſh of Baddow, near Chelmsford, to his great Surprize, perceived Money fall upon his Spade, from the ſide of the Hedge; and on ſorther Inſpection, found buried under a Tree, the Quantity of a Quarter of a Peck, when clean'd, of half Crowns, Shillings, and Six-pences, of Qu. Mary's, Qu. Elizabeth's, and King Charles the Firſt's Coin; ſince which, the ſaid Place hath been viſited by ſeveral curious Perſons to ſee the ſame, and many other Pieces of Antiquity, have been found. 'Tis remarkable, that the neighbouring People uſed to report, that the ſaid Place was haunted.

On Friday Evening left, a Fellow who had been employ'd ſome Time at Heybridge near Maldon, being at the Swan Alehouſe there, and a Farmer in the Neighbourhood coming in, he deſired the Farmer to let him ſee what a Clock it was by his Watch; who having no Miſtruſt of his Deſign, readily delivered it to him, and the Fellow in a jeſting Way, ran up Stairs therewith, and no body following him immediately, got out at a Chamber-Window, and went clear off with the Watch, and hath not ſince been heard of.

P's Colch. Journal: April 1739

EXTRAORDINARY CIRCUMSTANCE - On Friday morning, while some coalwhippers were employed clearing out a collier-ship off Blackwall, one of them, an Irishman named Sullivan fell overboard and

instantly disappeared. His fellow workmen immediately commenced a search for the body about the spot where he fell in, but without success. A fisherman who was about sixty or seventy yards from the ship and had just thrown his net into the river, unconscious of what had occurred, directly afterwards found it very heavy, and from the weight anticipating a great draught of fishes, drew it up and was greatly surprised to find his net contained the body of a man. He pulled towards the shore, but on passing the ship from which the coal-whipper fell, he was hailed by the Irishmen on board who ordered him to leave their companion's body there.

The body was hauled on deck and the coal-whippers, finding it still warm, stripped it and commenced using the means recommended by the royal Humane Society to restore suspended animation, and, by the aid of a medical gentleman who was sent for, their exertions were fortunately attended with success. In about twenty minutes, signs of life began to appear and in less than an hour after he had fallen into the water, he was enabled to converse, and the poor fellow eventually resumed his work. He was in the water at least ten minutes and this case affords a remarkable illustration of what may be done by prompt and judicious exertions in restoring persons apparently drowned.

ESSEX STANDARD: January 4th 1834

Even luckier, was...

John Rolfe, employed by Mr. Tanner in the construction of a well for the Halstead Waterworks, who fell from a ladder a distance of 100 feet. Fortunately Rolfe's fall was broken by the water at the bottom of the well and he was rescued by the well-borer (whom he passed in his fall) without sustaining much injury beyond a few bruises.

ESSEX STANDARD: May 1st 1863

One well-appreciated satisfactory outcome demonstrated how important it was for people to keep up with their paperwork...

The Essex Telegraph for June 16th 1863 described a case in which Henry Taylor, a boy, was accused of refusing to join the ship of George Miles Rayner to whom he had been apprenticed at Wivenhoe. Previously, the boy had brought a charge of cruelty against Rayner. When the apprenticeship documents were produced, it was discovered there was a blank where the boy's name should have been entered, so it seemed... *"he had apprenticed himself to nobody. The boy left the court as quickly as he could and when the complainant* [George Rayner] *departed, he was greeted with the hisses of the audience."*

A short time since, as a gentleman in Norfolk was walking over his estate, he perceived a poor woman breaking down his fences for firewood and addressing her, said he would endeavour to find means for preventing it in future. The poor woman returned home, under the expectation of receiving a visit from the Officers of Justice, but to her agreeable surprise, in a few hours afterwards, a chaldron of coals was sent by the orders of her injured reprover... If this humane example were followed in every parish of the kingdom, there would be less cause for complaint against wood stealers and fence breakers.

ESSEX UNION: July 21st 1809

Tuesday morning, a gentleman walking by the Serpentine river in Hyde Park was cross'd two or three times by a well-looking young man, who at last made a full stop before him and bid him stand. The gentleman upon this, demanded what he wanted, to which the poor man, bursting into tears, replied, "I want to rob you, but can't." The gentleman's humanity was moved to so great an instance of sensibility, and assuring the man he might be under no apprehension, enquired into the motives which induced him to take so dangerous a course. It appeared that the poor young fellow had been a midshipman on board a Man of War; but that his ship being paid off, he was out of all manner of employment, and reduced to the utmost distress, having an infirm mother to support, besides a wife and two children. The gentleman was so much affected at this story that he gave him two guineas and dismissed him with some cordial advice upon the proper methods to pursue, which the other one seemed to receive with the most lively marks of gratitude and satisfaction.

IPSWICH JOURNAL: April 30th 1763

The tale of John Saunders is one of the most remarkable turn-around stories I have read...

John Saunders, a remarkably well-spoken, mild young man of demure carriage and rather respectable appearance was placed at the bar under... a very violent suspicion of having stolen a horse, but it turned out that the suspicion was groundless and that instead of John Saunders stealing the horse, the horse stole John Saunders.

CHELMSFORD GAZETTE: January 3rd 1823

The story reveals that Mr. Stephen Marchant of Turnham Green was riding the horse when it became lame owing to a pebble wedged in one of its feet. Mr. Saunders came to his aid, offering to hold the horse while its owner searched for a large stone with which to knock the pebble out...

But while he was hunting about for the stone, he saw to his utter astonishment, John Saunders on the back of the horse and scampering away towards Kensington as if the deuce was in him... Mr. Marchant

*stood aghast for a moment, and then
followed crying, "Stop thief, stop thief!"
with all his might. Every horseman on
the road... and many foot passengers
scampered after him, and the hue and
cry resounded far and wide.*

*"Stop thief, stop thief, a highwayman,"
Not one of them was mute,
And all and each that passed that way,
Did join in the pursuit.*

*And still as fast as he drew near,
T'was wonderful to view,
How in a trice the turnpike men
Their gates wide open threw.*

He had soon left his pursuers behind, and Mr. Marchant was left with no easy means to get home. He came into London the next day and was amazed to see Saunders in Piccadily, mounted on his horse. John Saunders dismounted and offered him the reins, explaining that he had *'mounted it by accident and it had run away with him.'* He said he had come to town to advertise for the horse's owner to return it to him, but Marchant was not convinced and had Saunders arrested for horse theft. Saunders was in big trouble. Horse-stealing was still a capital offence.

John Saunders explained that at the time, he had just drunk some Scotch Ale, which, *'having got into his head, he supposed induced him to get on the horse's back, quite contrary to his intention. The horse ran away with him directly - directly contrary to the way he wished to go.'* He explained that his umbrella was damaged and a band-box he was carrying at the time wrecked, with his mother's bonnet and feathers inside. [He was actually carrying the wording for the advertisement he intended to put into a newspaper at the time he was arrested.]

Mr. Marchant in reply said he was inclined to believe his story, but thought it right he should be told he was not to play pranks with impunity. The Magistrate therefore gave John Saunders a suitable admonition and dismissed him.

E. PEACHEY,
1, George Street, High Street,
COLCHESTER
(Side of the George Hotel).

Cabinet Maker, Upholsterer, Carpet Factor,
AND
BEDDING MANUFACTURER.

A Variety of New and Second-hand Goods in all Departments always in Stock.

☞ A Visit of Inspection respectfully solicited.

GOODS LET ON HIRE.

BENHAM & CO.'S
Printing Works,
High Street and Culver Street, Colchester

BENHAM & Co., having erected NEW MACHINERY of the most improved kind, are prepared to execute

EVERY DESCRIPTION of LETTER-PRESS PRINTING,
INCLUDING
Handbills, Circulars, Prospectuses, Shop Tickets, Labels, &c., At the Lowest Remunerating Prices. ESTIMATES GIVEN.

Bill-Heads, Cards, Posting Bills (in one or more colours), Hand-Bills, Show Cards Sermons, Pamphlets, Bookwork of every Description
In the best Style and with the Greatest Despatch. [1881

FARMERS' ACCOUNT BOOKS.

This Season's Editions of the under-mentioned Farmer's Account Books are now ready.

SWINBORNE'S FARMERS' COMPLETE ACCOUNT BOOK
Fcap. folio, half bound, cloth sides. Price 7s. 6d.
EXTRA SIZE DITTO, FOR LARGE FARMS, fcap. folio, half bound. Price 12s

SWINBORNE'S BAILIFF'S ACCOUNT BOOK
Fcap. folio, half bound. Price 5s.

COMPANION DITTO (CORN AND STOCK ACCOUNT, WITH SUMMARY OF WEEKLY PAYMENTS OF WAGES), adapted for the use of the Principal, fcap. folio, sewed. Price 3s. 6d.

TAYLORS' IMPROVED FARMERS ACCOUNT BOOK.
The Plain Farmers' Book; fcap. folio, half bound. Price 6s.

The above are specially recommended to the attention of Agriculturists and others requiring a simple and effective mode of keeping account of the Work done on the Farm, Outgoings, Cultivation and Crops; Valuation of Stock; Poultry and Dairy Account, &c. In order to meet the arrangements of different Districts, the Labour Tables are prepared to commence the Week SATURDAY or MONDAY.

Published at the *Essex Standard* Office, Colchester ; and may be obtained either direct from the Office, or from SIMPKIN, MARSHALL, & Co., LONGMANS & Co., HAMILTON, ADAMS, & Co., and WHITTAKER & Co., London : and all Booksellers. [1889

WATERLOO
FEEDING
OIL CAKES.

Unequalled for all classes of Stock. Every delivery is guaranteed to Analysis. Price **£7..15..0** per Ton, free on Rails in Hull. [1893

Manufactured by the WATERLOO MILLS CO. (Limited), HULL.

NINETEEN GOLD AND PRIZE MEDALS AWARDED

CANTRELL and
Aromatic Ginger Ale
Lemonade.
Sparkling, Montserrat.
Refreshing Seltzer, Soda, Kali, Lithia Waters,
AS SUPPLIED TO
COCHRANE'S
MINERAL
WATERS.

Her Majesty's Imperial Houses of Parliament and to Connoisseurs of Aerated Waters in all Civilized portions of the known world.

Works—DUBLIN and BELFAST.

Agent :—J. C. SHENSTONE, Dispensing Chemist,
13, High Street, Colchester. [1890

ASPHALTE FLOORS.

THE Best for Bays of Barns, Malt-Houses, Threshing Floors, &c., laid in all parts of England for the past 40 years. Foreign Asphalte and other Materials for Tennis, as laid for the Wimbledon Match Courts, and in every part of the Kingdom. [1896
T. PRENTICE & Co., Contractors, Stowmarket, Suffolk.

At a GREAT SAVING to the PURCHASER !!!
Ladies, send letter or post card, and you will receive, POST FREE, Sample Patterns, with Prices, of all the LEADING NOVELTIES for the Autumn and Winter Seasons. NEW STYLES AT PRICES TO SUIT ALL PURSES.

DRESS FABRICS
BY THE
Bradford
MANUFACTURING
COMPANY
BRADFORD YORKSHIRE

The Bradford Manufacturing Co., by trading direct with the public, have effected a revolution in the styles and Fabrics of Dress Materials. This is testified by innumerable Press Opinions. Carriage Paid to any part of the United Kingdom, on all orders over £1. The Century Cashmeres, as exhibited at the Health Exhibition, are in ever-increasing demand. Be particular to address in full. Please write at once, and mention this Journal.

The BURGLAR'S HORROR.
CLARKE'S PATENT
PYRAMID NIGHT LAMPS
1s. EACH, SOLD EVERYWHERE.

CAUTION—TO PREVENT BURGLARIES.
A Pyramid Night Light should be lighted in a front and back room of every house, as soon as it is dark. Burglaries are more frequently perpetrated before bedtime than after. Householders have the greatest dread of a light. The police recommend a Night Light as the best safeguard. Almost all burglaries may be prevented, and much valuable property saved. If this simple and inexpensive plan is adopted. The Pyramid Night Lights are much larger and give three times the light of the common night lights, and are therefore particularly adapted for this purpose.
PATENT PYRAMID NIGHT LIGHT WORKS,
CHILD'S-HILL, LONDON, N.W.

KINAHAN'S
LL
WHISKY.

Gold Medal Paris Exhibition, 1878.
"THE CREAM OF OLD IRISH WHISKIES."
PURE, MILD and MELLOW.
DELICIOUS, and VERY WHOLESOME.

The Gold Medal Dublin Exhibition, 1865.
20, GREAT TITCHFIELD STREET, LONDON, W.

Reckitt's
Blue
"Largest Sale in the World"

NURSE	EDDA'S	BABY	SOOTHER.
NURSE	EDDA'S	BABY	SOOTHER.
NURSE	EDDA'S	BABY	SOOTHER.
NURSE	EDDA'S	BABY	SOOTHER.

Free from any Narcotic.
Free from any Narcotic.
Free from any Narcotic.
Free from any Narcotic.
Free from any Narcotic.
This unequalled remedy is entirely free from any opiate or sedative or strong acting Medicine; its effect is instant in relieving Infants from GRIPES, WIND, COLIC, &c. It is guaranteed a simple, harmless Medicine. It attacks the root of the disorder and no after ill effects are possible. No cost in charge of a Baby should be without it. Price 1s. per bottle at Chemists, or free on receipt of that sum by THOMAS KEATING, CHEMIST, LONDON.

HEALTH FOR ALL !!!

HOLLOWAY'S PILLS

A RIDE TO KHIVA
BY
CAPTAIN FRED. BURNABY,
Royal Horse Guards.
Page 13 says :—
"Two pairs of boots lined with fur are also taken

ESSEX STANDARD: October 25th 1881

214

In conclusion...

The elegant writing style of the old newspaper hacks never fails to amuse me. With no actual pictures to pin their copy to, their descriptions needed to be all the more colourful. The Chelmsford Chronicle for March 29th 1833 described Mrs. Caroline Cox, charged at the local petty sessions with attacking her next-door neighbour, as being *a very energetic-looking piece of rustic beauty.* The Essex Standard, reporting the trial of Joseph Smith and Stephen Hills for burglary at the Essex Quarter sessions in February 1842, described the prisoners as *two powerful determined-looking men, appearing like railroad men.* In August 1842, when a Mr. Simmonds, a farmer at Baddow tried to drive a group of female gleaners from one of his fields, he bit off more than he could chew.

[They] *swore at him in the most shocking manner and used the worst language he had ever heard - even from a man; in fact it was such as he should be ashamed to repeat. (Here the ladies looked at one another with much astonishment.) They attempted to pull him off his horse with intent to strip him. They said they would make a free man of him. They could not get him off, but stoned him, and incited a hundred more women to do the same. (We could not but shudder at this picture of the poor man's situation, and indeed it is surprising that he did not undergo the fate of Orpheus, who was torn to pieces by the Bacchantes because he would not accede to their wishes.) Complainant then went on to state that he escaped from the field of battle with great difficulty, leaving in the hands of his fair, or rather* unfair, *enemies a portion of one of his buskins...*
ESSEX STANDARD: August 26th 1842

The bizarre (and almost unbelievable) has continued to intrigue readers since local papers first came into being...

LEYTON - There were lately four persons named John Swann living at this place, not related to each other, having wooden legs. Neither has been in the army or navy. One is sexton of the parish.
STRATFORD TIMES: March 25th 1859

The Woodford Mail, reporting cases from the Stratford sessions in 1897 described how James Webster had amused himself outside the Railway Bell Inn by *'throwing haddocks at passers-by.' "...It was stated he had already been turned out of the Butchers Arms for attempting to sing in 3 different keys at the same time."* He claimed he had thrown the *'finny monsters about'* as others had thrown them at him. The case was thrown out due to lack of evidence. (Woodford Mail: November 27th 1897)

Often I find, one tale leads to another. In October 1890, a number of Essex newspapers picked up this story...

DISCOVERY OF A SKELETON AT SHOEBURYNESS

On Thursday morning, while a gang of 'checkies' in charge of a man named Sycamore were engaged in excavating sand... they discovered a skeleton, presumably that of a man about three feet eight inches below the surface. It was in excellent preservation and was found lying face downwards with the wrists crossed behind the back... Major Raban R.E. who is in charge of the works thinks that the man must have been buried 100 years. A rumour is gaining ground that he was one of the mutineers of Admiral Duncan's fleet at the Nore in 1797.

Shoeburyness, as this picture from the Graphic shows, was an important military training area. A number of other bodies were found in this area in the early twentieth century. Some may well have been the Nore mutineers...

In 1797, Britain was at war with France and large numbers of sailors recruited. They found it to be a harsh regime, harsher even than they could ever have expected. Many had been pressed into service. There were routine floggings, poor food and pitiful pay. Led by Richard Parker [pictured below], a large number of the sailors anchored in the Thames Estuary, rebelled. Another mutiny occurred at the same time at Spithead. The rebels saw it as a kind of strike for better conditions. Admiral Duncan and the powers-that-be saw it as treason and mutiny and after a long stand-off, Parker and over two dozen of the leaders of the mutiny were to be hanged from the yard-arm and buried *'without the benefit of clergy'* (Norfolk Chronicle: June 10th 1797). Though such indiscipline in our navy might have proved a bit of a problem in dealings with the enemy, the same paper was anxious to report, *'The French Navy are in a similar state of insubordination and mutiny as the British sailors at the Nore.'*

At that time, not every Englishman regarded Napoleon and the French Revolution as a bad thing. There were suggestions that Richard Parker had a political agenda that went beyond a fight for better conditions...

Whatever his former course of life may have been, he is now the avowed chieftain of the mutiny, and beyond all doubt has designs deeper than his deluded fellow seamen are able to fathom.
     IPSWICH JOURNAL: June 17th 1797

So, whilst we needed all the sailors we could get, and would eventually *'impress every heart with the warmest feelings of gratitude; it being the intention of His Majesty to proclaim his royal pardon to all those concerned in the mutiny at the Nore'* (Norfolk Chronicle: November 4th 1797), no such mercy would be shown to the ringleaders.

Parker's body was first buried at Sheerness, but, according to the Ipswich Journal and Norfolk Chronicle, his wife arranged by devious means to convey the body to the burying vault of Whitechapel Church, where he was finally laid to rest. Some of the other leaders of the mutiny however, may well have found that like other naval miscreants, they were simply laid in a shallow sandy grave on the Essex side of the Thames.

It was not unusual for all kinds of odd items to find their way to the surface at Shoeburyness. It was being used for testing artillery and the like, well over 150 years ago. When the Chelmsford Chronicle reported the deaths of seven men in March 1885, they also commented that this was the third similar accident in recent times.

Past centuries may not always have been full of cheer, but our old newspapers give us reminders that these were not all hard times and amidst it all people could still appreciate a joke...

Last Sunday evening, a gentleman... was sitting with his wife and friends at their parlour fire when the door bell was violently rung. The lady rose and then suggested to her husband that, as the girl was out, he had better go to the front door. Accordingly, he opened it and found... a nicely done-up basket covered with white linen... After looking up and down the street, he took the basket into the parlour. On the covering being removed, a beautiful little child appeared, some 5 months old... One of the lady visitors took up the baby and found a note pinned to its dress, which charged the gentleman of the house with being the father and implored him to support it. A rich scene ensued between the injured wife and the indignant husband... the latter denying all knowledge of the little one and asserting his innocence... At last, the wife was induced to forgive the husband, although he still stood to it like a Trojan that he had always been a faithful husband Finally, the lady, rather roguishly told her husband it was strange that he should not know his own child, for it was their mutual offspring which had just been taken from its cradle upstairs by the nurse for the very purpose of playing the joke. The surprised husband joined heartily in the laugh which was raised at his expense.

HALSTEAD GAZETTE: December 17th 1857

Somehow, in compiling this book a few items from past local rags have never quite fitted in, but still should never be left out...

The Pitsea Never Frets Society held their annual dinner this week.
GRAYS & TILBURY GAZETTE: May 31st 1884

ONANISM - or a Treatise upon the disorders produced by MASTURBATION or the dangerous effects of secret and excessive Venery. Translated from the last Paris edition by A. HUME M.D. Sold by J. Shave in Ipswich, W. Keymer in Colchester & M. Hassall at Chemsford.
IPSWICH JOURNAL: September 5th 1772

A tale related in an Essex Standard of 1876...
A gentleman riding a very ordinary looking horse asked a local the way to the nearest town. The local, looking at the animal with contempt said, "With that there hoss, it's jus' fourteen miles; with a good chunk of hoss, seven miles; but if you had Jimmy's hoss: gosh! You're there already."

Or how about this 'slightly' politically-aligned item from the very Conservative 'Essex Standard'...
The grand City Reform Feast of Wednesday was characterised by a little incident which was not recorded in any of the papers, but which may probably amuse our readers... The tables being covered and the general company seated, previous to the arrival of the Lord Mayor with Lord Grey... and the rest of the principal visitors, the Reformers, unable to endure a few minutes' delay, actually attacked and finished all the turtle within reach before any of the above-named personages made their appearance and before grace had been said.
ESSEX STANDARD: July 14th 1832

In times of war, many in Essex lived 'dangerously near' a threatened coast. So, you had to be prepared [for Napoleon]...

CHELMSFORD: Night signals have been lately established on the heights round the coast. Each signal-house is also supplied with a stack of furze which is to be set on fire on the first appearance of alarm...
(IPSWICH JOURNAL: September 15th 1804) ...which would be the signal for

other beacons to be lit, passing the message by flame until all in the kingdom had been informed.

And so we have it - just a hint of the marvels buried in our local papers. And of course, this does not just apply to Essex. Just over the border, some equally odd things seem to have been going on...

FINBOROUGH MARROW BONE CLUB - All members are requested to attend the Annual meeting on Tuesday 30th inst. on special affairs. Rev. W. M. Hurn in the chair.

IPSWICH JOURNAL: December 13th 1783

STRANGE IF TRUE.—A few years ago two gentlemen, who had been left executors to the will of a friend, on examining the property, found a scrap of paper, on which was written, "seven hundred pounds in Till." This they took in the literal sense, and examined all his apartments carefully, but in vain. They sold his collection of books to a bookseller, and paid the legacies in proportion. The singularity of the circumstance occasioned them frequently to converse about it; and they recollected among the books sold (which had taken place seven weeks before) there was a folio edition of Tillotson's sermons. The probability of this being what was alluded to by the word "Till," on the piece of paper, made one of them immediately wait upon the bookseller who had purchased the books, and ask him if he had the edition of Tillotson, which had been among the books sold to him; on his reply in the affirmative, and the volumes being handed down, the gentleman immediately purchased them, and on carefully examining the leaves, found bank notes, singly dispersed in various places of the volumes, to the amount of seven hundred pounds! But what is perhaps no less remarkable than the preceding, the bookseller informed him that a gentleman at Cambridge, reading in his catalogue of this edition to be sold, had written to him, and desired it might be sent to Cambridge, which was accordingly done; but the books not answering the gentleman's expectations, they had been returned, and had been in the bookseller's shop till the period of this very singular discovery.

CAMBRIDGE INDEPENDENT PRESS October 3rd 1840

An inquest was held at the West Herts Infirmary before F. J. Osbaldeston Esq. and a respectable jury on the body of Mark Wingfield who died from the effects of an injury he received by a wagon passing over his great toe.

HERTFORD MERCURY & REFORMER: March 18th 1848

The news, as reported in our old local papers never fails to amaze me, as it does in this Ipswich Journal story of August 7th 1784. [The Czarina, by the way, refers to Catherine the Great]

2. The Czarina has folicited of our court, that the Britifh criminals fentenced to tranfportion may, as long as may be thought expedient, be conveyed at her expence to the moft defert parts of the Ruflian territories; which having met the approbation of his Majefty's minifters, occafioned the Attorney General's moving a new act, to enable the King to tranfport fuch convicts to any parts, either in or out of his dominions. The moft defperate and incorrigible offenders, it is faid, are to be landed in fome defert iflands in the South Seas, having been firft fupplied with proper inftruments for fhooting, fifhing, &c. *St. James's Chron.*

To be RUN for,
On the Race-Ground at Dedham in the County of Effex, On Wednefday the 30th of May, 1739.

A Silver CUP of Two Guineas Value,

BY any Horfe, Mare, or Gelding, who never won the Value of five Guineas, by Way of Plate or Match, at any one Time.: No lefs than Three to ftart, each paying four Shillings Entrance; to run twice round the Ground at a Heat, and the belt in three Heats to have the Cup: To enter at the Ancbor on the Race-Ground, at or before Two of the Clock in the Afternoon of the fame Day; to catch Weights, and run fair. *。* The faid CUP is given by Mr. Lancelot Fuller.

CAUTION: Several persons are going through this county informing against the retail brewers for supplying their customers with beer after nine o'clock in the evening [and we thought our licensing hours were bad!] ... being contrary to the Act of Parliament... which inflicts a penalty of 20L for each offence, half of which sum the informer is entitled to.
KENT & ESSEX MERCURY:
July 15th 1828

Finally, isn't it wonderful to read predictions like this, with the advantage of hindsight...

The day will come, and it is probably not far distant when Bradwell-on-sea will be a place of great importance, a place of enterprise and commerce, a harbour where anchored navies proudly ride. It is most favourably situated with the German Ocean on the East and the wide estuary of the River Blackwater on the North...
CHELMSFORD CHRONICLE: September 15th 1905

My thanks are owed to the staff and members of...
Essex Record office at Chelmsford,
British Newspaper Archive at Colindale
Colchester Library
Suffolk Record Offices at Ipswich & Bury St. Edmund's
Saffron Walden Museum
Foxearth & District Local History Society
Little Baddow Local History Society
Bulmer Local History Society
and all the other people who have helped me to locate
a number of the stories published here

Braintree 1826

INDEX OF PLACES

Persons of a full habit of body or who are in any way subject to determination of blood to the head should avoid travelling by the railway trains, as several instances have recently occurred in which the tendency to apoplexy has been strongly developed and increased thereby. Such a consequence might have been anticipated from the rapidity of transit and the sideling motion of the carriages increasing the frequency of the pulse and hurrying the circulation.

ESSEX STANDARD:
January 18th 1839

The *North London News* for March 8th 1862 quoted from a regional paper published a century earlier, which had announced the marriage between a Grenadier belonging to the Yorkshire Buffs and the daughter of a chimney sweep, whose dowry was soot to the value of forty pounds.

...on Saturday night as police-constable Miles... was pursuing his dreary beat through the Dagenham marshes, where... another constable of the same division was mysteriously murdered a few years since, he discovered three carts led by two men and a boy, being heavy laden. He questioned the party as to their contents and was told they were potatoes, but not being satisfied with the answer, he told the men they must go with him to the Dagenham Station... He found the carts contained a number of packages stitched up in canvas and containing unmanufactured tobacco... To arrest single-handed on so lonely a beat three persons with so valuable a freightage was an act of no common daring.

SOUTH-EASTERN GAZETTE:
August 3rd 1852

Hornchurch	80, 132
Ilford	68, 74, 89, 206
Ingatestone	65, 198
Ipswich {Sffk.}	85-86, 169
Kelvedon	132, 198
Kentford {Sffk.}	78
Kirby	85
Lamarsh	53, 111,
Landermere	165
Langenhoe	196
Lavenham {Sffk.}	88, 168
Leaden Roding	148
[Wrothing]	52
Leigh	98, 180, 215
Leyton [Layton]	186-188
Liston	145, 172-173, 209,
Lt. Baddow [and Baddow]	215
Lt. Bromley	15
Lt. Clacton	149
Maldon [Malden]	29, 89, 90, 98, 103, 104, 138, 155, 160, 189, 202
Manningtree	84, 193
Margaretting	198
Marks Tey	19
Mersea	16
Messing	201
Middle Wycke	50
Nayland {Sffk.}	194
Newmarket {Sffk.}	63
Newport	85
Ongar	29, 178
Pebmarsh	102-103, 115
Pitsea	219
Plaistow	178
Prittlewell	107
Rayleigh	178
Ridgewell	180-184, 200
Rivenhall	174
Rochford	41, 81, 121, 202-203
Rollesby {Norfk.}	49
Romford	38, 62, 89, 94, 131, 132, 157, 164, 178, 179
Saffron Walden	13, 28, 60, 64, 90, 158
Shoeburyness	216-218
Sible Hedingham	180-184
South Benfleet	171-172

Tiptree House old mansion, was in the night of Tuesday, the 15th inst., reduced by fire to a heap of ruins; the bare walls only are left standing and even those are in a tottering state. So great a progress had the flames made before they were discovered, that no time was left to secure even apparel, money or valuables of any description.. Last week, a polard oak was peeled in the parish of Tendring... and fairly measured by Mr. John Golding... at 50 fathoms and a half.

IPSWICH JOURNAL:
May 26th 1810

HARWICH ROYAL MAIL
And TELEGRAPH COACHES.
W. COLLEN and Co. Proprietors of the above, BEG leave to offer their best Acknowledgments to their friends and the public in general, for the very liberal support they have hitherto been honoured with, and, in the assurance that no effort of theirs shall be wanting to merit their future favors, they venture to hope for a continuance of them ; they now inform their friends and the public in general, that their HARWICH ROYAL MAIL COACH, will set out for London from the Three Cups Inn, Harwich, every night at 7 o'clock, and return from the Spread Eagle Inn, Grace Church-street, every night at the same hour. They further acquaint them, that their HARWICH NEW TELEGRAPH COACH will set out for London, from the White Hart Inn, Harwich, every morning, and return from the Spread Eagle Inn, Grace Church-street, and King's Arms Inn, Leaden, hall-street, London, every morning.
Places and Parcels carefully booked at the Plough-Bradfield ; Thorn Inn, Mistley ; Packet Inn, Manningtree ; and Three Cups Inn, Colchester.
N. B. The Proprietors of the above Coaches, will not be accountable for parcels or luggage of any description whatever, above the value of 5 £. unless booked as such, and paid for accordingly ; nor any parcel of less value unless booked. *Harwich, 12th April, 1810.*

Dr. MENISH's
MUSEUM of NATURAL CURIOSITIES.
CHELMSFORD, ESSEX.
SALE by AUCTION
By Mr. KELHAM,

On Tuesday the 15th of May, 1810, and following days, At BISHOP's HALL, near Chelmsford,

A Genuine, distinguished, and valuable Collection of Natural History; exhibiting a splendid association of highly interesting minerals and fossils, British and foreign, petrefactions, crystalizations, &c. a rich display of brilliant specimens in native gold, and a variety of extraordinary insects; a most singularly astonishing tusk and bones of a stupendous Elephant, found by the late enlightened possessor in the separation of a rock at Walton on the Nase, an undoubted inhabitant of the Antidelnvian world; a curious mummy of the bird Ibis, an object of Egyptian adoration, a variety of ancient coins, select and scarce, and an inexhaustable store of other rare productions of nature and art, together with the appropriate cabinets, glass cases, and drawers, containing these celebrated remains of antiquity; the whole of which were decidedly the property of the late H. Menish, M. D. and were by him collected and formed with indefatigable application, philosophical research, scientific knowledge, and profound judgment.

Descriptive catalogues, 1s. each, will be ready for delivery ten days prior to the sale, at the Auction Mart, London; of Mr. Hodson, printer, Cambridge; Mr. Bird, jeweller, Bigg's-lane, Norwich; Mr. Bevil, goldsmith, Ipswich; Mr. Railton, Cups, Colchester; at the Angel Inn, Bury St. Edmund's; Post Office, Romford; Mr. R. H. Kelham's Phœnix Circulating Library, and of the Auctioneer, Chelmsford.